UNDER THE CARING EYE OF GOD

UNDER
THE CARING EYE
OF GOD

Finding God in Hospital

JOYCE HUGGETT

Eagle
Guildford, Surrey

Published by Eagle, an imprint of Inter Publishing Services (IPS) Ltd, Williams Building, Woodbridge Meadows, Guildford, Surrey GU1 1BH

Photoset by Intype, London
Printed in the UK by HarperCollins Manufacturing, Glasgow.

ISBN No: 0 86347 039 4 (hardback)
         0 86347 040 8 (paperback)

Acknowledgements

A whole variety of people have given me their time and support while I have been writing this book. I am most grateful to each of them but space allows me to mention only a few.

My first vote of thanks goes to Canon Peter Nicholson, the General Secretary of St Luke's. From the moment I first told him that I sensed God was asking me to write about St Luke's to the time when the manuscript was finally completed, he has given endless encouragement and help, allowing me to work at his own desk, to ply him with questions and to gain access to the documents I needed for my research.

Next, I want to thank my friend and publisher, David Wavre. David visited me while I was a patient in St Luke's, listened while I expressed my longing to write about the ministry of the hospital and believed in the book before I had even written the first chapter. As always, I have found his work partnership stimulating and creative. He and my editor Teresa de Bortodano, who also visited me while I was in hospital, have given me the benefit of their editorial skills and I am indebted to them both for their insights, their wisdom and their affirmation.

Without the home team, I could not have created the time or summoned the energy to write this particular book so my thanks flow once again to my husband, David, for his shrewd comments and support, to Linda, my friend and home help who kept the house in order while I wrote and to Sandie, who became my secretary while I was convalescing and who has worked long hours checking the footnotes of the manuscript and coping with my correspondence.

James Thomson, the Chairman of the Medical Staff Committee of St Luke's and his colleague Roger Springall have been most generous in their comments about my manuscript and in giving me their valuable time. I owe them both an enormous debt of gratitude. The Chaplain of St Luke's, the Rev. Trevor Morley and the Chaplain of the Queen's Medical Centre in Nottingham, the Rev. David Storer, also sacrificed valuable time so that I could interview them and I am glad to have this opportunity to thank them publicly for their help and their ministry.

Others connected with St Luke's were equally kind: members of staff who answered my many questions while I was visiting the hospital, ex-patients who responded to the questionnaire I sent them and people like the Appeal Director, Pam Hutchence and the receptionist, Alan Brown, who had not known me as a patient but who welcomed me so warmly when I worked on the manuscript in Peter Nicholson's office. Such obvious enthusiasm and interest has made this project a joy and not a chore.

Photographers Lorenzo Lees and Canon Coates have laid at my disposal their creativity and I am delighted that we have been able to publish some of their many superb pictures of St Luke's.

Librarians in the local library in Nottingham and at the headquarters of the USPG in London have also taken an interest in this project and have helped me to unearth invaluable information about Canon Cooper, his ministry, his travels and the plight of people condemned to end their days in the workhouse. In particular, I must mention Margaret Ecclestone at Partnership House in London who found and photocopied the articles written by Canon Cooper from which I have quoted.

My friends the Rev. Peter Williams, formerly Vice-Principal and tutor in Church History at Trinity Theological College and Martyn Offord, lecturer in English at Bilborough College, Nottingham, further guided my reading and research. Peter pointed me to books which helped me to understand the conditions faced by the clergy in the Victorian era and Martyn to literature which reminded me of conditions which characterised the London of Canon Cooper.

My final vote of thanks goes to the Most Revd. George Carey, the Archbishop of Canterbury, for taking the trouble to read the manuscript and to write the Foreword to this book; and to the Rt. Rev. Lord Runcie, the retired Archbishop of Canterbury and the Rt. Rev. Michael Baughen, the Bishop of Chester who similarly read the manuscript and sent the commendations which appear on the dust jacket. They are all such busy people that I was greatly touched by their willingness to express their support of the ministry of St Luke's by promoting this book.

I am aware that, in mentioning many of the people who have worked closely with me while I have been writing, I have omitted to mention others whose names should always be on the lips of those who talk of St Luke's. I think, in particular, of the consultants of whom, as my consultant frequently reminds me, he is but one and of the Chairman of the Council, General Sir Patrick Howard-Dobson who dedicates so much time and energy to St Luke's. Sir Patrick's welcome of me has always been courteous and kind and I have appreciated his interest in this book. Behind the scenes, too, hide those who have prayed this book into being and people in the parishes who pray regularly for St Luke's; hidden people who look for no other thanks than the privilege of being permitted to promote a ministry which, for one hundred years, has come under the caring eye of God.

Joyce Huggett

Contents

For
Roger Springall
and all the consultants, staff and supporters
of St Luke's Hospital for the Clergy

All royalties on the sale of this book will go to
St Luke's Hospital for the Clergy

Foreword by the Archbishop of Canterbury

This is a most fitting book for the Centenary of St Luke's Hospital for the Clergy. It gives intriguing glimpses of the life of the Founder, Canon Cooper, which shows how much St Luke's today owes to his original vision, yet how many developments there have been which have enlarged his ideas. But this is not dry as dust history. Joyce Huggett, one of St Luke's recent patients, begins with her personal experience and the gratitude she feels for the ministry she received. From her own story she leads us more deeply into the story of St Luke's as a whole and offers us many insights into how St Luke's cares for the carers and, in so doing, reflects on the nature of healing.

It's not only the medical skills which Joyce applauds at St Luke's, though these are freely and expertly given. It is the sensitivity of the pastoral and sacramental ministry also found there. Joyce tells us how she realised it was not merely that her illness was cured. She was healed, taken another step along her own pilgrimage as a Christian, and helped to use her experience even of illness as a means of spiritual growth.

I can testify, too, to the remarkable ministry at St Luke's, and how it benefits, in a quiet and frequently hidden way, the ministry of the whole Church of God. It is a particular delight that as Archbishop of Canterbury I am President of this Hospital. It has my warmest and fullest support and I hope that its Centenary Year will mean that many more people will come to appreciate its unique ministry.

George Cantuar
Lambeth, June 1991

Into the Eye of God

For your prayer
  your journey into God,
may you be given a small storm
  a little hurricane
  named after you,
persistent enough
  to get your attention
violent enough
  to awaken you to new depths
strong enough
  to shake you to the roots
majestic enough
  to remind you of your origin:
  made of the earth
  yet steeped in eternity
  frail human dust
  yet soaked with infinity.

You begin your storm
  under the Eye of God.
A watchful, caring eye
  gazes in your direction
  as you wrestle
  with the life force within.

In the midst of these holy winds
In the midst of this divine wrestling
  your storm journey
  like all hurricanes
  leads you into the eye,
Into the Eye of God
  where all is calm and quiet.
A stillness beyond imagining!
Into the Eye of God
  after the storm
Into the silent, beautiful darkness
Into the Eye of God.[1]

1

The Small Storm

'You begin your storm
   under the Eye of God.
A watchful, caring eye
   gazes in your direction
   as you wrestle
   with the life force within.'[1]

On the last Sunday of 1990 my husband and I attended a
service of Holy Communion in a sixteenth-century, stone-
built Byzantine church on the island of Cyprus. During that
service the vicar prayed: 'We thank you for the past year;
for blessings received and miracles perceived.' That short
prayer transported me away from sunny Paphos to one of
the finest squares in London – Fitzroy Square – which nes-
tles in the shadow of the British Telecom Tower in the
centre of London's medical heartland. More accurately, that
simple prayer took me, in my imagination, into number 14,
Fitzroy Square – into St Luke's Hospital for the Clergy –
the place where, during the summer of 1990, I had found a
shelter in my small storm.

   Aware that it would be possible to spend the rest of the
service reminiscing about the 'blessings received' in that
haven of healing, I forced myself to concentrate on the liturgy and the sermon but as I drove away from that little
church that night, and as I walked in the vineyards and
orange groves and tramped along the beach the next day,
New Year's Eve, I allowed myself the luxury of looking
back at leisure.

I recalled how, as 1990 dawned, several commitments demanded my attention: the book I was writing and a proposed trip to New Zealand, in particular, dominated my thoughts.

My reverie reminded me how much I had enjoyed working on the book, *The Smile of Love*, and how I had been particularly thrilled when, at the beginning of February, while my husband, David, was away from home, the opportunity had opened up for me to bury myself and my computer in a small, cosy, cottage in the countryside. There I had been able to be single-minded and concentrate on the one task in hand – the writing. During those two weeks, ideas had flowed freely and my Prayer Journal testifies to the sense of fulfilment I had enjoyed as I wrote. So far as I was concerned, the New Year had got off to a most promising start.

My husband and I returned home on the same day and, to celebrate our reunion, we visited a nearby restaurant where we enjoyed a simple meal as we caught up on one another's news.

The storm brews

That night, at 3 am to be precise, though I had been sleeping soundly, I was jolted into consciousness by a pain which was so severe that it took my breath away. It felt as though someone had kicked me in the stomach and winded me. Reluctant to wake David at that early hour, I slipped quietly downstairs where I sat, doubled up in front of the gas fire, wondering what could have caused this excruciating pain.

Three hours later, the pain disappeared as suddenly as it had arrived and I crawled back into bed and dozed until David roused himself for the new day.

That day, as I continued to work on the book I concluded rather ruefully that, after the frugal diet on which I had existed at the cottage, I must have eaten something in the restaurant which my digestive system could not quite cope with. I thought no more about the traumatic night.

Exactly one week later, our daughter arrived home unexpectedly. Anxious to give her as much time as possible, rather than spend precious time preparing a meal at home, I suggested we once again visit the same restaurant. Over a simple supper, we listened to her news and plans.

That night, soon after three o'clock, I was once more rudely awakened by the now-familiar pain. Again, I crept out of bed, went downstairs and repeated the process which had worked the week before. This time, bending myself double in front of the gas fire did not relieve the pain. It refused to go. When morning came, I was still by the fire, still trying to catch my breath and still writhing in pain.

Although our family doctor never minds being called, I hate to bother him. Perhaps this is pride on my part – the fear of being a nuisance or worse, of being thought neurotic. But when the hands of the kitchen clock showed that his surgery would, by now, have started, I telephoned, since I was still sick with pain, and appalled by my deathly white face.

As always, he came as promptly as he could. And, as always, he was courteous, kind and efficient. When I described what had happened, he pulled a face and said: 'Sounds like gall stones. We'll arrange for you to have X-rays and to see a consultant and if my diagnosis is correct, it will mean surgery as soon as possible. Major surgery – like the hysterectomy you had a few years ago.'

Memories of the hysterectomy flooded back into my mind: the pain, the prolonged convalescence, the depression and the question it had raised in my mind: 'Who cares for the carers when they need looking after?' But out loud I simply said: 'Surgery? But how long will that take? I'm supposed to fly to New Zealand in six weeks and I'll be there for another six weeks.'

He pulled a face again and suggested postponing the trip. I thought of the Holy Week Quiet Days near Wellington which David and I had been invited to lead, the Easter Convention where we were scheduled to speak and the post-Easter conference for clergy and their wives where we were to be the main speakers. I thought, too, of the marriage work which had been planned in Auckland – with the students at the Theological College, at the Christian Care Centre and in other places. Postponing the trip was quite out of the question. Perhaps we should cancel it all together and trust that other speakers would be found to step into our shoes even at this late stage?

'Don't do anything for a few days,' the doctor advised. 'First, let's see what the X-rays reveal and arrange for you to see a consultant. Meanwhile, I'll give you some antibiotics and some painkillers which you can take if you have another attack.'

I spent the next few days resting and was grateful, after all the trauma, for this enforced rest with the time it afforded to lift this perplexing set of circumstances to God.

The God of the storm

Five months earlier, I had embarked on exploring a method of prayer which has existed since the sixteenth century but which is attracting a great deal of attention today. The Spiritual Exercises of St Ignatius. On Quiet Days and retreats I had dabbled with this biblically-based, Christ-centred method of meditation and contemplation and found it both illuminating and life-changing. Now I wanted to give myself to The Exercises: to start at the beginning and work through to the end, a process which would, I realised, require a considerable commitment of time and energy for some nine months.

Undaunted by the commitment, I carved out of my diary time for daily meditation and reflection on certain Scripture passages; time, too, for the fortnightly sessions with my prayer guide whose task it was to listen to my discoveries and questions, to discern how God's Spirit was re-shaping me and to suggest further passages of Scripture accordingly.

I began this nine-month spiritual marathon voicing the kind of prayer made popular by a lyric from the musical *Godspell*: a prayer which is an adaptation of one attributed to St Richard of Chichester:

'Day by day,
Oh! dear Lord,
Three things I pray:
To see you more clearly,
To love you more dearly,

To follow you more nearly,
day by day.'

When I had the first gall bladder attack, the first part of that
prayer had been answered. As I had contemplated Christ, I
had not only found myself fascinated by this strong, vigor-
ous, upright leader, I had also found that my commitment
to him was being re-kindled. It was not that the Gospel
narrative was new to me. I had been brought up in a Christian home and read Theology at university. Yet through
contemplating familiar Gospel stories in this leisurely, consecutive, contemplative way, familiar truths were making
a fresh impact. They seemed to be affecting deeper layers
of my personality. Consequently, the more clearly I sensed
I saw Jesus, this man whose closeness to God seemed to
give birth to a genuine care for people and a determination
to expose injustice, the more I seemed to be drawn to him:
to see him more clearly, in my experience, *was* to love him
more dearly. Loving him more dearly gave rise to the longing to follow him more nearly; to be led by him – anywhere.
As I expressed it on one occasion:

'Strengthen within me this longing to follow you,
to become more like you,
to live my life in the way you would live it.'

A variation of this prayer punctuates page after page of my
Prayer Journal. It is interspersed with the kind of questions
I found myself asking at this time:

'How do I live my prayer?
What are the Kingdom values we pray for?
What is the Kingdom activity many Christians sing about
   in choruses like: "Make way . . . and let his Kingdom
   in"?
What did Christ come on earth to do?
And what did he mean when he made that curious claim:
   "Blessed (blissfully happy with a happiness that cannot
   be dented) are the poor in spirit"?'

In answer to the question, 'What did Christ come to earth

to do?' I realised that, among other things, he came 'to bring "shalom" to everyone; to make life on earth better for everyone; to *spread* love, joy, peace, patience, kindness, goodness; to stand against and challenge oppression, injustice, poverty, pollution.' I saw that, if I was to carry this caring, confrontational love into the world, I would have a strong gut reaction when brought face to face with poverty and injustice – just as he did. I found myself inspired, not just by the person of Jesus, but by the women who surrounded and supported him from their private means.[2] In them I was witnessing, I realised, a vibrant, self-sacrificing spirituality lived out in the nitty gritty of daily life. I was attracted by it and wanted to emulate it. At the same time, some words of St Paul brought me up with a jolt: 'I want to know Christ ... becoming like him in his death' (Philippians 3:10). They were words to which I would return many times in the days that lay ahead. At the time, I simply registered them and my reaction to them which prompted a pithy prayer: 'Continue to change me ...'

A challenge

'Spend some time meditating on the Wedding in Cana of Galilee,' my prayer guide had invited the Sunday before my first attack. By 'meditating', I knew what he meant. Picture the scene. Try to step into it. Interact with the characters in the Gospel narrative. Then reflect on what you have seen and heard and sensed and felt. Try to discern what God is saying to you as you reflect on your meditation. Let it result in appropriate action.

The day after the second gall bladder attack, I wrote in my Journal: 'With time in bed, and slowed down by the antibiotics ... I loved meditating on this passage today.' I went on to record how I was captivated by the character of Christ. Both his humanity and his divinity intrigued me. In his humanity, he seemed such fun to be with – the life and soul of the party. Yet through his humanity, a divine light seemed to shine so that in his hands, very ordinary things changed. This realisation prompted a prayer which I wrote down: 'I'm thrilled by the way you take the ordinary things of life: impure water, little loaves, small sardines, a chalice of wine and make of them something wonderful; symbols of your smile of love . . . Through this gall bladder business, take me deeper and deeper into you.'

I had no idea how that prayer was to be answered but, despite the uncertainty which now hung over the New Zealand trip and despite the physical weariness and emotional vulnerability which prevented me from applying my mind to writing my book, I felt held in a deep and almost tangible peace:

> In the midst of these holy winds
> In the midst of this divine wrestling
>   your storm journey
>   like all hurricanes
>   leads you into the eye,
> Into the Eye of God
>   where all is calm and quiet.
> A stillness beyond imagining![3]

Next day, again I contemplated the fun-filled Christ, and as I marvelled at the miraculous way in which, at Mary's request, he had turned water into vintage wine, I sensed that I saw him wheel round, face me, call me by name, remind me of Mary's request and ask the question he so often asked those he met: 'What do you want?'

At first I was completely taken aback; but such a blunt, direct question, even though it was laced with great kindness, seemed to demand a reply. My instinctive reaction was to ask that the New Zealand trip might not have to be cancelled, that I might be saved from the need for surgery, that health should be restored to my body. I then added a rider which came from somewhere deep inside me: 'Lord, what I most want is whatever you perceive will draw me closer to you and be best for your Kingdom', I wrote. 'I really am prepared to live with sickness or health – whichever will give you most glory.' That prayer, although from time to time I was to regret uttering it, filled me with a curious sense of freedom. Jesus, I knew from experience, can cure all kinds of diseases today just as he did when he lived on earth. Equally, I am aware that he sometimes speaks eloquently through the language of suffering. I sensed he spoke to me now: 'Leave it with me. I will show you what to do – one step at a time.'

I thought back on what I had been discovering about Christ as I had encountered him in my meditations and through writing *The Smile of Love*: that he was someone who had the best interests of people at heart. He did not merely claim to hear the cry of the poor, he set up home among them and championed them. When such a loving person says, 'Leave it with me. I will show you what to do', a sense of excitement and anticipation permeates perplexity and pain. So I waited. And resolved to heed his mother's advice: 'Whatever he says to you, do it' (John 2:5).

A haven

As I reflected on my doctor's kindness and his efforts to contact a consultant at our local hospital to arrange an early appointment for me, a seed-thought took root in my mind. I shall never know whether *God* said: 'I want you to go to St Luke's' or whether I merely thought: 'I could contact St Luke's'. What I do know is that this seed-thought startled me because, at that time, I knew almost nothing about St Luke's Hospital for the Clergy in London. I had never been a patient there and knew only one person who had: Wendy, a vicar's wife.

I recalled standing on a bridge in Durham with Wendy five years earlier. As we drank in the Sunday stillness and gazed at the glut of autumn colours: the browns and bronzes, the golds and russets of the leaves shimmering in the unseasonal warmth of the sunshine, she told me that soon she was to go into hospital and that she had chosen to become a patient at St Luke's. I remembered wondering why I had never registered the existence of this hospital and asked her why she had chosen to go so far when it meant that her husband and parishioners would be denied the joy of visiting her. I recalled the look on her face when she explained how wonderfully she had been treated on a previous visit. 'I'm a nurse, remember,' she laughed. 'And we nurses are very choosy when we have to become patients.'

I must have hung that conversation on a peg in my mind. To my knowledge, I had never taken it off its peg until this moment when the memory was as vivid and clear as the original conversation. I toyed with the idea of telephoning Wendy but did not put this plan into action.

Next day, although I was still feeling somewhat fragile, I felt well enough to meet a clergy couple who come to me for counselling from time to time. The wife is also a trained nurse. When they heard my saga, her immediate response was: 'Have you thought of going to St Luke's? I was a patient there last summer and was so impressed with the level of care and nursing.' Again, I was tempted to telephone Wendy, but I did nothing about it. Even so, the seed-thought continued to germinate. It was to be watered a few days later.

At that time, members of our church's contemplative prayer group used to meet in our home once a month. That Saturday, as we drank coffee before the meeting, I told them what had been happening to me, whereupon one of the members – a chaplain at one of the Nottingham hospitals – muttered: 'St Luke's. If I were in your shoes, I'd go there. They really know how to care for the carers. Given a choice, I would always opt to be a patient there.' The look on her face as she spoke added weight to her words. I could see that, for her, too, St Luke's had earned a special place in her esteem and affections.

I could no longer ignore that fast-growing seed-thought. 'Lord, do *you* want me to go to St Luke's?' I asked in my prayer time the next day. In response, a still, small voice seemed to say: 'I want you to go to St Luke's and I want you to write about your experiences there.'

I could no longer resist. That weekend I phoned Wendy. She was, as always, concerned for me and enthusiastic when I mentioned the hospital for the clergy. 'Oh, yes,' she said. 'I definitely think it would be right for you. You'll be so drained when you return from your six-week tour of New Zealand. You'll need that extra care they give you there. Instead of feeling that you're a patient in hospital, you'll feel at home – as though you're having a rest in a big, Victorian Rectory. It even has its own garden where you'll be able to sit out when you're convalescing, its own library where you can browse and borrow books and a lovely chapel where you'll be able to be still. You'll really love that.'

'But what about visitors?' I protested. 'London's a long way from Nottingham. David won't be able to come every day and neither will people from the parish. Didn't you feel lonely?' 'Oh no,' Wendy responded. 'People really have time for you in St Luke's. The nurses and the consultants, the chaplain and the domestics – and even the Matron come and sit with you and chat to you. There's no chance of being lonely. You're treated as a person not just a patient. It really is fantastic. And it's possible, you know, to have too many visitors when you're not feeling well. They can drain you so there are advantages in being so far away – especially when you're a clergy wife.'

What Wendy was saying was making perfect sense but I voiced another fear. 'Wendy, it all sounds rather elitist,' I protested. I went on to tell her about the spiritual journey I had embarked on five months earlier and how contemplating Christ had high-lighted for me his love of the poor, the marginalised, the deprived. 'I've been asking God to make me more like Jesus,' I confessed, 'to help me identify with the poor and those on the fringe of society – the people he lived with when he was on earth. This feels like the other end of the social spectrum. It smacks of private medicine and privilege and though I can see that that feels right to some people, it doesn't feel right for me at this moment.'

Looking back, I admire Wendy's patience as she continued to deal with my questions and qualms. She explained that what was on offer was not private medicine but pure gift. Charity. Private medicine is a privilege the patient pays for, charity is a gift a needy person receives. Charity (*charis*) quite literally means grace – unearned, undeserved love. 'The consultants who work at St Luke's see you and operate on you in their own free time,' she explained. 'They all work in London teaching hospitals but this is their gift to the clergy and their dependants. They're not paid a penny for the work they do at St Luke's. If you go there, you'll simply be on the receiving end of their compassion and kindness and I know you won't regret it.'

Wendy had given me a great deal to contemplate. The choice was mine. For several days I was in turmoil. A large part of me wanted to remain in Nottingham to become a patient among the people with whom I live and work; I did not want to be treated as a special, privileged person. Yet I could not resist the deeper draw, which I believed to have come from God, to accept humbly and gratefully, what was being offered by the staff of St Luke's.

The eye of the storm

I telephoned the medical secretary at St Luke's and discovered that if I wanted to explore the possibility of becoming a patient there, my doctor would need to write on my behalf. My doctor wrote. Within two weeks I was travelling to London to see a consultant.

The arrival of Spring seemed to coincide with the date of this first consultation. Blackbirds and chaffinches chirped lustily and harmoniously as I walked from my home to the station. And as I ambled from the Underground to the consulting room, I relished the warm, spring sunshine and lingered in Regent's Park to gaze at 'God's grandeur'[4]: the carpet of blue-bells and hyacinths which embalmed the air with their heady scent. I marvelled that here in the heart of the capital, the Creator's handiwork could be obscured neither by the noise nor the senseless way people and traffic rushed through the overcrowded streets.

Despite these flashes of pure pleasure, I detected within myself the nervousness I normally experience when I suspect that I shall be invited to present my own medical case history. Was it this nervousness which drove me out of the sunshine and into the consulting room half an hour before the time of my appointment? Probably. Although on the train journey I had jotted down the notes I felt I would need if I was to paint an accurate picture for the consultant, I still lacked confidence in my ability to give him the necessary information.

No one seemed to mind that I arrived early. I was welcomed with kindness and courtesy before being shown into the consultant's tastefully furnished waiting room. The inviting armchairs, the neat pile of magazines and the restful decor helped me to relax and unwind. I was just beginning to savour the peace (there were no other patients there), the pleasing surroundings and the magazine I had thumbed through when I heard voices in the corridor outside. A patient came into the waiting room and jerking her head in the direction of the consulting room, whispered reassuringly, 'He's very nice'! Before she had time to elaborate, 'he', a slight man with greying hair and twinkling eyes stepped into the room. He stretched out his hand and shook mine warmly, introduced himself, smiled and said: 'You've come a long way. Your reward for being early is that I can see you straight away. My next patient seems to have been delayed.' And he led me into his consulting room.

The consultant was not wearing a white hospital coat, but a smart, pin-striped suit and a red tie. Neither did he invite me to exchange my clothes for a shapeless hospital gown. On the contrary, he commented approvingly on what I was wearing as he invited me to take a seat opposite him. Sheila Cassidy, herself a doctor, underlines how important such seemingly-simple gestures are for the patient:

'A patient coming up to see the doctor for the first time will consciously or unconsciously dress themselves in such a way as to present themselves as they would wish to be seen. Their clothes are body language which declare who they are, individual people with their own tastes and ideas. If we ask people to remove their clothes and put on a uniform before they meet the doctor, we are removing from them some of the protective armour they need for this difficult interview. We are in fact depersonalising them, treating them as objects and we make them less able to communicate effectively because they are nervous and embarrassed.

In the same way, if a third party is present at the medical consultation the patient is frequently inhibited. It matters nothing that the third party is a nurse, that she is a professional, that she is friendly: her presence will alter the interaction between doctor and patient and reduce the communication.'[5]

Was it the absence of the hospital gown and the customary 'third party' which made it easy for me to respond to the consultant's invitation to tell him my story in my own way and my own time? Or was it the fact that he looked, not blank or bored, but interested while I was talking? I suspect that each of these gestures played their part in freeing me to pour out my story precisely as I remembered it – without referring to my notes.

From time to time the consultant made an entry in his medical file but his eyes and face conveyed to me a vitally important piece of information – that he was listening attentively and compassionately; that he was listening, not just to my medical history, but to me; that he was concerned, not just about a diseased gall bladder, but about my person. Such listening is an art form which, as a counsellor, I am attempting to master. Being on the receiving rather than the giving end, I was discovering, is a most healing, liberating experience. Despite my limited medical vocabulary, in the presence of such a caring listener, instead of becoming inarticulate as I normally do on such occasions, I found it comparatively easy to trace the events which had resulted in this consultation.

By the time the consultant invited me to go through to the examination room, the patient–doctor bond of trust which is in itself so healing, had been well and truly forged. Even so, I squealed when the consultant prodded the still-tender area surrounding the gall bladder. We both laughed as it seemed to confirm the correctness of the diagnosis which had already been made. The presence of gall stones made surgery seemingly inevitable and urgent.

'Put your clothes back on and, when you're ready, we'll talk about the options,' he said kindly.

By this time, I was feeling so secure in the relationship which had been established that I was able to air the questions which still bothered me. Was surgery really necessary? What about laser treatment? And what about the trip to New Zealand which was now only days rather than weeks away?

He dismissed none of these questions but dealt with them one by one.

He explained why, in this instance, he took the view that surgery would be preferable to laser treatment and, by this time, I trusted him sufficiently to accept his judgement without further question.

I also voiced my anxiety about the New Zealand trip. He allayed my fears by giving me a safe framework in which to operate: 'I want you to go on a strict no-fat diet,' he instructed. 'By no-fat, I mean no fat – not even giving yourself the luxury of spreading butter or margarine on your bread. It sounds rather boring, I'm afraid, but it should help to keep the problem under control. I will also prescribe pain killers just in case you have an attack and write a covering letter so that, should you have any trouble taking them through customs, you can show that you have these drugs in your possession for medical reasons.' We went on to explore possible dates for the surgery which, he insisted, should take place as soon as possible after my return. And he warned that I must clear the diary so that after the operation there would be time 'to queen it' and to convalesce.

Suddenly I felt safe; confident that, not only was the New Zealand trip right, but that I could cope with it and that, in some strange way which I could not yet foresee, the impending experience of hospitalisation was to be an adventure and the enforced convalescence a God-given time of 'hiddenness'.

I had no more questions, so the consultant rose from his chair, shook my hand again, said a warm and sincere goodbye and said, with a genuineness which added to the surprises he had already given me that day: 'I'll be pleased to do the operation for you at St Luke's and I look forward to working with you.'

I walked out of his consulting room to be dazzled by the spring sunshine which was still warming the streets of London. I was dazed, too, with joy. I felt so energised by the sense of well-being I was enjoying that I walked at a brisk pace from the consulting room to St Pancras Station where I waited for my return train to Nottingham.

As I sipped coffee in the cafeteria, I glowed with gratitude. I had been heard, understood, cared for, respected and I felt strangely whole, valued, glad to be alive. I kept turning over in my mind the realisation that what the consultant had heard was not simply my medical history but my hopes and fears, my uncertainties and questions. What he had been treating was not just another gall bladder problem but a person called Joyce. Me. And what he had given me was not just his competence as an eminent surgeon, though he had given me that, he had given me compassion, human warmth communicated through touch and smiles, caring eyes and tone of voice, the compassion which carries healing in its wings because *com* (with) *passion* literally *suffers with*. His genuineness had conveyed to me a healing message. I mattered. It mattered what happened to me. Yet he had heard from me nothing that he did not already know. My notes had been sent from Nottingham and he had seen the result of the scan. What he was doing, I realise in retrospect, was establishing with me a rapport which Sheila Cassidy describes so beautifully:

'It is in the telling of the story that I meet my patient and in my listening to him that he meets me. This first meeting is a pivotal one in establishing a therapeutic relationship and it may take up to an hour – sometimes longer. But it is time well spent for in that hour one can establish bonds of trust and confidence which are the practical tools for later "work". Everything depends on the quality of my listening: the patient must understand clearly from my verbal and non-verbal cues that I am interested in him as a person as well as in his physical problems. This means not only paying careful attention as he speaks, but asking him to clarify issues which I do not understand. As his story unfolds I make notes and if it does not emerge spontaneously, I ask not only what happened . . . but how he *felt* about it then – and how he *feels* now. This exploration of the emotional as well as the physical component . . . is the key to establishing a supportive relationship. It is often the first time a patient has been asked by a doctor – or indeed by anyone – how he feels.'[6]

I had been with my consultant for less than thirty minutes but, as I wrote in my Prayer Journal in the cafeteria on St Pancras Station, 'I feel cherished'. Being heard had changed the water of a visit to London into the wine of a healing encounter.

Awakened to new depths

'I wish everyone could be on the receiving end of the kind of care which I've just received,' I muttered to myself while I continued to mull over the events of the day. 'I wish everyone had someone who would listen, not just to their words or what they project but to their innermost needs and feelings so that they feel loved and cherished, accepted and supported as I do.' I was still in the coffee shop; still sipping my coffee. At that very moment, I became aware of a commotion near the door. Looking up to see who was creating the disturbance, I saw a shabbily dressed man shove a scantily dressed woman into a chair near the window. The woman, who looked as though she was in her early fifties, was trembling all over. From pain? From cold? From fear? I had no way of telling. What I could tell was that she was one of London's powerless people.

The man, whose gestures were rough but whose intentions were obviously kind, shuffled off in the direction of the food counter and I presumed he was going to buy her a drink. After he had moved, there was no one between the woman and me so I could see her clearly. I noticed that her lined face bore the hallmarks of intense suffering. Lumps of her thin, dyed hair had already fallen out leaving her hair dishevelled and incapable of disguising the ugly, bald patches disfiguring her head. As I gazed at her, I felt the pain of her helplessness and, to my embarrassment, I found myself weeping for her. Huge tears rolled down my cheeks and dropped into my coffee. When I was able to focus through the blur of my tears, I noticed the woman was staring at me. I longed that *she* should feel as cherished as I had felt that day so I smiled – a weak, watery smile. At first she looked startled. Suspicious. Eventually, she smiled back. Gradually, she stopped shaking and relaxed and when her companion brought her a steaming hot drink and a hamburger, she ate and drank and from time to time looked in my direction. Each time she did so, we both smiled and I prayed that my smile might convey to her at least a fraction of the compassion I felt for her and her plight.

Some ten minutes later, I had to tear myself away to catch my train. Should I give the woman money? Should I say something to her? These questions bothered me. Even though I sensed that it would be unhelpful to do either, the questions continued to plague me as the train sped from St Pancras to Nottingham. The picture of that woman plagued me, too. She personified powerlessness and helplessness, conditions with which, like others in pain, I now readily identified.

I had forgotten, until the gall bladder storm demolished my defences, how the prospect of surgery paralyses people; how it leaves them feeling stripped of their independence, at the mercy of others, utterly dependent on well-wishers, not simply for their sense of well-being but for their survival. I had forgotten, until I went through the agonies of waiting for hospital appointments and X-ray results that such uncertainty snatches the controls of life from the patient's hands and forces them to hand over the reins to people they neither know nor necessarily trust. I had forgotten that this is not only unnerving and frustrating but that it is both terrifying and threatening.

There in the train, I closed my eyes and recalled how, a few days before, I had been contemplating the Christ who fed the five thousand; how I had seemed to see Jesus besieged by a rabble of unruly people each with their own handicap: of blindness or deafness, lameness or bearing the burden of a sick or dying relative. The words which drew me were: 'Jesus was full of compassion.' The realisation had dawned that he healed them and fed them because he loved them. That realisation prompted another prayer: that he would increase in me his compassion for the poor and the hungry and help me to discern how to help them appropriately.

On St Pancras Station, one of my prayers had been answered. I had suffered with that powerless woman in some small measure. And in the consulting room, I had discovered what such compassion conveys. There I had been the powerless one, the one needing help. Through his compassion, my consultant had given me acceptance, understanding, hope of deliverance. These are Kingdom words. They had been communicated in a Kingdom way. And they were healing.

A few days later, I met my prayer guide. When I told him

what had happened on St Pancras Station, he pointed out that what I was identifying with in this woman was the fear and frustration, the helplessness and uncertainty which characterises more than two-thirds of the world every day they exist: victims of famine and war, violence and rape; the unemployed and the homeless, the bereaved and the depressed, those destined to sleep in cardboard city or in bus shelters, those locked up in prison, the childless, relatives of the dying, couples contemplating divorce, thousands whom society has rejected as well as the lonely rich. This changed my attitude towards the impending hospitalisation and convalescence. I began to look on them as a challenge and a privilege as, suddenly, I saw that my small storm of pain and uncertainty was not simply giving me a glimpse from a position of strength into the problems faced by powerless people, they were providing me with insights which can only be gleaned from the inside, from in-touchness and identification. These insights had brought me face to face with one way of living my prayer: I could come close to those in need simply by offering them my own vulnerability. The incident in the cafe was showing me how healing this could be. My small storm, I sensed, was not only under the watchful, caring eye of God. It was a gift.

2

Many Ports in the Storm

'We all need those people in our lives whose acceptance, understanding, and love for us creates an atmosphere that feels like home . . .'[1]

In the weeks that spanned my first consultation and my admission to hospital, my eyes were opened to a spirituality which is lived rather than spoken about. Such a spirituality, I discovered, creates a safe harbour where the vulnerable may find support and shelter. Through it and the people who flesh it out, God comes.

Some people expressed their support through prayer. One of the house groups attached to our church, for example, promised that while we were on our travels in New Zealand they would pray for us every Tuesday when they met for their evening time of fellowship. When the winds of worry or disappointment or home-sickness threatened to demolish my peace of mind, the awareness of their commitment seemed to anchor me in the love of God and the home fellowship.

Members of a church on the outskirts of Nottingham, some of whom we have never met, also covenanted to pray for us every day. They asked for details of our speaking engagements so that they could be as specific as possible as they interceded on our behalf.

Whole communities, similarly, generously offered to make a prayer priority of our trip to New Zealand. These, too, asked for details of the tour though I knew they would not be unduly concerned about the sparcity of the information we gave. They had learned that to intercede does not mean to plead with a God who is reluctant to give good things to his people. Rather, to intercede simply means to come before a good, loving, generous, all-knowing God with people and situations on our heart.

Many not only prayed, they wrote to remind us of their love. Their letters were lifelines: they reminded me of an observation once made by Henri Nouwen: 'A good letter can change the day for someone in pain . . . can create a smile and bring joy to the heart.'[2]

Thoughtfulness

When we broke our journey in Singapore, we were to discover that Christians there were praying for us too and, as always, translating their prayer into action.

We were met at Changi Airport by our long-standing friend, Keith Chua. Keith owns the hotel where we were to stay for three days. Despite a hectic schedule, he had come himself to meet us rather than merely send a hotel car. 'I knew you would be tired from the trip,' he explained when we expressed our thanks. 'And, anyway, you're not here for long this time and I wanted to spend as much time with you as possible.' This thoughtful gesture touched us deeply. And so did the warmth of the welcome expressed by our many other friends on the island; young people who used to worship in our church in Nottingham when they were students. Though they now hold down responsible positions, they still make time to express care for us each time we visit Singapore.

Three days seemed frustratingly short for this visit but, thanks to the kindness and efficiency of the girl who used to live with us and who still seems a part of our family, we met most of our friends over a celebratory no-fat meal in one of Singapore's famous sea-food restaurants. There we all enjoyed reminiscing and catching up on the news of years. One couple was unable to spend that evening with us. Late one evening, they took the trouble to visit us at our hotel bringing with them their four-year-old daughter and their little baby – an addition to the family we had not heard about but whom they wanted to introduce to us because they have called her Joyce to remind them of our friendship.

As well as meeting friends, addressing a group of Christians and doing a little counselling, David and I carved out time to relax and pray. I continued to contemplate Christ as he is portrayed in the Gospels and as I explained to my prayer guide in the taped messages I sent him, I was discovering that my prayer and my life were becoming inextricably intertwined rather than compartmentalised as they had been in the past. My prayer even seemed to penetrate my dream world.

One night, just before I left home, a vivid dream had made an indelible impression on me. I dreamed that a tramp had stumbled through our garden gate and vomited all over my herb garden. Instead of feeling outraged as I might normally have done, I felt full of compassion for him and wanted to go to him because I saw him, not as an intrusion, but as someone whom Christ loves. Recording that dream in my Journal next morning, I observed: 'I went further. I *believed* (in the sense that I accepted without being able to fully understand) what Jesus meant when he said: "Whatever you did for one of the least of these brothers of mine, you did for me" ' (Matthew 25:40). This belief hit me with the force of a revelation. It made a very deep impression on me. I was reminded of this one day while David and I were enjoying a chicken-rice lunch. I found myself staring, first at the other customers who were sampling the special dishes offered by the enthusiastic and welcoming fast-food stall-holders and then at the elderly woman whose task it was to clear and clean the tables after the customers had left. I looked at her skeleton-like limbs and at the face which seemed lined with anxiety and my heart began to bleed for her. While we were all eating more than we needed, I wondered whether she ever sat down to a nourishing square meal. If she did, there was no evidence of this in her physique. If she did not, what did following Christ mean in this and similar situations?

I continued to turn this question over in my mind as we tore ourselves away from Singapore and its people and as we re-discovered that compassion kiwi-style is no less lavish than the Singaporean expression of it. Once again, people seemed to have projected themselves into our shoes and anticipated our needs – for privacy and fellowship, to meet stimulating people and to spend time together as a couple and I was moved when I discovered that our many hostesses had taken my no-fat diet seriously and had used their creativity to concoct colourful, attractive and appetising fat-free meals. Such thoughtfulness, in one sense, seemed so simple. Yet it indicated the love with which we were enveloped throughout the trip.

Whether we were staying in the home of stranger, or of people we knew, whether we were leading Quiet Days or speaking at large conferences, whether what we were saying proved popular or controversial, the attitude toward us as people was always the same: one of warmth and generosity; one of genuine hospitality Henri Nouwen describes so well when he claims that 'hospitality is the creation of a free and friendly space where we can reach out to strangers and invite them to be our friends.'[3]

Within the free and friendly spaces of North Island, we forged many firm friendships – so much so that to leave felt like a real wrench. As we flew from Auckland, we recalled some of the people who had assured us that they had been drawn closer to God through the Quiet Days we had led, some who claimed that their marriages had been touched through the marriage retreats we were privileged to conduct and the young people whose love and understanding of God had so evidently deepened during our time together at the student conference in Auckland. I reflected, too, on what the Christians in New Zealand had conveyed to me: that giving expression to our prayer often involves us in giving unobtrusive, hidden help just where we are. As someone has put it, 'blooming where we are planted'.

Despite the love which had been lavished on us, both David and I were exhausted.

Such ministry sounds romantic but is, we find, costly and draining as well as rewarding. John Sanford explains one reason in his helpful book *Ministry Burnout*:

'the energy drain that comes from working with people who are in need is subtle. One hardly uses one's physical energy in working with such people, but mentally and spiritually one becomes depleted. It is like having a small but constant loss of blood . . . energy is used up in supplying energy to the other person. This is so even if the person in need is a fine person whom we like; it is all the more so if the needy person is difficult, demanding, or clinging.'[4]

Another reason is that 'relationships require energy . . . A true relationship is an effort; we must put energy into it in order to get energy from it.'[5] On a trip of this nature, one meets many needy people who seek help. This trip had been no exception and at the same time we had invested a great deal of ourselves in forming warm and close relationships. Although we returned home in two stages my energy level remained at a low ebb. Suddenly, the impending operation loomed large on the horizon and the thought of it filled me with horror.

The sacrament of the laying on of hands

This sense of alarm deepened during my first weekend at home. I was co-leading a retreat for the contemplative prayer group in our church. I had long looked forward to meeting members of this group and to sharing with them some of the good things God had done in answer to their prayers. But I found, when I arrived at the retreat house, that, though my body had been jetted back to England, my heart was still in New Zealand and, as we went into silence for the second part of the weekend, fear, like an oil slick, edged its way towards me. Like a seagull caught in the sticky substance, I found myself incapable of doing anything to combat the paralysing and terrifying consequences.

Up to this moment, I had been buoyed up by people's prayers and love. Surgery had seemed nothing more than a far-distant obstacle to be negotiated in due course. Now 'St Luke's' was the next entry in my diary and I knew I was not ready. I was due to leave for London two days after the end of the retreat but I had not yet unpacked from the overseas' trip. To add to this pressure, I became increasingly troubled by a ticklish cough which caused me to question whether the hospital would admit me as planned. And now terror compounded the problem.

'Everyone is afraid of pain,' Sheila Cassidy claims in her book *Sharing the Darkness*, 'and well they may be for it saps the strength and crowds the consciousness'.[6] What people in pain want 'more than anything is that this thing should not be happening to them, that it should turn out to be a bad dream, that they should be rescued, cured, kissed better, made whole.'[7] Those who suffer 'are a bottomless pit of longing. They long for healing, for wholeness, for comfort, for affirmation, for love.'[8]

This was certainly my experience that weekend. As I expressed it in my Journal a few days later: 'On the Sunday afternoon, while the retreatants were doing their collages, I went up to the chapel, and, lying prostrate on the floor, I nose-dived into a deep and terrible dread of the impending physical pain. Every part of my being cried out, screamed out against it. But eventually I was brought to that place of submission which could say with integrity. "Not my will, but yours be done. If it is not possible for this cup to be removed, then I will drink it."'

I love the verse in St Luke's Gospel which reminds us that when Jesus said his yes to the Father in Gethsemane, 'an angel from heaven appeared to him and strengthened him' (Luke 22:43). I treasure, too, the memory of those rescuing hands which reached out to me in that prayer-saturated chapel.

The retreatants and the other retreat giver, Margaret, concerned about my cough as well as the gall bladder problem, had expressed a desire to give me the sacrament of the laying on of hands before the end of the retreat. In his thoughtful and thought-provoking book *Touch: An Exploration*, Norman Autton reminds us that 'the laying on of hands is no magical gesture. It is a sacramental act of much spiritual significance.'[9] He reminds us that 'in sickness physical touch can be seen as an antidote to fear and anxiety, freeing and mobilizing the body's natural healing and calming the troubled mind and spirit.'[10]

In the Church of England's service for the sick, the laying on of hands is described as an act of obedience: 'Our Lord

Jesus Christ went about preaching the gospel and healing. He commanded his disciples to lay hands on the sick that they might be healed.'[11]

And Bishop Morris Maddocks stresses that 'the laying on of hands, accompanied by the prayer of the Church, is a spiritual ministry of great power ... When used for healing ... [it] draws the sufferer more closely into the Body of Christ so that the health of Jesus Christ may be received by the sufferer through the body. It is a linking into the life and vitality ... which find their source in Christ. Those who minister are used as the channel for this healing power, as the link in this chain of grace.'[12]

There in that chapel, the retreatants formed the links in my chain of grace. Gathering round me, they laid hands on me, anointed me with oil and prayed that God would grant his 'healing and peace according to his loving and gracious will'.[13] As they prayed, it was as though gentle hands were rescuing me – lifting me out of the slime of the oil slick and bathing me in a cleansing, liberating detergent. I stopped struggling and simply soaked up the powerful peace in which I now felt held. I experienced what Macrina Wiederkehr describes so beautifully:

> 'In the midst of these holy winds
> In the midst of this divine wrestling
>   your storm journey
>   like all hurricanes
>   leads you into the eye,
> Into the Eye of God
>   where all is calm and quiet.
> A stillness beyond imagining!'[14]

Sensitivity

The laying on of hands can take place anywhere: in the home or in hospital, during a service or at some other time. Part of its power is that, through the touch of another person, the love and care of God is powerfully and mysteriously conveyed. This means, of course, that such a ceremony must be conducted with the utmost sensitivity bearing in mind the particular person on the receiving end of this ministry. There are times when this sacrament is best given in complete silence. While one person lays their hands lightly on the head of the person being prayed for, the others gather round and pray silently and lovingly. On other occasions, the use of liturgical prayer or quiet, spontaneous prayer may make a moving and meaningful contribution. Sometimes the person being prayed for might appreciate some singing such as some of the quiet worship choruses which are popular in many Christian circles today or one of the plaintive Taizé chants which have taken so many thousands of Christians deeper into an awareness of the love of God.

When such sensitivity characterises the people and the occasion, the laying on of hands almost always proves to be a most moving experience where God's power and presence and the sense that he is at work in some hidden way can be felt. When such sensitivity is absent, on the other hand, the ceremony can scar the memory of the person being prayed for. Norman Autton explains that one reason for this is that touch reduces the distance which divides people: 'Each person lives as if with an invisible fence around his body, a fence that keeps others at that distance with which he feels most safe and comfortable. We know little . . . about the conditions under which a person will permit another to touch him, and little of the consequences of body contact.'[15]

We know that each person is unique in their response to giving and receiving touch. Some feel threatened by physical contact – even the laying on of hands. Others can be crushed by it. Many, on the other hand, welcome it. When we judge the situation accurately, discerning both the desire and the need for such touch, we give to the person the sense of well-being and peace I have described from my own experience. When we misjudge or mistime the situation, and particularly when touch is not gentle, even the laying on of hands can seem like an invasion of privacy, an intrusion, even a 'put-down'. The sufferer then experiences, not the prayed-for 'shalom', but the forfeit of peace.

Burden bearing

Because people in pain feel so vulnerable, they frequently fail to give clear messages to those trying to help them so that it is not clear whether touch will or will not be acceptable. The ability of one retreatant to exercise sensitivity was fully stretched by the mixed message I gave her just before the retreat began. She was someone who had prayed for our trip and whose letters I had valued while I had been 'down under'; I valued the closeness this correspondence had fostered. Before we went into silence that weekend, we walked through the meadows where, sitting together to marvel at the beauty of England in May, I began to describe some of the highlights of our tour. I also found myself pouring out some of the anguish I felt now that our travels were over. And I wept. Seeing my tears, she placed her arm around me and allowed me to continue to cry quietly until the tears subsided.

As I look back, it still puzzles me that I felt able to share with her only a portion of my pain. Was it that she was a retreatant and I hesitated to spoil her retreat? Was it the age-old problem that clergy and their wives often find it hard to receive support from members of their own congregation – partly because it was drummed into many of us during training that it is inappropriate to make friends with one's parishioners? Was it pride? Was it that I was too sore to give or receive any more love at that moment, homesick as I still was for friends in New Zealand? Was I still fighting my own helplessness rather than receiving it as a gift and a trust? I don't know. I do know that, even though I drew this retreatant with one hand and kept her at arm's length with the other, her partially expressed and partially accepted offer of tenderness touched and strengthened me reminding me that caring is an offering which carries a powerful, persuasive message even when it is seemingly shunned or only half-accepted.

I also remember the sensitivity with which she wrote to me when the retreat was over. On her lovely card she reminded me that she remained in the wings waiting, loving and praying. If I needed or wanted her, she would come at any time. On the other hand, she would not feel offended if

I looked elsewhere for the help I needed. I knew she meant what she had written.

Many months later, she wrote to me again:

'I just wanted to tell you something of what [your sharing on retreat] had meant to me. Firstly, I felt privileged to be whatever support I was being to you at the time. I didn't understand what was happening but God used the situation to speak to me deeply again of what "bearing one another's burdens" is about. Somehow, in the way we were sitting, as I held you, your tears were trickling down my face and into the corner of my lips. So I was literally tasting your tears. And it seemed to me that the Lord was reminding me that I didn't have to understand or know about the source of someone's pain – sometimes I would simply be asked to enter into it without knowing the whys and wherefores. So the bitter taste of your salty tears was a reminder of all that and I am happy to be able to be available to be alongside you if and when it helps without making any demands or knowing things it may be neither helpful nor appropriate for me to know. I can't always think of the right things to say – maybe that's a good way of stopping me saying the wrong thing and encouraging me to listen rather than speak.'

'We all need those people in our lives whose acceptance, understanding, and love for us creates an atmosphere that feels like home',[16] claims Macrina Wiederkehr. We need them because they touch the running sores of our innermost being. As Henri Nouwen rightly observes:

'When we honestly ask ourselves which persons in our lives mean the most to us, we often find that it is those who, instead of giving much advice, solutions or cures, have chosen rather to share our pain and touch our wounds with a gentle and tender hand. The friend who can be silent with us in a moment of despair or confusion, who can stay with us in an hour of grief and bereavement, who can tolerate not-knowing, not-curing, not-healing and face with us the reality of our powerlessness, that is the friend who cares.'[17]

Such people are, I discovered, more than a port in the storm, they are the lifeline which enable the powerless to reach the sanctuary of the harbour.

A different kind of touch

The night the retreat ended, I hardly slept. By this time the ticklish cough which had troubled me all weekend had turned into a hacking one. Again, the dread of surgery swept over me. I felt ill-prepared for hospitalisation. Physically I was not ready because of this cough. Emotionally I was not ready because I had scarcely had time to unpack and insufficient time to re-orientate. Spiritually I was not ready because I was too tired from the trip and drained from leading the retreat to enjoy the stillness before God which re-energises me.

I phoned St Luke's to report my cough. The Sister who answered the phone thought that, in spite of it, there would be no problem in admitting me, as planned. 'The problem is,' she said, 'you're not on my list for this week's operations!' It transpired that, while I had been away, the date of my operation had been changed. A letter had been sent to my contact address in New Zealand but it had never reached me. The hospital staff were expecting me to arrive, not this week, but next.

Suddenly I was faced with the spaciousness of a week at home I had not expected to have. My anxiety vanished, the anger which had made me irritable with my husband disappeared and, although my case was partly packed, I felt gloriously free – the kind of freedom I imagine a penned-up sheep must feel when it is allowed into the meadow to graze.

I worked on my correspondence, cleared up the house and telephoned the friend with whom I had hoped to spend the Thursday of that week before the date of the operation had been fixed. We had cancelled that arrangement but, to my joy, he rearranged his diary yet again to make himself available for our time together. We agreed to meet in Derbyshire. This friend, Ian, is a monk and an experienced Spiritual Director. He and I had met only twice before. On both occasions we had been speakers at large Christian conferences. Ian is a Roman Catholic. I come from the evangelical wing of the church. Nevertheless, at one of these conferences, we had been making in public such similar claims about the nature of prayer, that our spiritual oneness had been joked about by the delegates. We determined that, at the first opportunity, we would meet.

We sat in the warm sunshine for the entire day, soaking up the sun and drinking in the exquisite freshness and greenness of Derbyshire in June. We talked – and talked and talked. Our minds and spirits touched and met in a quality of sharing which is rare in my experience but so infinitely precious when it happens. This gave birth to the kind of relationship Heather Ward, an author whose insights had helped both of us, describes so powerfully as 'Christian brotherhood':

> 'Christian brotherhood enables us to see ourselves as belonging to, and with, all others; to know that we share with them both our divine inheritance as a son of God and the unloveliness of the Prodigal Son among his pigs, and that we owe one another both reverence and the fellowship so often uniting beggars.'[18]

Perhaps it was because I sensed that we both knew that we were spiritual beggars that, when Ian asked the seemingly-innocent question, 'How are you really, Joyce?' I responded with a degree of honesty which even took me by surprise. 'I'm empty. Lonely.'

Ian looked neither surprised nor disapproving. It was as though Christians in positions of leadership made this kind of confession to him every day of his life. But I do not admit to such inner emptiness easily and the confession proved a most liberating one. Until I made it, I had not realised that since my return from New Zealand, a terrible loneliness and sense of spiritual impoverishment had been feeding the exhaustion. Or was it the other way round? That loneliness and spiritual bankruptcy were expressions of exhaustion? It did not really matter. What did matter was that, until this moment, I had not carved out the time to reflect on the spiritual hunger which had been gnawing away inside me.

Now, as I spread it before a perceptive, caring person, I saw it clearly.

As we talked about this poverty of spirit, Ian did not come across as a person who had never experienced such inner emptiness for himself or as one who had found all the answers. On the contrary, there was such a sense of mutuality and shared vulnerability between us that I sensed, in discussing these mysteries, we were both groping for an exit from a spiritual fog. Together we were exploring some of the reasons why Jesus claimed that such poverty of spirit was 'blessed'.

As the day wore on, we seemed to stumble on insights which excited us both. We thought of Heather Ward's claim that spiritual growth does not mean increase in size or 'in the number or quality of attributes, but increased responsiveness to God, increased receptiveness to his Spirit.'[19]

We talked of Pascal's term, 'the God-shaped vacuum' – by which he meant that inner chasm within each person which only God can fill. What was happening in each of us, we discerned with a growing sense of awe and excitement, was the realisation that inner emptiness need not be negative. It can be, and often is, the kind of capacity for God that Eric Abbott, one-time Dean of Westminster, describes when he claims that 'our soul is an emptiness for God to fill. . . . It is a loneliness for his divine friendship . . . And because we are *capax dei*, because we have a "capacity for God", we can receive Christ in ourselves; and we can receive that most characteristic of all his gifts, the gift of Peace.'[20]

Discovering with Ian this positive face of loneliness and emptiness certainly served to fill me with this peace. That night, I wrote in my Prayer Journal, 'I feel so glad, so joyful, so grateful, so excited. Thankyou for showing me that this gnawing emptiness is a gift – your gift; that you are carving out within me a greater capacity for you.'

The circumstances had not changed but I had changed. I had found, not just a port in the storm, I had re-discovered that my ship has an anchor. I had stopped feeling seasick. And I had entered once more into the eye of God and experienced his indescribable peace and light. I suddenly saw that the longing my emptiness was expressing was the yearning Evelyn Underhill describes when she speaks of the life which is a real life – 'being wholly for *thee*'. If I had known of the following prayer at that point in my pilgrimage, I would have used it. It portrays so much more eloquently than any words of mind, the positive face of the emptiness which was still there:

'O Holy Spirit of God –
come into my heart and fill me: . . .

I offer to Thee the one thing I really possess,
My capacity for being filled by Thee.
Of myself I am an empty vessel.
Fill me so that I may live the life of the Spirit,
The life of Truth and Goodness,
The life of Beauty and Love,
The life of Wisdom and Strength.

But, above all, make Christ to be formed in me,
That I may dethrone self in my heart
and make Him King;
So that He is in me, and I in Him.
Today and Forever.'[21]

The day spent with Ian gave me further evidence that my storm was not only under the eye of God, it was coming to me as a gift to nurture my person and my prayer:

'For your prayer
 your journey into God,
may you be given a small storm
 a little hurricane
 named after you,
persistent enough
 to get your attention
violent enough
 to awaken you to new depths
strong enough
 to shake you to the roots
majestic enough
 to remind you of your origin:
 made of the earth
 yet steeped in eternity

frail human dust
yet soaked with infinity.'[22]

Touch

When Ian left, other people took over as carers. This time
friends in the church seemed like valued and welcome gifts
from God. I think, in particular, of my last afternoon in
Nottingham.

A small group of middle-aged to elderly women meet
together in our Church hall on a Monday afternoon. I no
longer lead this Women's Fellowship but I do try to speak
at their meeting three times a year. Because my operation
had been postponed, I was able to honour my original agree-
ment to be with them on Monday, June 4th.

I have known many of these women for nearly eighteen
years. I love them and, although I see little of them, I know
that their affection and prayerful support is as strong as it
has always been. At the end of the meeting, as one by one
they said their personal goodbyes, I realised how important
non-demanding, sensitive touch can be. I am not the kind
of extrovert who thrives on enthusiastic or enveloping bear
hugs. These usually leave me feeling ill at ease. Smothered.
I am the kind of person who needs to feel loved and affirmed
and these women seemed to know, that day, how best to
express the concern they felt. Some just squeezed my hand
as they said goodbye. Others kissed me tenderly on the
cheek. Others gave me the kind of gentle hug I can cope
with. I came away feeling loved and joyful and walked home
relishing the sense of well-being their affection had given
me. I now felt ready in body, mind and spirit for the operation.

Physical contact had told me what I knew already but so
desperately needed to have underlined that day: that these
women were not only on my side, willing as well as praying
me back to wholeness, they were actually with me, alongside me in prayer and care. Their gestures of solidarity and
affection said so much more than even the most carefully-
chosen words could have communicated that day. Someone
has expressed it in a powerful though simple diagram:

Tension		Urge/need to		Act of		Soothing[23]
	→	be caressed	→	contact	→	effect

The prayer and the care, the burden bearing and the perceptive listening, and the tenderness of touch all expressed love *par excellence* and poured into me a strength I would not have enjoyed had I been left to struggle on alone.

This strength and sense of well-being remained with me as I finished packing on the day I left Nottingham. So much so that my friend and 'cleaning lady' laughed: 'You look as though you're about to go on holiday rather than into hospital', she said. I smiled. There was so much to smile about. God was answering that prayer I had written months before: that he would take the ordinariness of my gall-bladder problem and make it special. It *was* special. It was opening my eyes to the variety of ways there are of living one's prayer as opposed to simply saying one's prayers. I had known, in my head, the theory of this. Now, I was experiencing the power of it; learning in an unforgettable way what it means practically to incarnate the compassion of Christ. The realisation was creating a sense of anticipation as I made my final preparations for the now-imminent departure for St Luke's.

A Second Home

'You find power when you are at home because it is there that you are loved, cherished, and accepted just as you are, with all your frailty, fears, and flaws. It is there in that lovely dwelling place called home that you discover you don't have to be perfect to be loved.[1]

The 9.37 am from Nottingham to St Pancras seemed unusually crowded on June 5th, 1990. While I was looking for a suitable place to sit, I found myself 'drawn' to a particular couple without understanding why but since there was an empty seat opposite theirs, I settled myself into it.

As the train pulled out of Nottingham station, I thumbed through a computer magazine, made an entry into my Prayer Journal and then took out my New Testament. I had almost completed The Spiritual Exercises and this train journey seemed an excellent opportunity to meditate on one of the Resurrection appearances of Christ. I had read only a few lines when the man opposite me wandered off to the buffet car. Left on her own, the woman smiled at me and started a conversation: 'Do you do this journey often?' she asked. Not many sentences later, she explained that she and her husband were on holiday and that they lived in Auckland. My face must have lit up as I told her that I had only recently returned from there. She asked me what I had been doing in her homeland. And when I explained, *her* face lit up. She had heard about our visit from the pastor of the church she attends. We discovered that we had many friends and acquaintances in common and chatted happily about them and New Zealand all the way to St Pancras.

My case was heavy so I took a taxi to St Luke's. As the taxi driver inched his way towards Fitzroy Square, I detected within myself feelings of apprehension and excitement. But as I crossed the threshold of the hospital, the apprehension vanished and was replaced with a curious feeling of well-being which I can only describe as a sense of home-coming. It was as though I belonged; as though I had returned from a long journey to take a much-needed rest in a beloved place. Yet I had never even seen St Luke's before.

This sense of home-coming deepened as I made my way to the receptionist's desk. There, I was asked, not for my hospital number as I am when I attend my local hospital, but for my name. The receptionist smiled a warm, welcoming smile as she handed me a 'welcome pack'. She smiled again as she opened a drawer in her desk and drew from it a pile of cards and letters addressed to me. She then explained that my room was on the third floor.

I was just about to carry my case to the nearby lift when a priest appeared as though from nowhere. 'Let me carry that for you,' he offered. 'It looks heavy'. As we walked the few yards to the lift, he smiled and said, 'Didn't I see you at CRE?' (The Christian Resources Exhibition – an annual, four-day, interdenominational event which takes place at Sandown Park, Esher, Surrey and aims to bring under the same roof some three hundred exhibitors representing almost every aspect of the church's work including caring, mission and prayer as well as practicalities like travel and training. Two days after my return from New Zealand, I had spoken on prayer at the Exhibition.) I admitted that I had been at CRE whereupon he teased: 'Come to write another book have you? You'll find all yours in our library. They're very popular here.' Continuing to chat in this jocular, friendly way, he summoned the lift and accompanied me to the Third Floor. I was to discover later that this person who had greeted me so heartily and increased in me the sense of home-coming was Canon Peter Nicholson, the General Secretary, who takes competent charge of the hospital.

Welcome

The welcome did not stop there. Another member of the team now took over: the slim, fair-haired Staff Nurse on duty on the Third Floor. I had arrived at a busy time for her. Nevertheless, she made time to come into my room, welcome me personally, tell me about the hospital and give me yet more mail adding with a smile which revealed the dimple in her cheek: 'All the post seems to be for you today.' What she said next touched me very deeply: 'You can call me Katherine or Staff Nurse – whichever feels most comfortable to you.'

This comment was healing. It brought us both onto the same level. We met as two adults not as helper and helped. This not only warmed me to Katherine, it contributed to the sense that here I was being treated as a unique individual rather than a number, or worse, 'the gall bladder on the Third Floor'.

Sheila Cassidy has helped me to understand how important it is to the patient that they sense this:

'We have to learn to be whole person doctors because our patients are whole persons. It takes so much more time and energy. It is destroying our protective hierarchies, our sense of omnipotence. Our corridors of power have been invaded and we are having to learn humility! . . . Patients are liable to be treated as objects, rather than people. Perhaps I should rephrase this for neither I nor my colleagues would ever consider a patient as an "object". What happens is that, for a number of very complex reasons, doctors and nurses sometimes treat people in a way that makes them *feel* as if they are considered as objects. I have experienced it myself and I have heard the complaint from many patients. The nicest quote on the subject comes from a lady who died in our hospice a couple of years ago; she spoke angrily of junior hospital doctors as "underlings who argue about you as they go by".'[2]

There was nothing about Katherine which led me to believe or feel that I was an object rather than a person. Rather, she treated me as an adult – a responsible, intelligent human being. Before she handed me various forms to fill in and sign, she took the trouble to explain why they were needed and where they would go after I had completed them. She also explained what I could expect from the next few days. After I had filled in the forms, I should unpack and change into my nightie and dressing gown because a doctor would be doing various tests. After that, I could change back into my own clothes, enjoy the library, the garden or even go for a walk because I would not be under-going any other tests that day. The physiotherapist and the anaesthetist would visit me on Wednesday (today was Tuesday) and my operation would be performed on Thurs-day. Having explained carefully what was about to happen, she then left me to fill in the forms in my own time and at my own pace.

As I answered the questions on the forms, I thought over the surprises Katherine had given me. She had communi-cated the message that, although she was busy, she could create time for me – time to explain, time to respond to any questions I might have. She had also given me a glimpse of the freedom from rules and regulations which I was to appreciate so much in this hospital. More importantly, she had treated me with respect and shown me that, as far as it is possible to do so, the hospital would allow me to keep my hands on the reins of my life.

Sheila Cassidy explains why this is so important in the patient–nurse relationship:

'[Patients] want to have their illness explained to them in words that they can understand and to be consulted about its treatment. They want to retain their dignity as individuals and keep some control over their lives. They want to participate in their care and share in our decision-making. They want us to be honest with them, warm and humble. More than anything, they want us to combine our competence with compassion . . . to share the frightening darkness with them. More than anything, they need our love.'[3]

Katherine had begun to communicate this to me. I was soon

to discover that she was not the only one to do so. I had scarcely filled in the forms when a knock on the door heralded the entrance of another nurse. She introduced herself as Stephanie and explained that she had just popped in to welcome me. Her tell-tale accent told me that she was from New Zealand which increased the feeling that here on the Third Floor I had found a home from home.

Unceasing prayer

While I waited for Katherine to return to collect the forms, I opened my 'welcome pack'. It contained information about the hospital, the Annual Handbook for 1990, details of the services which are conducted twice weekly in the chapel and a leaflet called 'The Patient's Round'.

I opened this leaflet first and as I read it, I began to sense that it concealed a secret – the chief reason why the building conveys not simply a welcome, though it does do that, but a sense of shalom – a feeling of well-being, the assurance, to borrow the language of Mother Julian of Norwich, that 'all shall be well'.

In the left-hand margin of the leaflet a clock face reminds the reader of the various punctuation marks in the hospital day. The first was 7 am

'. . . day begins, everyone is beginning to rush around. Night staff off, day staff on . . . the first cup of tea. Pray for all the domestic staff who keep the hospital running day by day. Offer your whole day to God . . . your hopes and fears . . . pray for the patients next to you. . . .'

The next clock showed 11 am

'. . . ward rounds. Thank God for all the nursing staff and doctors . . . the physio and occupational therapists. Pray for the team in the operating theatre . . . surgeons and anaesthetists . . . for all those having oper-

ations today. Pray for courage and healing
for others and yourself . . . remember you
are part of the healing team too. . . .'[4]

and I found myself praying my own version of the familiar
prayer which appeared next on the sheet:

'Lord, make me an instrument of your peace,
where there is despair, let me bring hope;
where there is darkness, light;
where there is sadness, joy. . . .'

As I prayed this prayer, a holy hush seemed to fill the entire
room. It was the kind of hush which stuns me sometimes
when I enter a place where the unceasing cycle of prayer
being offered transforms a seemingly ordinary building and
turns it into holy ground. It was the kind of hush which
brings with it an awareness that the God who always
enfolds us with love is communicating that love so powerfully that he intends that we should tune into it, experience
it and be strengthened by it.

All I could do was to stop reading and simply relish the
sense of the divine presence.

'Holiness comes wrapped in the ordinary. There are burn-
ing bushes all around you', claims Macrina Wiederkehr in
her book *A Tree Full of Angels*. 'Glory comes streaming
from the table of daily life.'[5]

There, in the stillness of this hospital ward, while my
case was still full of my belongings and my letters remained
unopened, I experienced this for myself. Having dropped so
easily and unexpectedly into the kind of profound stillness
I associate with being on retreat I began to wonder whether
one of the reasons why I had tuned immediately into the
peace which transcends the busyness of this place was that
prayer is offered as unceasingly and faithfully in the hospital as it is in a convent, monastery or any other place that
has been 'bathed' in prayer. It is offered by the patients who
enter the hospital with their own discipline of prayer, it is
offered by the staff in their times of stillness before God and
through their work, it is offered by many of the supporters of
St Luke's who remember the unique ministry of this hospi-

tal in their personal and communal prayer times. This realisation filled me with a sense of awe and reminded me afresh of the power of that mysterious ministry entrusted to us by God – the ministry of intercession.

Freedom

Sounds from the kitchen which was opposite my room reminded me that lunch would soon be served so I started to unpack. It was then that I began to appreciate the sense of freedom which St Luke's offers its patients.

I had put in a request for a single room and this request had been granted. I wanted to make the room 'mine'. Home. And I had brought various treasures to help me: a small cross I had acquired in a convent in Blackpool which reminded me that the sisters there were praying for my hospitalisation, an exquisite cut-crystal candle holder with its tiny candle which had been given me by two special friends who would, I knew, be praying for me also, and a card which had been sent to me by the monks of Mount St Bernard Abbey in Leicestershire as a tangible reminder that they, too, were praying. This card is a favourite of mine. It has on it a picture and a verse. The picture is of a person resting in the cupped hand of Christ. The verse is a comforting one: 'See! I will not forget you. I have carved you on the palm of my hand' (Isaiah 43:15).

I had brought with me a large, blue, bath-sheet. I draped this over a stool I found in the room and, by placing on it my cross, my candle and my picture, found I had created a prayer corner which gave the room a feeling of home straightaway. The arrival of lunch interrupted my unpacking so while I ate, I opened the letters and cards which had arrived at the hospital ahead of me. I read each letter slowly, feasting on the messages of care and concern they conveyed. And I treasured each card: the two which had been hand-drawn for me by artistic friends, the hand-painted one with the purple violets, the carefully-chosen ones which also carried messages of love and affection. Each letter and each card contributed to the sense of well-being which now seemed to be flowing into me and by the time I had stood some of these treasures on my dressing table, others on my bedside locker and yet others on the top of my wardrobe, the room was transformed from a bare hospital ward to a cosy, comfortable home which seemed to be papered with tenderness.

After I had unpacked and changed into my night attire, I stretched out on my bed to doze. As I did so, I thanked God for all that I had received through the ministry of St Luke's so far: the welcome, the competence, the compassion and the comfort – and I had only been there for two hours!

> 'May you be given a small storm
> a little hurricane
> named after you . . .
> majestic enough
> to remind you of your origin
> made of the earth
> yet steeped in eternity
> frail human dust
> yet soaked with infinity'[6]

prays Macrina Wiederkehr. In giving thanks for my small storm, I became conscious that it was already highlighting for me answers to my questions: What are Kingdom values? What is Kingdom activity? I was seeing them enfleshed by members of the staff of St Luke's.

All-embracing

By the time the doctor had completed his tests, it was visiting time. My first visitor was a friend of mine, a priest who lives in London and with whom my husband and I enjoy a deep, spiritual oneness and rapport. He had offered to come to pray with me on this first day in hospital. Like me, he is someone who is very susceptible to atmospheres. As we sat and exchanged news, he suddenly said, 'This is a very special place isn't it? I sensed it as soon as I stepped inside the door. It is as though you can feel the presence of our Lord.' I thought back to my own encounters with that almost-tangible presence as I stepped across the threshold of the hospital and as I prayed in my room and nodded to indicate that I sensed I knew what he meant.

That afternoon, my room became even more like holy ground because this priest not only prayed for me with the laying on of hands which I have described in chapter 2, he had also brought with him a little phial of oil with which he anointed me. Again, as he prayed and laid his hands on me, the sense of the presence and compassion of God was so strong that, for a long while after he had gone, all I wanted to do was to remain still and to soak up this energy. I no longer needed to gaze longingly at that figure leaning on the cupped hand of Christ, I felt myself being held in his hand and supported by his love. The sense was so over-powering that even while I chatted to my next visitor, my daughter, about mundane matters, the sense of the divine presence did not evaporate. Tea arrived while my daughter was with me. To our surprise, instead of tea for one, tea for two was brought. I was to discover that this concern for the well-being of visitors as well as patients was typical of the all-embracing hospitality offered at St Luke's.

While we were enjoying our tea, Stephanie, the nurse on duty, appeared again. This time she was clutching a large bouquet of flowers. She stayed to admire them with us and then, without being asked, went off to find a suitable vase in which I was able to arrange them a little later that afternoon. 'Isn't she nice?', my daughter observed, sensing that I would be well cared for in this healing environment.

My daughter left and I explored the possibility of tele-phoning my husband to report on the many good things I had received that day already. A pay phone was brought immediately and I marvelled that nothing seemed too much trouble for the nursing staff or the domestic staff. They seemed to see themselves as servants of the patients.

Facilities

That evening, after my third visitor had left me, I discovered the hub of the hospital: the chapel. Situated on the ground floor, not far from the office and reception, Canon Nichol-son's room, the library and Matron's office, it is both an integral part of the building and yet set slightly apart. As I pushed open the door, that same stillness I had already encountered in my room met and almost over-powered me. It was so marked that it seemed to draw me deep into a restfulness of body, mind and spirit which nothing could disturb – not the regular rumblings of the trains which rush under it nor the sound of someone polishing the corridor outside, nor even the awareness that surgery was now imminent. In this place of prayer, nothing mattered except the consciousness of the love which seemed to be flowing from the heart of God himself.

I gazed at the beautiful reredos with its symbols of Love: the figure of Christ hanging on the Cross and the icon of the Creator holding the world in his hand. And I turned over in my mind some insights I had gleaned from a book I had been reading in my room: *A Year Lost and Found* by Michael Mayne, Dean of Westminster.

In this book, the author, reflects on his prolonged period of illness and on the Passion of Christ and highlights the power of powerlessness. He shows that in Gethsemane even when Jesus abandoned himself to others and allowed his hands to be bound, he was just as powerful as when he was free to roam the countryside exercising his teaching and healing ministry. 'Nowhere is Jesus more powerful than in his passive suffering on the Cross'[7] even though here he is 'not the one who *does* but the one who is *done to*.'[8]

That phrase, 'not the one who does, but the one who is done to' struck a chord in me. This is the condition of every patient. It was about to become my experience. Michael Mayne makes this connection and observes:

'The image of God is to be seen in us – as it was in Jesus – equally in our *active* lives, in our work and our creativity, and in our *passive* lives, by the way we accept and respond to things that are done to us. Or . . . as we endure illness, by our response to the things which are done for us. This means that those forced to be inactive by lack of work or handicap or illness or old age need not feel they are of any less value as human beings. Rather, this time can be seen as a true and creative sharing in the nature of a God who himself became powerless and vulnerable.'[9]

I pondered on these claims which had come to me with the power of a revelation. Was I on the verge of plumbing the depths of that curious prayer of St Paul: that he might become like Christ in his death? Could this provide me with a goal for my convalescence? Could I expect Christ to shine through my helplessness?

Helplessness! There, in front of me, in that figure on the Cross, I could see helplessness and brokenness personified. For nearly half an hour I simply gazed at that crucified figure and allowed these embryonic insights to trickle from my head into my heart. Within forty-eight hours, I would be one of the passive, inactive ones having things done to me by the surgeon and his team. I prayed that I might discover the power of powerlessness and, like Michael Mayne, so learn the lessons of my illness that I would value them and view them as a vital part of my journey into God.

After I had prayed this prayer, I again luxuriated in the stillness and identified with the hero of a story I often tell when I speak on prayer at meetings, retreats or Quiet Days.

The story is of a peasant who lived in Ars in Southern France; a person who was drawn as by a magnet to the love of God. So much so that on his way to the fields in the morning as on his way home in the evening, he would leave his shovel and axe at the church door, enter the building and sit soaking up this love.

The regularity of his visits did not go unnoticed by his priest who asked him one day: 'Tell me, what do you do when you come and sit in the church like this?' The peasant simply replied: 'I look at him and he looks at me and we tell each other that we love each other.'

The 'Communion of Saints'

Still sensing that oneness with the French peasant, that night, as I prepared for bed, I turned again to the leaflet which had formed a part of my 'welcome pack'. On the last page, the hands on the face of the clock marked 9.30 pm:

 'evening ... sun sets ... you are by yourself with your thoughts ... remember those in pain, those frightened of death.... All day long you have been surrounded by the love of God ... it has been in the surgeon's knife ... the eyes of your friends ... the nurse's hands ... and now it is in the solitude of the night ... sleep now.'[10]

I prayed one of the prayers from the leaflet: another favourite of mine; a prayer which comes from the Office of Compline and which would, I knew, be echoing round the whole world:

'Be present, O merciful God, and protect us through the silent hours of this night, so that we who are wearied by the changes and chances of this fleeting world, may repose upon thy eternal changelessness; through Jesus Christ our Lord. Amen.'[11]

As I switched off the light, I thought of some of my friends who would already have prayed that prayer and I felt humbled to be a part of God's great family; part of the 'Communion of Saints'.

Sleep did not come at once. But it did not matter. I was at peace, content to enjoy the calming atmosphere which penetrated the night hours just as much as it transformed the day-time; content, too, to know that night-time in England marks day-time in New Zealand where more friends would be praying. As John Ellerton, a hymn writer who died just after St Luke's was founded put it:

'We thank Thee that Thy Church unsleeping,
While earth rolls onward into light,
Through all the world her watch is keeping,
And rests not now by day or night.

As o'er each continent and island
The dawn leads on another day,
The voice of prayer is never silent,
Nor dies the strain of praise away.'[12]

I prayed for the other patients none of whom I had yet met, for the night staff who had been as kind and welcoming as the day-time team, for Matron who was working such long hours and for my husband who would have no idea how enriched and re-energised I was already feeling.

I became aware, as I prayed, that I was not alone. It was not just that the God who has promised 'I will never leave you or forsake you' was with me, though I still sensed his presence. Rather, there was the awareness that others in the hospital were praying; that others had been praying year in and year out, day in and day out, night in and night out for nearly one hundred years. I was but a very small drop in the great ocean of prayer which flowed into and out of this place. It was such a humbling and awe-inspiring realisation that I found it a privilege to be there – just one of the thousands who had discovered in this building that we live the whole of our lives under the caring eye of God – even when we are sick.

Consistency

What I was not aware of that night as I turned over in my mind the kindness with which I had been welcomed in this hospital which already felt like home was that so many of my own experiences had been expressed by former patients in letters of thanks. These, I was to discover later, are stored in files on the ground floor in the General Secretary's office.

Had I had access that night to the letters and reports which I have since been privileged to read, I might well have worked into the small hours attempting to piece together parts of the jig-saw which make up a fascinating and moving picture of the ministry of St Luke's and show so clearly that the care which was being expressed to me has been offered to countless others down the generations.

From the very beginning, for example, patients seem to have found in St Luke's a second home. I think of a letter penned by a patient as early as 1894: 'I came here much broken down, and thanks under God, to the skill and kindly care bestowed so unweariedly upon me, I am going out quite another man . . . One thing I am quite sure will last my life – the remembrance of the graciousness with which I was welcomed, as to a real home, and with which I have been nursed and cared for, as though by the oldest and dearest friends.'

A year later, in 1895, a patient wrote; 'Allow me to send the committee of St Luke's House my very sincere thanks for the kindness and attention given to my child and for the surgical skill obtained through your institution. "Home" let me rather call it, for in every way Mrs . . . and I found this to be no mere paper claim, but a most happy and comforting reality.'[13]

This word 'home', like an ever-recurring theme, appears year after year. It comes again in a letter from a grateful missionary who was admitted as a patient in October 1899: 'Please convey to the Committee of St Luke's Hostel my great appreciation of their kindness in admitting me at a moment's notice, and for all the attention and careful nursing I received from the staff. To a Missionary arriving in England ill, as I did, the Hostel is indeed a home, and I shall never forget the great debt I owe it.'[14]

The word is used again sixty-five years later when, in the aftermath of the introduction of the National Health Service, the need for the ongoing ministry of St Luke's was being questioned. Among several other reasons given to show why St Luke's was still needed was this: 'It is never forgotten that the Nursing Home is for the clergy, and every endeavour is made to ensure that patients' surroundings are in harmony with their vocation, and to provide an atmosphere in which they can rest and feel at home.'[15]

In 1990, just before I was admitted for surgery, another patient used the word in a letter of thanks: 'This is to express, however inadequately, my gratitude and appreciation for my stay in St Luke's. The warmth of the welcome from all the staff made me feel as if I were a member of the family coming back home after an absence, rather than a first-time patient! The kindness and care I received on the Third Floor was overwhelming. Everyone and every moment made me see how blessed we are to have St Luke's to put us on our feet again so lovingly and effectively. Thank you.'

'Home', claims Macrina Wiederkehr, is that place where you feel 'loved, cherished, and accepted just as you are, with all your frailty, fears and flaws.'[16]

A sense of welcome and belonging

Home is also that place where you feel you belong. A clergy wife who was a patient in the 1980s recalls how she was made to feel 'part of a family, of being special and not just a number on a temperature chart'. She remembers 'a night when sleep deserted me, and the night staff-nurse came and sat and chatted, made tea and saw me through the long, quiet hours in a relaxed and comforting way.'

As Michael Baughen, the Bishop of Chester, explained in his address at the 96th Annual General Meeting in May 1990 this kind of care underlines the uniqueness of St Luke's. Patients are treated with excellence and skill in countless other hospitals in our country, but 'in St Luke's you feel you belong'. Home is not only that place where you feel you belong and where you feel loved and cherished, home is where you always sense a welcome. And, as Bishop Michael rightly observed, 'Here at St Luke's the nurses, from the Matron down' express such care and love to patients and visitors alike. 'A former patient in our diocese said, "I arrived at the Hospital feeling rather apprehensive and far from home. I was received with a personal, warm welcome." '[17]

A deacon who was a patient with me recalls with gratitude the warmth of the welcome she received: 'I was met by Sister Thomas on the afternoon that I was admitted and felt welcomed immediately. I had two friends with me and we were all made welcome with a tray of tea. Nothing was too much trouble for the Staff whether they were agency or permanent. I was told that I would not be able to have anything by mouth after midnight on the night of the operation. At 11 pm I was brought tea and toast . . . this was going the second mile. As the gates were pulled across the lift and I lay on the trolley to go up to theatre, one of the nurses said "I will be waiting for you when you return". Another waved me off!'

Unstuffiness

The freedom from petty restrictions, 'the sheer unstuffiness of the place', was what helped one clergy wife most. She explains in her letter; 'I arrived from Derby by train on a Sunday afternoon and no one minded that I was late (42 to Pentecost Sunday lunch!) and no one wanted me into bed immediately as if I were ill. In fact and this was wonderful for me, when my daughter and her fiancé came to see me, I was allowed OUT of the hospital for a walk with them. I found that super – to be free of regulations and routine.

'I was also very helped by the availability of the telephone, both the one that could be wheeled into my room and the pay box downstairs. I really needed to keep talking to my family and going over the awesome possibilities looming ahead of me.'

Spiritual environment

Even the spiritual environment which was making such an impact on me is spoken of frequently. As early as 1896, in his address at the Third Annual General Meeting of the hospital, the Bishop of Marlborough referred to it:

'It seems to me, ladies and gentlemen, that Christ Himself is indeed present in the work, and therefore filling it with sympathy and love ... I would ask you all to bear in mind that this is a practical, necessary and blessed work. It is carried out distinctly on Christian lines, and is, in its very highest aspect, a reproduction of Christ's own work.'[18]

Thirteen years later, in thanking Bishop Ryle for his address at the Annual General Meeting, the Archdeacon of Winchester, Archdeacon Atlay, said:

'[The Dean of Westminster] has spoken about the spiritual atmosphere of the Hostel. That is an element about which we take a great deal of care. The patients not only receive great medical and surgical skill and tender nursing, which are essential for their recovery, but they find themselves in a spiritual atmosphere which is a great help to them in smoothing the difficulties which they encounter whilst lying there.'[19]

If I had been able to put together those pieces of the joyful jig-saw that night, I might have caught a glimpse of what makes St Luke's so special. In the words of one of the Sisters, it is simply this: 'St Luke's cares for the whole person not just their ailments.' Or, as one of the night Sisters expressed it, 'St Luke's recognises the uniqueness of each individual patient. Every person is different. We try to take the time to discover who they are and what they bring with them in terms of anxieties and pressures.'

Had such realisations taken root in me that night, I might have recognised that here I was to witness an answer to one of my questions: 'How do I live my prayer?'

Caring for the Carers

'Compassion asks us to go where it hurts, to enter into places of pain, to share in brokenness, fear, confusion, and anguish.'[1]

The smell of freshly-made toast wafting from the kitchen into my room persuaded me to stir next morning. I could have washed and dressed. I chose, instead, to enjoy a touch of luxury: breakfast in bed watching the news. A further touch of luxury came in the form of the newspaper I had ordered the day before.

I rarely make time to read a newspaper from cover to cover. Today there was time. There was time, too, to turn over in my mind the advice and information which I had been given by the nurses and the physiotherapist the day before:

- my operation was to be performed on Thursday at 6 pm;
- I would therefore have my pre-med at 5 pm;
- I should prepare for this by having a bath at 4 pm;
- I would be given no food after breakfast;
- after the operation, I would be on a drip, have a drain and be fed intravenously until Sunday or so;
- I might feel sick or sleepy and would be given regular pain-killing injections because it was important for me to get up and move around from the first day after the operation;
- I should use my head to help me get up from bed;

64

- I should wiggle my ankles regularly as an aid to recovery.

I found these facts, not daunting, but reassuring. Knowing what to expect gave me confidence in the team. The fact that they had taken the trouble to communicate the plan gave me the sense that I mattered. It also helped me to plan the time and feel in control of it instead of wondering and worrying what might happen next.

'There won't be any visitors today,' I thought to myself, 'so I can enjoy a kind of Quiet Day. It can start with the service of Holy Communion in the chapel.'

The service, I remembered from the information gleaned from the 'welcome pack', began at 10 am.

Katherine had told me that there was no need for me to stay in bed as though I was ill and no need to wear night attire so I dressed and, on my way to the chapel, explored the library. This, I discovered, is a large, light, welcoming room full of the smell of the fresh polish which is lavished on the shiny, spotless, parquet floor. Comfortable armchairs invite patients or visitors to linger and the shelves bulging with books rejoice the heart of any bookworm. Since I am one of those bookworms I browsed to my heart's content and noticed, to my joy, that many of my favourite authors appeared both in the theology section and the general section. Elizabeth Goudge was there, and Mary Stewart and Evelyn Underhill, to mention a few. Some of the titles I spotted are now almost unobtainable so I relished the thought of the rare treat of being able to read for the pure pleasure of reading rather than in preparation for the next talk, sermon, magazine article or project.

I thought of the many patients who, like me, find reading the greatest relaxation and felt grateful that St Luke's had anticipated our need and provided for it in this sensitive and generous way.

Spiritual nourishment

I also felt grateful that each Wednesday morning and Sunday afternoon, there would be the opportunity to attend the Eucharist and be nourished by the sacrament.

As I made my way to the chapel, memories of the time spent there the previous evening came flooding back. Would that same sense of powerful stillness hit me when I entered, I wondered. It did. And since I had arrived well before the service was due to begin, I was able to take in the simplicity but effectiveness of my surroundings. This morning, I was not dependent on the dim light of dusk as I had been the evening before. The chapel was brightly lit and I drank in, not only the silence which had not evaporated overnight but was still there, as powerful as ever, but the aids to worship which make the room so pleasing and powerful for those of us for whom the visual 'speaks' a language of its own.

The first thing that struck me was that the blue chairs, the matching blue kneelers and the gentle grey-blue of the carpet were attractive and restful. The coving with its clusters of grapes and vine branches then caught my eye. I also felt drawn to the altar on which lay an open Bible beside a brass cross flanked on either side by two simple candlesticks. This visual focus reminded me that the suffering Christ still shines his light into our darkness and still comforts and instructs us through his Word. But, as on the previous evening, the reredos and the altar frontal captured my attention. Both of these take up the theme of John 15: 'I am the vine, and you are the branches. Whoever remains in me, and I in him, will bear much fruit; for you can do nothing without me.' (v.5 TEV).

The altar frontal is olive green. In the centre, an embroidered white dove hovers over an embossed, gold circle. From the circle come threads of gold which become branches of the vine. In turn, these bear bunches of black grapes. Above the altar, or holy table as some prefer to call it, rises the reredos itself. The bottom panel is gold. In the centre stands an icon of Christ the Intercessor facing his world. In one big, strong, brown hand he holds that world which looks both tiny and heavy. The other hand is outstretched in blessing. He sits on a throne within a frame created by sturdy vine branches. Shoots stem from these branches giving birth to leaves and clusters of grapes. On the left hand side of the kingly figure stands an angel who has eyes for no one but Christ. And on the right stands Mary whose gaze is also fixed on Jesus. Another dove – this one in gold – descends onto the figure of Christ.

The sound of fellow patients slipping into the silent chapel caused me to turn my attention from the reredos to the people. I noticed that most of them were men – clergy, not dressed in the customary dog collar but wearing that great leveller: the dressing gown. It was impossible to tell whether any were bishops or archdeacons, men experienced in ministry, or whether they were curates or vicars in their first living who were just learning the ropes. In this place, it did not matter. What did matter was that, for some reason, we had all been brought to this place where we had become 'those for whom things are done or to whom things are done'[2]: those who had become powerless and vulnerable, who were therefore required to learn the 'stature of waiting.'[3]

The service was most sensitively led by the Chaplain and it thrilled me to think that these nurturing words of the liturgy were feeding, not just those of us who felt strong enough to make the trip to the chapel, but also patients who cared to tune into the service on their bedside radios. These patients could also receive the sacrament from the Chaplain who is always prepared to visit the bed-ridden after the service is over.

The gospel reading was John 21: a favourite passage of mine where Jesus, after his Resurrection, stands on the seashore watching his friends fish. I love the way he shows them where to find the shoal of fish. Even more, I love the way John records how he cooked breakfast for these disciples. And I find the way he re-commissioned the crestfallen Peter most moving.

My mind went back to that reading after the service was over. Reluctant to leave the prayer-saturated chapel on this my Quiet Day, I lingered to gaze once more at the symbolism of the reredos. The message which seemed to be conveyed by the gospel reading and the reredos was heartening. In the gospel reading, it was only after Jesus had lovingly served, fed and consoled his heart-broken disciple that he re-commissioned him. Similarly, in the reredos, Jesus, the life-giving vine, could clearly be seen to be the source of the energy and fruitfulness pulsating through the branches.

The implications for the patients were reassuring. We would not be sent back into our parishes and ministries until our depleted resources had been replenished by God through the sacrament and the Word and the care of an attentive staff.

Flora Wuellner, author of *Prayer, Stress and our Inner Wounds*, shows how vital this assurance is to the well-being of the clergy:

'For three years I served on a committee of my denomination that interviews pastors in order to hear and share their problems and explore ways of helping them through their difficulties. I was impressed by the hard working sacrificial quality of the lives of many of the pastors, but I also became aware of the unhealed wounds of the past and pain of the present that many of them were carrying around. I noticed that many of them were in a state of serious exhaustion . . . In the thirteenth chapter of John we see Jesus kneeling before his friends taking their tired, dusty feet tenderly into his hands and washing them . . . Only *after* he had lovingly served and ministered to each one of them did he challenge and command them to reach out and lovingly minister to each other. He was not just being a role model of service to them. I believe he was bringing each of them the nurturing, healing touch, so that they, as healed persons, could be free to touch others lovingly . . .

Just as he knew they could not wash the feet of others, with all that that implies, until they themselves had been ministered to, so they could not be sent as nurturing shepherds to the hungering, hurting world until they had been comforted, fed, given strength and the assurance of his presence, the Bread of Life always with them.

This is hard for us. It is hard to learn to receive. We like to be on the giving end. We like to be in control. It is not easy to admit that we are vulnerable, we have needs, limits, and wounds. It is hard to admit it to others, and it is hard to admit it to God. Perhaps it is hardest of all to admit it to ourselves.'[4]

She goes on to explain why this realisation is so vital:

'A christian leader is a person who feels called by God through Christ to expend his or her centre life and strength channelling and manifesting this transforming love of God on the frontier where creation meets chaos.

One of the main causes of leadership fatigue is our temptation to feel that it's all up to us. This is the problem of super-responsibility. We feel that God's kingdom stands or falls according to the extent of our will-power, our righteous efficiency, and our power to love and heal. Perhaps we have learnt to delegate responsibility outwardly, but we have not learned it inwardly. We carry the burdens of all upon our hearts and never take an inner vacation. We overlook Jesus' challenge to be the branches of the vine (John 15:4–5), and try to become the vine ourselves. Without realising what has happened we are trying to become the generators rather than the transmitters of the divine energy.

Even prayer itself can become exhausting if we approach it as an activity willed by us and initiated by us rather than as a response to the God who has already loved us forever and who holds us even when we turn away from prayer.

One major aspect of super-responsibility is the difficulty we feel in letting others serve us and minister to us. For so long we have thought of ourselves as the nurturing ones, the loving, giving, strong ones that it is a real struggle with our guilt to let ourselves be helped and served by others.'5

Here in this chapel, we, the carers, were being cared for. Here in this hospital, we no longer needed to masquerade as mini-Messiahs nor was there a need to assume the role of the life-giving vine. No. We could relax, admit the limitations of our humanity and revel in the rare luxury of knowing ourselves cherished, supported and re-equipped for whatever the future held. The reredos reminded us of this with its visual images of those ancient yet ever-new truths: Christ has died, Christ is risen, Christ will come again. It was communicated by the crucifix which hangs over the icon, by the feet of the figure hanging from the cross which point to the dove and the icon below and by the size of the nails in the hands and feet of the dying Christ. These showed us, pictorially, that the Christ who died for those of us who are learning the 'stature of waiting' still intercedes for us, that he gives us his Spirit to be our helper before sending us back to bear fruit for his Kingdom.

This hospital, I sensed, would become for us, not simply a refuge, a haven, an oasis, but would also prove to be the womb where we patients were hidden, not because we had been cast on a spiritual scrap heap, but because we were being re-born in some curious, indefinable way and for some purpose which, as yet, was known only to God himself. While we were in this womb, just waiting, we were being fed by the chaplain whose voice I could hear greeting personally each of the patients, by the secretaries working in their office, by Canon Nicholson and Matron, by the receptionist and kitchen staff, by the surgeons, the nurses and the domestic staff, by the anaesthetists and the physiotherapist, the cleaners – and by Jimmy, the much-loved porter.

Companionship

I was the last patient to leave the chapel and, though I had lingered for some considerable time, the chaplain was still there greeting in a leisurely way each of the twenty people who had attended the service. His sensitivity and care impressed and touched me – especially since, having greeted the more mobile patients, he still had to visit the bed-ridden ones who had requested the sacrament in their rooms.

By Sunday, I realised, I would be bed-ridden, but the prospect now held no terror for me. In this house of healing, I felt safe. Held. Understood and protected. This is what happens to a patient who is surrounded by the kind of care I was receiving. As one patient put it: 'Your care is what makes me feel safe and secure in your hands. It is when you show me I am special among a hundred others who are also special.'[6]

Peter Nicholson, the General Secretary, made me feel special that day. As I walked past his door, though I could see that he was busy at his desk, he still invited me in. We chatted about the hospital. 'It's very special', I offered. 'It makes me feel as though I'm on a post-Pentecost retreat.'

Sensing my interest in the establishment, Canon Nicholson interpreted this as an invitation to tell me about the hospital: its needs, its foundation, and the way he had come to be appointed as General Secretary. Peter Nicholson is a gifted story-teller and I sat, spell-bound, as I listened to a man who so obviously loves his work and believes in the ministry of St Luke's.

'Tell me,' I asked when there was a lull in the conversation, 'has anyone ever written a book about St Luke's?'

'That's our desperate need', he responded energetically. 'We need someone to write the story for our 1991–1992 Centenary.' My mind went back to that moment four months earlier when I sensed God had said to me, 'I want you to go to St Luke's and I want you to write about your experiences there.'

I told Peter about that moment. 'That's the way it happens – the way God does things', he said enthusiastically as he opened the drawer of his desk and drew from it a sheaf of papers and a booklet which he invited me to take to my room and to read at my leisure. Just as some women love to knit, so I love to write. I frequently find myself suffering from withdrawal symptoms when writing time is squeezed out. So I spent the remainder of the morning reading about the founder of the hospital; grateful not only for the fact that my spiritual needs had been met but that my need for intellectual stimulus was also under the caring eye of God.

Researching

Little seems to have been written about Canon William Henry Cooper whose compassion for destitute clergy gave birth to St Luke's. The little that is known has been summarised in a short memoir written by Dr A. Tindal Hart, which I started to read while I ate my lunch.

William Henry Cooper seems to have sprung from an Anglo-Irish family who probably lived in Tipperary in Southern Ireland and who had strong Church and military connections. While the names of his parents and the date and place of his birth remain a mystery, it seems certain that, on leaving school, William Cooper did not enter university but went straight into the army. Records show that on May 5th, 1855, he was commissioned as Ensign in the Second Royal Cheshire Militia. Shortly before this he had been married by special licence to Anna Matilda Wilson. Two years later, he transferred himself to the Second Staffordshire Regiment in Plymouth.

In 1857, the Staffords were sent to Ireland and by the time they returned to England two years later, William had been promoted to the rank of lieutenant.

By 1859, however, any military ambitions were well on the wane. His thoughts were now turning away from the dizzy heights of a military career to ordination. William's regiment was disbanded in July 1860 and in the following December he was ordained a deacon of the Church of Ireland by Bishop Robert Daly of Cashel in Waterford Cathedral.

He served his title at Doon in County Limerick and after being priested on December 22nd, 1861, was put in sole charge of a key parish: Tallow in County Waterford where he served from 1862 until 1864. But towards the close of 1863 he wrote, 'I determined to offer myself for missionary work. My bishop approved of my decision.'[7]

On leaving Ireland, William Cooper was accepted by the Society for the Propagation of the Gospel and in 1864 he and his wife set sail for Australia. Here, despite his wife's failing health and seemingly insurmountable problems, 'living in one room, without a servant, and frequently a scarcity of proper food', he proved indefatigable. As incumbent of Woodspoint, Victoria, he threw himself into the work with energy and verve, building two churches and a parsonage, laying the foundations for a third church and not only collecting sufficient funds for the completion of that third church but 'procuring from the people a guarantee for the entire stipend of a missioner.'[8]

William Cooper's 'parish' expanded to include the whole of Victoria. His new responsibilities entailed travelling vast distances and encountering many hardships and dangers. He described one missionary tour in the gold fields and agricultural townships:

'During five weeks I rode 751 miles, held twenty full services ... administered holy baptism to thirty seven children, visited 105 families ... conducted family worship wherever I stopped, and distributed a number of sound tracts. Many of the stations had never before been visited ...

I was much pained by the deplorable state of ignorance in which the bush children are being brought up: the majority know absolutely nothing of the rudiments of religion: they are ignorant even of the existence of GOD: very few know the Lord's Prayer, a small portion can repeat the Creed, but I did not meet one child who knew the Ten Commandments. I gave away twenty-five First Steps to the Catechism, and if a grant of simple Catechisms were made from the Sunday School Depot for the Mission work, I am sure the distribution would be attended with good results.'[9]

By 1868, he felt in much need of a rest and therefore accepted more settled work in the form of an incumbency near Melbourne.

For a short while, William Cooper made a significant contribution to the work of this thriving diocese. But the intrepid Irishman was soon on the move again: this time accepting an offer from the Bishop of Christchurch in New Zealand.

As he left Australia to take up his new work, he took with him outstanding tributes to his person and work which indicate the way in which his ministry was developing under the caring eye of God. The Bishop of Melbourne praised the missionary's 'zeal and ability together with an unusual degree of power and willingness to endure fatigue and privations of every kind in the fulfilment of his duties. His powers of endurance in this at times trying climate has enabled him to do an amount of journeying and take a series of weekday as well as Sunday services, to which few men would have proved equal.'[10]

Recreation

Thoughts of William Henry Cooper occupied my mind that afternoon as I obtained from Matron the key to the gate of Fitzroy Square's delightful garden. 'What prompted such a man to set up The Hostel of St Luke?' I asked myself as I made my way across the paved area outside the hospital and unlocked the large, black, iron gate.

Thoughts of the world of Oliver Twist also crowded into my mind: the London where, according to a journalist of the time, 'the houses are so full of children that ... you can hardly shut the street-door for them.'[11] The London where many men, women and children appeared to have abandoned all hope, where there was 'a desperate, ferocious levity in the air; and the thin, wan, woe-begone faces laugh and jeer at you as you pass by.'[12] The London so full of ruffians, waifs and strays, 'ragged wretches who crouch like vermin against the walls'[13] which convinced Lord Shaftesbury and others that God had called them to dedicate everything they had to improve the lot of the weak and the helpless. Lord Shaftesbury campaigned on behalf of thousands of such children: little children who were compelled to work impossible hours in the textile mills, children who were continually brutalised by their factory owner employers, 'children were employed as chimney-sweeps' so-called 'climbing boys'. Their bodies were prepared for work by being rubbed all over with salt water in front of a hot fire to harden their skin. They were then forced to carry bundles of rods and brushes on their bent backs and coerced into climbing naked up the crooked, narrow chimneys to dislodge the soot. Girls were commandeered into working alongside naked men in the mines and were chained to the heavy carts which carried coals up the long, low, narrow, underground passages: they were frequently subjected to sexual abuse by the men with whom they worked. Children of five and under worked without light in the rat-infested mines. There were children in the brickfields whom Lord Shaftesbury observed: 'three parts naked, tottering under the weight of wet clay – some of it on their heads and some on their shoulders – and little girls with huge masses of wet, cold and dripping clay pressed on their abdomens'.[14]

I thought of the London of 'the Refuge': the only shelter open to hundreds of the destitute who swarmed the dark and noisy back streets of the ever-expanding capital. The Refuge into which, night by night, were filtered tattered and tired out creatures who, as one observer put it:

'pass in one by one: the father and his footsore boy – the mother with her whimpering babe in her arms, that are so lean they must hurt the flesh of the little imp. The superintendent ... distributes the regulation lump of bread to the guests, and they pass on, by way of the bath – rigorously enforced for obvious reasons – to the dormitories set out like barracks, and warmed with a stove, which is always the centre of attraction ... The women and children have a ward apart. Some are reading: some are sewing rents in their clothes, some are darning: some have cast themselves to rest under the leather coverings and, with inexpressible weariness, are in the land of dreams. I have paced these dormitories early and late, and have been with strong men who have burst into tears as their eyes have fallen upon the rows of sleeping mothers, some with two – some with three infants huddled to their sides for warmth, or folded in their poor arms. Young and old are here – houseless, and with babes to carry forth tomorrow into the east wind and the sleet. This story is told by the coughs that crackle like a distant running fire of musketry – all over the establishment.'[15]

That a committed Christian like Lord Shaftesbury should dedicate his life and risk his reputation to alleviate the suffering of the sick and needy was reminiscent of the compassionate, confrontational Christ. I wondered why so few Christians seem to be like him today; why the church seems to encourage a narcissistic, 'bless-me' form of spirituality which has no cutting edge; why the need to express our spirituality is rarely spelled out in Christian circles, why we seem to wear blinkers and have a blind spot about the urgent needs of the poor which are as great as ever. Pride in Lord Shaftesbury's achievement was dislodged in a surge of anger and divine discontent with my own life-style. 'Give me a cutting edge for you,' I prayed. 'May I be as a sharp tool in your hand. Continue to challenge *me*. Teach me what this means in practical terms.'

Canon Cooper had such a cutting edge. Conscious that destitute clergy of his day were among the impoverished who resorted to the Refuge, and worse, the Workhouse, he determined to rescue such men and their families from such appalling conditions. That is why he drew up his plans to provide both a hostel where sick clergy and missionaries could receive professional care and a home where they and others could convalesce and where such faithful warriors of the Kingdom could spend their old age.

Recalling how hard I find it to adjust to life in England when I have been on a teaching tour abroad, I wondered how Canon Cooper had felt when he had been obliged to return from the mission field and how, practically, he had established the hostel of St Luke's.

I felt humbled to be enjoying the benefits of his vision and hard work. I was also enjoying the garden rather than being cooped up inside. It felt liberating to be free to watch a pair of sparrows enjoying a mud bath, to observe a colony of pigeons flock around a Pakistani man who was sitting on a bench outside the garden tossing crusts of bread onto the paved, pedestrian precinct. I paused to stroke the smooth bark of a plane tree, to finger the leaves of the variegated ivy which was beginning its climb up a forest-sized tree trunk and I watched, fascinated, while yet more pigeons devoured the flowers of an unknown bush with frantic flutter and flourish of wings. At the same time, I thrilled to the song of the blackbirds which nest in this oasis at the heart of the metropolis.

'Time', I had explained to our Women's Fellowship just before I left Nottingham, 'is to be savoured, relished: to be lived tick by tick. Time, according to Pierre de Caussade, is to be prized.'

The spaciousness of this day, free from tests and surgery, was giving me what I imagined William Henry Cooper rarely enjoyed: quality time to appreciate God's gift of the present moment. To let go. To really rest. As I wrote in my diary later that day: 'St Luke's provides clergy and their dependents with time and space to "stand and stare". Here they are cared for – not just their bodies but their whole person. They are ministered to, loved. I am excited by the concept.'

Having explored the nooks and crannies of the garden, I wandered round Fitzroy Square. This square is a stone's throw from the hectic pace and pollution of Tottenham Court Road and Euston Road and yet, as a conservation area, its Georgian charm is well preserved.

I gazed, in admiration, at the ingenuity of the famous eighteenth-century architect, Robert Adam, whose idea it was to build forty pleasing, imposing dwellings in a square around a circular garden. I marvelled at the buildings on the south and east of the square all of which he designed to be faced with Portland stone brought by sea from Dorset. Recalling how, as a child, I had watched iron railings being ripped out at the beginning of the Second World War, I was delighted to discover, not only that the railings had been replaced but that they matched the originals. I drank in the wonder of the window boxes which looked magnificent against the warm, white stucco façades of the buildings and which overflowed with trailing ivy, pink and purple petunias, yellow and purple pansies and scarlet geraniums. And I stroked the smooth curves of the sculpture which has been erected on the fringe of the garden and discovered from the nearby plaque that this had been created by Naomi Blake and placed here as a token of thanks to the citizens of London for the hospitality granted to wartime refugees. The setting of the statue, in the shadow of St Luke's, seemed fitting. Both the building and the sculpture are reminders that the needy are never hidden from the *caring eye of God*; that when men and women are prepared to express Christlike compassion, the helpless are rescued, the powerless strengthened and the starving fed.

But as I continued to explore the exquisite square my thoughts turned away from the plight of the poor, past and present. I tried, instead, to imagine what Fitzroy Square might have been like when all forty homes were finally completed in 1830; what life was like for the inhabitants later during Queen Victoria's reign.

Had I been standing in the square then, I imagined, I would have heard, not the thunder of fast-moving cars and taxis, the wail of ambulances and police cars or the roar of people revving up powerful motor-bikes but the rattle of carriages, carts and horse-drawn omnibuses, the iron wheels of bicycles and the sound of horses' hooves on the cobbles, the organ grinder's music or the cry of street vendors like the newsboys, the lavender girls or the orange sellers. Had I been exploring the square then, I might have been mesmerised by 'the dreamy Paradise of the rich'[16]: the elegant homes, the dignified ladies being transported in their carriages to fashionable balls, the opera, art galleries, museums, garden parties or sumptuous dinners. For London at that time was not only a sombre city, it had a charm all its own; a magnetic quality captured so powerfully by writers and artists alike. In the words of Wordsworth:

> 'This City now doth like a garment wear
> The beauty of the morning: silent, bare.
> Ships, towers, domes, theatres and temples lie,
> Open unto the fields, and to the sky:'[17]

Or as a journalist of the time expressed the magic:

> 'Society appears a fairy tale . . . Ladies on horseback glide through a Park whose air is warm and hazy; their veils and their horses' manes float on a gentle breeze; the elms . . . make a feathery back cloth. Not one ugly face, not one figure that is not finely turned . . . the men are always handsome and dignified, the women young and lovely.'[18]

As my imagination conjured up visions of Victorian fashionables at home and at play and contrasted their wealth with the plight of the poor, I became suddenly aware again of the rumble of the traffic rushing up to Marylebone. As then, so now, London is a city of contrasts. As then, so now, while some people live in luxury, others make of themselves and their possessions an offering which benefits the deprived. I did not realise it at the time, but during my walk around the square, a seed-thought had been sown which would grow and provide me with an answer to my question: 'What does it mean to be poor in spirit?' Such seeds best germinate and grow when we pull off the fast lane and rest. Michael Mayne's book, *A Year Lost and Found*, underlines this:

'Part of waiting on God, learning to be passive in a way creative for your inner life, is not a question of *thinking* about God, but of growing in stillness. It has to do with prayer, and with that interior silence which may come from listening to music or from the simple contemplation of the world about you.' During the solitude of illness, 'If you are a priest, for a while it is not possible to spin round the parish like a whirling dervish. You are no longer conditioned by time and people and events. You can let go, and begin to observe the world around you with its own different kind of rhythm of birth and death and rebirth, and learn again the truth you have once known – perhaps on retreat or on holiday – but forgotten: that in the words of Jeremy Taylor, "There should be in the soul halls of space, avenues of leisure, and high porticos of silence, where God walks."[19] For there is a different kind of passivity, one that is not necessarily forced upon us by illness or old age, but one that is chosen because it goes to the very heart of what it means to be a follower of Christ – and certainly the very heart of what it means to be a priest. Stillness is a rare and precious quality. "Nothing in all creation," wrote the fourteenth-century Germany mystic, Meister Eckhart, ". . . is so like God as stillness." Stillness has to do with seeing, with the opening of our eyes to another dimension, to the mystery of God that lies all about us; and it is the specific task of the priest "to keep the mystery of God present to man".'[20]

While I was reading this page from the book. I recognised the importance of this Quiet Day to my sense of well-being. When I first discovered that I was to be a patient for a full forty-eight hours before my operation, I felt frustrated and irritated. It seemed a waste of time. But now I thanked God for the pure gift of this opportunity to stop spinning, to let go, to relax – simply 'to be'.

At that moment the sun began to shine and I sat enraptured by the radiance of the evening sky. Turning out my lights, I listened, on my personal stereo, to the monks of

Mount St Bernard Abbey chanting the consoling, plaintive Office of Compline. I could picture them, in their cream-coloured cowls, standing in the choir stalls of *their* hushed chapel. I could see, too, what was happening to the world outside. The skies had been black and threatening all day. Although it was June there was a cold wind but now the threatening clouds were scudding across the sky revealing patches of blue and a silver sun which beamed its rays into my room. It shone for a full hour – the first sign of sun that day.

I continued to sit in my chair peering out at the chimney stacks and the scaffolding, the high rise buildings and the roof tops. In this 'desert in the city', to borrow Carlo Carretto's phrase, I reflected on the way nature often mirrors our personal circumstances. That evening, nature seemed to whisper, 'no matter how dark the sky seems, behind the clouds, the sky *is* still blue; the sun is still shining'. Through nature, *God* seemed to reinforce a message from Scripture: 'I am with you always.'

'I . . . you . . . always.'

Like a parched person, I drank deep draughts of this promise. Resources replenished, I turned my attention once more to the founder of St Luke's and determined to discover a little more about William Henry Cooper and the reason why he resolved to establish the original Hostel of St Luke's.

5

A Succession of Storms

'God's Spirit wastes nothing'[1]

After three years in the Canterbury province of New Zealand, William Henry Cooper suffered the traumas of what would be described today as 'burnout'.

'Burnout', according to John Sanford, a psychologist and an ordained Anglican clergyman, 'is the word we use when a person has become exhausted with his or her profession or major life activity.' The symptoms include 'a chronic tiredness of the sort that is not repaired by sleep or ordinary rest and only temporarily alleviated by vacations.'[2] 'If we apply the dictionary definition of burnout to human beings, we must imagine a man or woman who has been devoured from within by fiery energy until, like a gutted house, nothing is left. Or we may imagine a person who once carried a current of psychic energy but now, like a burned out electrical conductor, cannot supply power any more. Or an individual who, like a burned out forest, feels that their power to renew themselves has been destroyed.'[3] This seems to have been the condition that dogged William Cooper for the next seven years. That is not to say that he stopped working. Far from it! It simply meant that the little energy which was regenerated from time to time was channelled differently.

When he first collapsed, he was given the 'less exacting' task of combining an incumbency at Akoroa with the supervision of the Missionary District of the Peninsula. Even this substantial clipping of his wings left him exhausted, however. So much so that, in 1876, he was forced to confess: 'I had to confine my labours to the town of Akoroa and the immediate neighbourhood.' Even then, life seems to have been a struggle. The day came when he discovered that he could no longer ride a horse and his doctor advised him to seek a change of climate.

Meanwhile, Anna Cooper's health was steadily deteriorating. The couple returned to Australia where William was put in charge of several important missions in New South Wales but their health gave continuing cause for concern so in 1880, they returned to Ireland.

The sea-storm

After two years as a member of the Home and Foreign Staff of the Society for the Propagation of the Gospel (SPG), William's old zeal and vigour returned. His recovery coincided with the arrival of 'very touching'[4] appeals for help from several bishops in the far north-west of Canada. Concerned that the spiritual needs of the hordes of immigrants settling in the prairies were not being met, the bishops wrote to the SPG for help. Despite Anna's continuing ill-health, William volunteered to sail to Canada to spend four or five months conducting missionary tours under the direction of the bishops of Rupertsland and Saskatchewan. His offer was accepted and he was given the additional task of taking charge of the six hundred emigrants who were to set sail from Liverpool on April 12th, 1883.

His original plan had been to take with him an assistant missioner-cum-companion-cum-organist and a large church tent to be kept standing for a week at a time in small country places where young people had never seen a church. He believed this would not only meet the needs of the unchurched but would also bring joy to the newly-arrived immigrants who would value services which were as much like services at home as possible.

To his disappointment, sufficient funds were not forthcoming so he was forced to travel alone and to reduce what he calls 'his outfit'[5] to what he could carry on horseback.

His own description of this 'outfit' reveals a great deal about the man, his priorities and his attention to detail:

'There is, first, a little case containing a paten, good sized chalice and baptismal bowl . . . a leather bag, hung over my shoulder, carries a Prayer Book, Bible, and a variety of things necessary for a ride of some weeks. . . . I have not time to describe my riding dress but I think it is as perfect as possible, especially the hat which a friend says is a triumph as it is respectable enough to wear about town, and in a few seconds can be turned into either a solar topee, or a sou'-wester.'[6]

In his water-proofed valise he carried the Order of Service containing the following information:

'Sunday
Morning Prayer and Celebration of Holy Communion – 10.30 am
Litany and Scriptural Instruction – 3.00 pm
Evening Prayer and Sermon – 7.00 pm
    Remember that wherever the service is held, that place for the time being is *the House of God.*
    There, be reverent in your conduct, *kneel* at the Prayers, *stand* at the Psalms, creed and Hymns. Bring your Prayer and Hymn Books.
    Answer the responses and join in the singing.
    Those who intend to communicate are requested to send their names, or see the Missionary before the service.
    Holy Baptism will be administered at all services after the second lesson.
    Churching of women before or after any service.
    If the service is held in a private house, women are requested to wear hats or bonnets: 1 Cor. xi. 5 and 13.'[7]

The same sheet said that William wanted to visit the sick and to provide people with literature: prayer books, hymn books and catechisms could be bought from him.
    Among the six hundred passengers sailing with him were three hundred and sixty Scandinavians who held their own

services on the voyage. He assumed pastoral responsibility for the rest.

The Captain of the ship gave him permission to hold services for those who spoke English but it was to be five whole days before these could begin because:

'On Friday night the wind . . . freshened into half a gale, and . . . a heavy Atlantic swell on the quarter knocked us about so unmercifully that Saturday morning saw almost all passengers suffering the horrors of sea sickness. On Sunday I attempted a morning service: the captain appeared in "full rig", a passenger who was to act as organist was at the piano, I was on my way to the saloon vested in cassock and surplice, when a heavy sea struck the ship, making her tremble from stem to stern. The organist was pitched off his stool and shot under a seat in the music room; I was thrown violently against a table; and then came roll after roll, which put any further attempt at service out of the question. We were not able to meet again till the Wednesday, when the weather moderated.'[8]

Land storms

Having weathered the storms endured by *The Sarnia*, William went on to face storms of another kind: frustration, delays, tiring travel by train and racketeering. After a long journey across Canada, he describes his first impressions of Winnipeg, Manitoba 'the metropolis of the North-West':

'Crowds of people, evidently newly-arrived immigrants, were lounging about the railway station, and walking in groups through the streets. There were large blocks of handsome shops and warehouses, and side by side with them wooden shanties, the primitive buildings of the early inhabitants. . . .

Everything in Winnipeg is charged for exorbitantly; the newly-arrived immigrant is preyed on by "landsharks", cab-drivers, hotel and lodging-house keepers, washerwomen etc. . . . House rent is very high: I was in a miserable little wood hut – only one room, and most scantily furnished with a rough table, a few stools, a bedstead and a stove, and the rent was 14s a week.'⁹

A helping hand reached out to rescue him from the storm. The rescuer was the Bishop of Rupertsland 'who received me most kindly, and asked me to be his guest until he had completed the arrangements for my Mission tour in his diocese.'¹⁰

Travelling traumas

While in Canada William seems to have re-gained his ability to ride. This resulted in frequent scrapes which he describes with relish. On one such occasion when he was riding his pony, Peggy, a threatening thunderstorm prompted him to press the pony to travel faster so that they could reach shelter before the storm broke. The ground was very hard for travelling and he feared that Peggy would fall. She did. Catching her foot in a badger hole 'she came down on her nose and sent me yards over her head. Scraping the wet clay off my hands and clothes as quickly as possible, I jumped into the saddle, and, turning Peggy's head to the storm, pressed on.' They rode on for a quarter of an hour when they reached the edge of a lagoon and found that a sedgy sheet of water separated them from shelter. Riding into it, the mare began to sink in the soft mud before falling into a 'boggy hole'.¹¹ Turning over onto her side to keep herself from sinking, Peggy threw her rider into three feet of water. Only time and a great deal of hard work extricated the pair from that hole.

In addition to taking all kinds of risks William spent time attending to the needs of English emigrants. He founded the Emigration Society and became its Honorary Secretary from 1886–1887. Such was the success of his mission and ministry that he was made a Canon of Saskatchewan and, according to his own records, was created Archdeacon of Prince Albert. Although a letter proposing his appointment as archdeacon was read to the Standing Committee of the

SPG in October, 1883, it would appear that William never took up this appointment.

Instead, he returned to England where he resumed his work with the SPG.

It would appear that Anna Cooper did not accompany her husband on this mission to Manitoba. One reason may have been that her health continued to give cause for concern and that it was feared that she might not survive if subjected to the primitive living conditions which William encountered on his travels.

When William was placed in charge of the SPG's Mission of Kamloops in British Columbia, however, she did go with him. Even this seems to have been too much for her. The couple travelled to Canada in 1887 not realising that a crisis was brewing. By 1889 they were forced to return home. William explained:

'In 1889 I was reluctantly obliged to resign my charge of the SPG Mission in British Columbia and return to England in consequence of my wife's illness. I had to take her, in a dying state, 2500 miles by rail to Montreal for surgical treatment. She lingered on for eighteen months and died in 1891, after five years of suffering. Her disease and suffering were much intensified by the hard life and privations she bore so bravely in the Mission Field, and the want of proper medical and surgical treatment.'[12]

Few references are made to Anna Cooper. The fragments we do have form a pathetic picture of a woman who married a soldier turned clergyman who whisked her off to the Australian outback where immediately she became ill. This was hardly surprising since, as her husband himself admitted, not only were their living conditions unsuitable but the couple were frequently under-nourished. Although she received treatment for her illness in Melbourne, the rest of Anna's stay in Australia and later in New Zealand left much to be desired. While her energetic and enterprising husband conducted one successful missionary tour after another, she lived the life of a lonely invalid.

Did she share his vision to help people find God? How did he feel after she died? How did he cope with his bereavement? How did he assess those years when she had sacrificed so much to support him in his ministry? We do not know.

What we do know is that, shortly after her death, he met and married a nurse whose Christian and maiden names have not been traced. Although the date and place of their marriage remains a mystery it would appear that the couple lived in Westminster and that, shortly after their wedding, they embarked on the joint enterprise which was to consume their time, energy and resources for the next eight years.

The storm of conflict

This major undertaking was to develop into St Luke's Hostel, a London Nursing Home for clergy and their dependants and the Homes of St Barnabas at Lingfield in Surrey: dwellings for destitute and disabled clergy both from home and abroad.

Just as William had once poured himself into the task of pointing thousands of un-churched, un-evangelised people in the outbacks of Australia, New Zealand and Canada to God, so now, he and his second wife dedicated everything they had and everything they were first to the founding of a hospital where clergy, their wives and children could receive the best of medical attention in a day and age when poverty would have deprived them of these necessities and second a home in the country where destitute, incurable and convalescent clergy from home and abroad could live.

Neither of these tasks was easy. The Coopers were faced with the problem of financing the projects and of renting suitable accommodation.

They appear to have been undaunted by the enormity of the undertakings and succeeded in renting a house in 57, Beaumont Street which was where St Luke's Hostel for the Clergy made its small beginnings. According to the first Annual Report of the Hostel, this temporary nursing home gave them an excellent start. It quickly became apparent, however, that the Beaumont Street house was too small and in August, 1894 the Council succeeded in acquiring another property, 16, Nottingham Place, Marylebone Road 'which is, in all respects, suited for the purpose, having been formerly a Nursing Home, and fitted up accordingly. The Committee also succeeded in purchasing a good deal of the furniture, which was in excellent condition, and in every way suitable for the work of the Hostel.'[13]

The Coopers worked, first in the Beaumont Street Hostel and then in the larger Nottingham Place house: William as the Honorary Secretary and his wife as Lady Superintendent. Although they appear to have had only a small private income of some £20 per year, they would accept no payment for the work they did at St Luke's.

Despite the seeming success of the Hostel, the Coopers and the Council of St Luke's were soon locked in conflict. The problem centred around the convalescent home in the country. William wanted to establish this immediately. The Council of the Hostel protested that this was premature; that plans for the second home would be detrimental to the success of St Luke's. William set up two funds, Canon Cooper's Special Fund and The Country Branch Fund, to collect money from private sources for the home in the country. When the Council announced in public that these funds should cease and that the donors should be informed that their gifts would be returned unless they could be appropriated to the London Nursing Home, the Coopers grew disillusioned and disappointed. Although there appears to have been no open quarrel, there can be little doubt that this battle of wills resulted in the Coopers' resignation from the St Luke's Staff in January 1895.

St Luke's was sorry to lose such a gifted, generous and great-hearted couple. The Council admitted they could not speak too highly of 'the great service rendered to the Hostel by Canon Cooper, who has been untiring in his labours in the cause'. Of Mrs Cooper they said:

'Mrs W. H. Cooper, wife of the Hon. Secretary, who has had considerable experience in nursing institutions, kindly undertook to act temporarily as Lady Superintendent . . . She took the entire superintendence of the Hostel during that time, and the Council cannot speak too highly of the work done by her, or the benefits the Hostel derived from her help. . . . The domestic arrangements had been carried out in the best possible manner and with exemplary economy during the final months that she had placed her services at the disposal of the Hostel, and they felt she had earned the warm praise and thanks of all who were interested in the welfare of the Institution.'[14]

The Council requested that Mrs Cooper should accept an honorarium but she refused, not wanting, she said, 'that any portion of the fund, which had been collected for the Institution, should be appropriated to that purpose.'[15] Instead, the Council subscribed among themselves and presented her with a farewell gift 'as a mark of appreciation of her services'.[16]

As soon as they had handed in their resignation, William and his wife appear to have contacted their wealthy friends and acquaintances once more and appealed for funds to establish the home in the country. Their efforts met with immediate success. On October 19th, 1895, a meeting was held at Church House, Westminster where William was appointed Honorary Secretary and Warden of a newly-rented temporary home. A Council was formed to run the Homes of St Barnabas, funds began to flow in, the venture enjoyed the support of many distinguished people, including the Princess Christian and, while William undertook the entire management of the project, his wife once again assumed the role of Lady Superintendent. In December, the first resident was admitted: 'William Fulford, a graduate of Pembroke College, Oxford, a distinguished poet and writer, who had never received a benefice and, when struck down by illness, found no other refuge than the workhouse.'[17] Once again, neither of the Coopers would receive any financial remuneration for their services even though they were obviously struggling to make ends meet and were appealing to the SPG for financial help.

In his first report in 1897, William expressed how encouraged they felt by the progress made and outlined his dreams for the future: 'I accepted the entire responsibility [for the homes], although only a small sum had at that time been collected; but the work began in Faith and Prayer, progressed rapidly and has, under God's blessing, passed in a most encouraging way through the most trying period to the success of the new institution.' He warned that 'it was virtually impossible to continue indefinitely in a private house'.[18] Wards were needed with modern sanitary appliances, and the aged wanted more privacy. More rooms for single men were required together with small houses for married couples, an infirmary, dining room, sitting room, kitchen quarters and accommodation for the staff. The work continued to grow and, by 1899 the Coopers had acquired a site for the Homes of St Barnabas and work on the building had begun.

The Coopers were not to live in that house, however. On November 14th, 1899, William wrote: 'I hereby resign my office as Hon. Warden of the Homes of St Barnabas. . . . I deeply regret having to give up my work at the Home, but am compelled to do so through ill health and under medical advice.'[19]

Was this a recurrence of burnout? Or was it the gout, the kidney trouble and the hernia problem which plagued him later? We are not told. What we are told is that William's wife was also ill. Since she was suffering from a mental breakdown, it seems probable that the task of founding, first, St Luke's, and then the Homes of St Barnabas, had drained them of all their resources. They moved to Chew Magna in Somerset for a year where the rest and the course of Bath waters appear to have restored their energies. In the autumn of 1900, they travelled to Australia where William became the vicar of Tamora in New South Wales. When they returned to England, in 1904, he accepted the chaplaincy of The Lansdown Hospital in Bath. Two years later, the couple retired to Worthing.

In the Spring of 1909, William fell seriously ill and, at his own request, was taken to the Hostel of St Luke's which, by this time had moved once more – this time to the newly-acquired premises in Fitzroy Square. On April 13th, aged 75, he died in this hospital he had worked so hard to establish.

What had prompted him to found such a refuge for the clergy and their dependants? Was it primarily a memorial to his first wife, Anna Cooper? Was he recalling his own breakdown and hers; making of his memories the springboard for providing the medical care and spiritual support they so sadly lacked when they most needed it? Or was this simply an extension of that Christlike compassion for people which shines through his life? Was he so finely tuned to the pain and emptiness suffered by many of his fellow clergy that he felt compelled to act?

The only clue comes in a letter which he wrote on March 17th, 1893 when his mind was full of plans for the home in the country for those 'returning from foreign stations' and for 'men who have broken down in their work'. What he most wanted for them was a home whose wards open onto the chapel 'so that the patients can have the comfort of the services and a place where rest and medical care can be provided.'[20]

The storm of destitution

It would appear from this expressed desire that he had not forgotten the cost to himself and his first wife of those years spent abroad. Neither had he lost sight of the fact that strength from God so often comes to our souls through stillness and the sacraments and to our body and spirit through caring people and congenial surroundings. What is equally clear is that the clergy at this time in our nation's history were in desperate need of the kind of establishment which William envisaged and whose plans, according to the Venerable Atlay, the Archdeacon of Willesden, he first mooted at a drawing-room meeting in the archdeacon's parish in 1891.

The need for a hospital like the Hostel of St Luke's was urgent. The plight of the parson has been well documented by historians who have shown how the rapid growth in the number of the clergy so outstripped that of new livings that the pool of unbeneficed clergy without a parish of their own grew steadily. In 1841, for example, there were 14,613 ordained men in England and Wales whereas by 1891, the number had increased to 24,374. Of these 24,374 only some 13,000 had their own parish, leaving more than 11,000 curates to join the queue for an incumbency.[21]

The result was that hundreds of these curates waited for sixteen years or more before they were offered a living.

Hundreds more never became beneficed; they remained curates all their lives. So we find Flora Thompson describing
the elderly curate who came to serve the parish of Lark
Rise: 'as strange a curate as ever came to a remote agricultural parish. An old man with a long, grey beard which he
buttoned inside his long, close-fitting, black overcoat.'[22]

Yet, the plight of the beneficed parson was serious during
'the hungry forties' and the years that followed. Clergy
stipends were on the decline so that the average incumbent
was half as well off at the end of Queen Victoria's reign in
1901 as he had been in 1837 at her accession to the throne.
In 1837, for example, the average income for an incumbent
amounted to £500 per year, but by 1897 clergy stipends had
dwindled, on average, to £246 per year. The situation seems
to have grown steadily worse for in 1902, the Bishop of
London claimed:

'It is computed by statistics that there are nearly 1,500
beneficed clergy with less than £67 a year from their
benefices upon which to live. There are nearly 5,000 more
where income is under £155 per annum. I want you to
picture to yourselves the slowly drawn out misery of
trying to keep up for society a respectable appearance
(rural clergy were given large Victorian Rectories and
expected to live like gentry) especially in the case of a
married man with a wife and children on such a pitiful
income as £67 a year. The thing is impossible ... When
we think over this terrible struggle with poverty we
cannot but realise how it incapacitates a man from doing
his proper work.'[23]

Canon Hinds Howell, at a meeting held in Norwich in connection with the founding of St Luke's, similarly high-
lighted the crisis faced by impoverished clergy. He 'supposed
there was no body of people in the world who were more
helpless when poor than the clergy of the Church of England.'[24] Poverty was the reason why it was necessary to
establish such an institution as St Luke's. At the same
meeting, the Dean of Chichester claimed that 'such a hospital would save many a valuable life ... to the Church. Too
often a clergyman has to work on, with breaking health,

until he is worn out, when an opportune rest in such a home as you propose might re-establish him.'[25]

If the predicament of the clergy caused concern while they and their families were enjoying good health, the concern deepened when the man needed a serious operation or when his wife or one of his children fell ill. 'How can he pay for a really dangerous and difficult operation?' asked the Bishop of London in 1902. The answer was that he could not pay. He was therefore faced with a choice: to continue to suffer or to watch a member of his family suffering or to seek medical aid in the nearest workhouse hospital.

Horrifying though this was, at least an incumbent could remain in his living until he died ensuring some kind of annual income and a roof over his head whereas the curate's position was much more precarious. Curates were at the mercy of the incumbents who employed them. The incumbent paid his curates' stipend from his own private income, and since curates' houses were few and far between, a curate had no secure roof over his head. From his meagre stipend he not only had to feed his family but also pay rent for his accommodation. Curates, the majority of whom, in 1853, received on average £79 per year, found it impossible to make ends meet. Stipends rose only slowly so even in 1873 most curates were earning only a little over £100 per annum. To add to their problems, curates rarely stayed in one parish for more than two years and no financial help was given to them when they moved to a new area. Condemned to a nomadic existence in grinding poverty, there was only one refuge for them when they could no longer work, or when they or their families fell sick – the dreaded workhouse.

In 1896, Canon Cooper and his friend, the Rev. C. W. Bond, the Vicar of St Nicholas', Brighton, had visited several workhouses in the locality to discover for themselves whether it was true that numbers of destitute clergy were ending their days in the squalor of these establishments. In one small geographical area alone, they discovered that twenty-seven clergymen had had no option other than to take up residence in these notorious asylums.

Conditions in the workhouses appalled such a vast variety of people that they were vividly and variously described. Most records reveal that they were crammed full with the aged and infirm who had no relatives or whose relatives were unable or unwilling to look after them. These lived alongside the sick of all ages: the blind and deaf, the lame and 'lunatics' as well as people with broken limbs. The workhouse also became home for unmarried mothers and other women with children whose husbands had deserted them leaving them unable to support their families. Children of all descriptions crowded into the workhouse too: illegitimate children, abandoned children as well as orphans.

So crowded were these dwellings that in some of them, it was estimated that the space allotted for standing and sitting in day rooms measured less than two feet per person. The average space assigned as sleeping room measured three and a half feet. As one observer expressed it, since the average measurement of an adult's coffin was eight feet, it was clear that the dead were given far more space than the living. When five 'medical gentlemen' inspected one workhouse in the Midlands, they expressed their astonishment 'to find so many as sixty-five children sleeping in an apartment 42 feet by 13 feet and only 8 feet high.'

When families were forced to move into the workhouse, they were immediately split up. Male adults were segregated from females and were placed in separate dormitories and separate dining halls. Male and female children were similarly treated. Men, women and children alike were dressed in the degrading and dreaded workhouse uniform and compelled to eat their meals in silence.

As to the conditions in the workhouse hospitals, these were so revolting that when they were brought to the notice of Florence Nightingale, pressurised though she was, she spent much time and energy campaigning for their reform. Her interest was triggered off by the conditions in the Liverpool Workhouse Infirmary where, 'twelve hundred sick paupers were accommodated'.[26] These were nursed by ablebodied women who happened to be inmates of the workhouse. None of them were trained. Many of them were drunken prostitutes. Her interest was further incited when, in 1864, the papers took up the case of a pauper called Timothy Daly who died in Holborn Workhouse. Death, it was discovered at the inquest, was caused by 'filthiness caused by gross neglect'.[27] Agnes Jones, Florence Nightingale's star pupil, became Matron of the Liverpool Work-house Infirmary in August 1864. Two years later, Florence Nightingale wrote an article describing the conditions under which her 'best and dearest pupil' was working.

> 'The wards were an inferno, the hordes of pauper patients more degraded than animals. Vicious habits, ignorance, idiocy, met her on every side. Drunkenness was universal – thirty-five of the pauper nurses had to be dismissed for drunkenness in the first month. Immorality was universal. Filth was universal. The patients wore the same shirts for seven weeks; bedding was only changed and washed once a month; food was at starvation level; alcohol entered the infirmary freely. The number of patients was very large, 1350, rising at times to 1500. . . . The task of training the pauper nurses was hopeless.'[28]

Comparing it to conditions in the Crimean War, Florence Nightingale commented that this particular infirmary was 'like Scutari all over again'.[29]

No wonder Canon and Mrs Cooper refused to rest until the Hostel of St Luke's was established. No wonder the early letters of thanks glow with gratitude. One of the earliest on record asks:

> 'What shall I render unto the Lord for all His benefits to me? Great has been His goodness to me and mine through your noble Society. What I should have done in my serious illness had I not made application to the Hostel of St Luke I cannot tell. My income is but £140 a year, with four children depending on me for everything; and now to your excellent Committee, and my skilful devoted medical man, I tender my warmest gratitude.'

Another reads:

> 'I have now a very difficult if not impossible task to perform, one that I feel utterly unable to accomplish as I could wish – viz., to thank you personally and the Committee in general for the successful treatment which my dear son has received at the Hostel of St Luke. I am a

poor man, having nothing beyond my salary, but when I get back to Canada I should like to be an annual subscriber of 10s towards the Hostel, if only to show my gratitude for what I owe it.'

Yet another says:

'I came here much broken down, and thanks, under God, to the skill and kindly care bestowed so unweariedly upon me, I am going out quite another man . . . one thing I am quite sure will last my life – the remembrance of the graciousness with which I was welcomed, as to a real home, and with which I have been nursed and cared for, as though by the oldest and dearest friends.

The Coopers must surely have been moved when, within the first few weeks of the hospital's ministry, a vicar with a gross annual income of £143 on which to support a wife and four children was admitted as a patient. They must have felt that their sacrificial self-giving was well worthwhile when this man, after spending forty-eight days in the 'home' was discharged, 'cured'.

This incumbent had been rescued from the workhouse, as was the fourteen-year-old son of an SPG missionary who was admitted as a patient almost as soon as the home was officially opened. He had been suffering from a severe hernia since childhood but his father had been unable to pay for him to have the necessary surgery. He remained in St Luke's for nearly a month until, he, too, was discharged 'cured'.

As I settled down that Wednesday night I realised that Canon Cooper's story had disturbed and challenged me. Concerned as I am for the well-being of clergy marriages, his seeming neglect of his first wife disturbed me greatly. But increasingly conscious as I now was of Christ's compassion for the poor, how finely tuned is his ear to their cry, I recognised that here was a man who could be my teacher in that, wherever his travels took him, his chief concern was to express the compassion of Christ to those he met. His prayer, deep and real and sacramental as it so obviously was, was always translated into action. He never fell into the trap of escaping from the world. Rather, his prayer burdened him with the needs of others. His brokenness also intrigued me. Was it a coincidence, I wondered, that from the brokenness of his breakdown and bereavement, he should give birth to a hospital as unique as St Luke's? While placing those questions on the back burner of my mind, I turned my thoughts to another: If Canon Cooper were alive today, would he still sense that such a hospital for the clergy was a pressing need?

6

Professional Pitfalls

'How much kinder is God to us than we are willing to be to ourselves!'[1]

'Is St Luke's still as necessary to the clergy now as it was when it was founded?' I thought about that question as I lingered over breakfast next morning. 'After all', I reasoned, 'although clergy stipends are so low that few of us could pay for private medicine, we now have the National Health Service and though this particular service is undergoing a period of turbulence, it could be argued that the need for St Luke's is less pressing than at the turn of the century'. I continued to turn this question over in my mind as I began to anticipate the unfolding day.

The highlight of the first half of the day was to be a visit from my husband. I thought of him making his own breakfast, travelling to London then returning to Nottingham in time to speak at a church meeting and I wondered how many members of the congregation were recognising that, while I was in hospital, he would be under all kinds of pressures. How many people, I wondered, would invite him to a meal or bring him a ready-cooked casserole to save him time and effort? How many would recognise, that it is not only the patient who goes through times of anxiety and fear prior to surgery: that close relatives have to face their own fears at such a time, that they need the same kind of support and care and prayer which was being lavished on me? And how many of them, while expressing concern for me, would expect business as usual from him?

98

David arrived looking tired and strained. But the sun was shining and I was grateful to Matron for suggesting that we should go out for a walk. I showed him the well manicured garden opposite the hospital and we sat and relaxed on one of the seats on the lawn enjoying the sun and the space as well as the privacy which gave us the opportunity to exchange news and share feelings. We walked around Fitzroy Square enjoying the cosmopolitan flavour of the area with its Cypriot and Italian restaurants. We watched tourists of all nationalities tossing crumbs to the clamouring pigeons or sipping coffee outside the colourful cafes dotted along the pedestrian precincts. We even went shopping in the local florist's and browsed among the bookshelves in the SPCK Bookshop. And I enjoyed giving my husband a conducted tour of the hospital which had become 'my second home'.

From time to time we would remind ourselves that this was not our day off despite the way in which we were spending it, but that within a few hours, I would be undergoing major surgery. Nevertheless, being together was proving therapeutic for both of us. By the time he left, David looked more rested and reassured. He, too, had sensed the concern and care of the staff. He had seen for himself how healing the environment was proving to be for me and he had commented on the way in which I had been given the freedom to make my room 'mine' – with my cards and flowers, books and 'prayer corner'. This, I could tell, was adding to his peace of mind.

Even so, it was not easy for either of us to say goodbye. By the time we met again, my operation would be over and I would doubtless be feeling much more fragile. While I had my pre-operation bath and prepared myself for the now-imminent surgery, I thought of David travelling back to be thrust into another round of meetings. I thought, too, of those in full-time ministry who have sought our help over the years. And I knew that I had found the answer to my own question. The need for a hospital like St Luke's is as urgent today as it was when it was founded, for, although few clergy or their dependants are reduced to living on the breadline, they are impoverished for other reasons. When the need for surgery is added to their already existing pres-

sures, the unique ministry offered by St Luke's comes as a
pure and unexpected gift from God. One clergyman
expressed this well at the 1984 Annual Meeting.

'When I came into Fitzroy Square ... I thought I knew
what St Luke's existed for. I fondly imagined I would be
here for an operation and recuperation so I could return
to my parish and continue my work as before – I was
wrong! It was far more than that. St Luke's exists to
enable operations and treatment to be carried out on us;
but to believe that it returns us to our parishes to continue
our work as we were before is entirely wrong. My experience was that we here become more than we were before
we came in! Healing and wholeness mean more than cutting out the cancer or the haemorrhoid, or whatever.
Healing is putting something in its place which wasn't
there before. Wholeness is more than curing a disease
which is a return to the status quo. Healing is moving
forward to the next stage. It is building something beyond
the physical, beyond the mental, and right through to the
spiritual – and that is precisely what I experienced at St
Luke's. Last summer I felt the touch of Jesus, and my
heart is full of gratitude to St Luke's for that touch.'

Stress

Had he still been alive, Canon Cooper would surely have
been moved by this stirring testimony. I find it moving too
because, as I have tried to show in chapter two, when I was
admitted to St Luke's, I needed not only surgery but also
spiritual sustenance. And just as tell-tale signs of stress had
reared their heads in me before I became a patient, so many
other patients coming to this particular hospital similarly
display symptoms which suggest that they have been over-
stretched for some considerable time. This problem is not
new. The ordained ministry seems to have produced its
stress casualties for the past hundred years at least.

The reports of the Annual Meetings of St Luke's makes
this abundantly clear. I think, for example, of the report of
the meeting held in 1895. Here I found a fascinating com-

ment made by the Bishop of Truro in which he claimed that: 'The number of clergy who broke down owing to the devotion with which they ministered to their people was very large, and they were the very best of the clergy.'[2]

Or I think of the testimony given at the Annual Meeting two years later. The Rev. F. Lawrence travelled from Yorkshire to register his thanks to St Luke's:

'I have come today from the East Riding of Yorkshire, not to make a speech, but simply to show myself as an example. About eighteen months ago, when, owing to long and continued mental work, my health broke down, the Hostel of St Luke took me in for nothing. They treated my case, and prescribed for me for nothing. And I have come today to be looked at as an example of what can be done for a patient close upon sixty years of age, at the Hostel of St Luke. And very glad I am to come such a long distance in order to give expression to my gratitude. All that the cure of which I have charge produces is £200 a year. With that, two Vicarages have to be maintained. How, with that small income could I go to an eminent physician, and ask him to give me the result of many years of experience.'[3]

The stress level had not dropped a decade later. At the Annual Meeting in 1909 the Bishop of Stepney observed:

'I am beginning to know in East London what I have known for a long time in East Anglia, the very great stress under which so many of our clergy are living: and of course this is immeasurably increased in times of sickness when a man may quite unexpectedly be told that he is to undergo a serious operation, which means a heavy expense.'[4]

Three years earlier, those attending the Annual Meeting had been told that fewer patients had been treated that year. One reason given was that 'there has been a larger number of patients suffering from neurosthenia, or nervous breakdown: these cases always require a long stay in the hostel and a costly course of treatment.'[5]

The Bishop of Winchester, in his address at the Fourth Annual Meeting of the Hostel attempted to explain why the stress level among the clergy was so high:

'there are difficulties – which do not suggest themselves at first – belonging to the homes of the clergy, that do not belong to the homes of other men. There is, in the case of other professional men, complete separation of the home from the work of the office, and in time of illness, he is able to shut out from his home all intrusion of business affairs which would be so inconvenient at such a time. But in the case of the clergy it is altogether different. Of course a vast amount of the work of every parish priest is done outside, in his parish, but no small part of it is transacted within the walls of his own vicarage, or the parish room adjoining it.'[6]

The situation has scarcely changed seventy years later. Most clergy live 'over the shop' with all the stresses and strains this imposes on the individual and his or her family.

Workload

In her helpful book *Living With Stress: A Guide for Ministers and Church Leaders*, Sarah Horsman, who has worked for many years with the Society of Martha and Mary, an interdenominational organisation which exists to express care for people in full-time ministry, writes:

'There is no doubt that the job of a minister has many inherent stresses: some of them are shared with many other jobs, others are specific to it. One of the stresses most often commented on is the twenty-four hour availability. Most "helping professionals" these days have a buffer between them and the outside world, in the form of a receptionist or secretary. At the end of the day they leave their place of work and go home, where they are not normally accessible to clients. By contrast, a minister is often the first port of call for everything from the most trivial administrative or practical matters, to pastoral care in an emotionally charged emergency. Even on a day off or at home in the evening, it is more than likely that he will be called upon for something.'[7]

This round-the-clock, seven-day-a-week availability takes its toll on the most dedicated, energetic person and their family.

Added to this problem, as Sarah Horsman goes on to explain is the problem of the never-ending workload:

'When it comes to workload, the simple fact is that there is always more work to be done than there is time in which to do it. The work is potentially never ending, and it is never possible to put your feet up at the end of the day and say, "I've finished". This of itself is a difficult situation, but add a pinch of justification by works, a dose of self-criticism, a smattering of guilt, a hint of fear of failure, and problems start to loom large.'[8]

One of these problems, as John Sanford points out in his book *Ministry Burnout* is exhaustion. Yet even when the ordained person is exhausted, they cannot escape from the relentless 'onslaught of services, weddings, funerals, crises, parish conflicts, holy day celebrations, sick persons to see, shut-ins to visit, classes to teach, and administrative tasks.'[9]

The Rt. Rev. Michael Whinney, Assistant Bishop of Birmingham, referred to this unending pressure in a moving sermon on one occasion. Describing ordained ministers as 'shepherds', he explained that this 'calling' is often far from comfortable. Peter and Paul and so many giants of the Church knew this only too well. Bishop Michael highlighted the risk of 'doing' at the expense of 'being': 'Ezekiel speaks about searching for the lost, bringing back the strayed, binding up the cripples, strengthening the weak. Paul urged Timothy to preach the word: to convince, rebuke, exhort: to be unfailing in patience and in teaching. At times I have allowed that list (and other such lists) to "drive" me and to produce a high anxiety level since it focuses mind and effort on all that shepherds are called upon to *do* rather than on what they are to *be*. It has been said, "Anxiety does not empty tomorrow of its sorrows, but only empties today of its strengths." So I have found in my own strength.'[10]

Involvement

If the non-stop availability and the incessant workload exert an increasingly intolerable pressure on the ordained person, their spouse and family, how much more does the nature of the work leave the caring 'shepherd' drained; with resources depleted. Again, Sarah Horsman puts this well when she refers to the 'minister's deep involvement in emotionally demanding situations'. She continues: 'Many helping professionals are taught to avoid getting too involved, but part of the essence of Christian ministry is this sharing in people's suffering.'[11] And, of course, she is correct. As servants of Christ, what we most want to demonstrate when people are in any kind of crisis is the compassion of Christ. We want even more than that. We seek to become channels of that compassion. This cannot happen without a costly involvement in people's pain. Henri Nouwen makes this clear when he defines Christ-like compassion:

'The Greek verb *splangchnizomai* reveals to us the deep and powerful meaning of this expression. The splangcha are the entrails of the body or as we might say today, the guts. They are the place where our most intimate and intense emotions are located. When Jesus was moved to compassion, the source of all life trembled, the ground of all love burst open, and the abyss of God's immense, inexhaustible and unfathomable tenderness revealed itself.'[12]

In other words, when Jesus saw the sick and the lame, the blind and the deaf, the leper and the dying, he hurt 'at gut level' as he absorbed some of their pain. Those of us involved at parish level, if we really care for those in our charge, must expect to suffer the same kind of 'gut' reaction when faced with other people's crises. When one of the wonderful prayer warriors of our church suffers a stroke, falls in the street and lies, disfigured and almost unrecognisable in the local hospital, we shall weep – at least inwardly. When a couple confide that their marriage is in crisis: that the love they once had for each other has turned to hatred and pain, we shall suffer with them. When a parishioner dies, whether a few hours old or in their nineties, we shall not only mourn with the mourners, we shall be faced with our own grief to work through, knowing that we have lost a member of our own extended family.

Would we want it any other way? This was the work to which we were called. We counted the cost, as far as we were able, before we responded to Christ's call. Yet it sometimes feels as though the price we pay is not less than everything we have and are.

The battering continues when we are required to lurch from funeral to wedding, from sick visiting to baptisms, from weeping with those who weep to rejoicing with those whose joy knows no limits: like the occasion in our own parish when the entire congregation reeled with shock in the aftermath of three unexpected deaths. First came the death from skin cancer of one of our leaders: a young man in his twenties. Three days later, came the death of the first child of another of our leaders: a baby, only twelve hours old. The day after that came the death through a head-on car crash of a member of our PCC: a young man in his twenties who was about to give up his career to become an ordinand. On the Sunday following the week which saw one funeral after another and while we were all still struggling to come to terms with our grief, a baby was baptised and we found ourselves being propelled out of sorrow into the joy of receiving into the fellowship this new little person. No one would have wanted to deprive the parents of the new-born child the celebration of baptism but the cost, especially to my husband whose responsibility it was to lead the services concerned, was immeasurable.

The Gospel writers make it quite clear that not only did Jesus take upon himself the pain of those he met, he also felt energy leave him when he ministered to them. St Luke recalls an occasion when a woman who had suffered from haemorrhaging for twelve years crept up behind Jesus and simply touched his garment. 'Immediately the bleeding stopped.' Whereupon Jesus asked: 'Who touched me?' Peter protested when no one owned up. Wasn't Jesus' question rather unreasonable? The entire crowd was touching the Master as they pressed round him. But Jesus insisted. 'Someone touched me: I know that power has gone out from me.'[13]

As the Master, so his follower. Just as Jesus' resources were continually depleted so those who have been called to go to people in Christ's name must expect that, when they counsel couples in crisis, or individuals in need, give spiritual direction or preach, they, too, will experience strength flowing from them. Such self-emptying is part of the price pastors pay for the endless privilege of extending Christ's Kingdom in the here and now.

Criticism

This self-sacrificial life-style would be easier to bear if it was met with gratitude. Sometimes it is. Often it is not. Just as Jesus was wounded so the clergy and their families are frequently wounded by well-meaning people and such emotional injuries sometimes break the camel's back. I shall never forget the clergyman David and I once counselled in Australia. He had just resigned from his church prior to being admitted to hospital for an operation and he was a broken man. He sobbed like a little boy as he told us tale after tale of the comments of his congregation which had cut him to the quick. It was as though he had been stabbed in the back by those he had sought to serve. Or I think of the elderly lady who once told me how dissatisfied she and other members of her congregation were with their vicar. 'We're meeting together regularly to pray him out of the parish', she declared vehemently and my heart bled for the vicar, a man known to me who was facing heart-rending personal problems at that moment. What he most needed was to be understood, cherished and loved, not criticised and ostracised.

The timing of certain criticisms can catch clergy and their families off their guard and are particularly painful. I think, for example, of an occasion when I had been invited to preach at a large, interdenominational service. During the week leading up to the service I had been speaking at a conference for clergy wives where I had spent hour after hour listening to one person after another pour out the despair which was crippling their lives and ministry. So I was tired and drained before the service began. Nevertheless I had prepared the sermon carefully in the hope that all the denominations represented would be able to grasp what I was saying about the adventure of prayer and how it affects our journey towards God. As soon as the service was over, an elderly but wiry woman pushed her way through the crowds, came to where I was standing, took me by the hand and began her vitriolic, verbal attack. 'What's the way into the journey?', she asked, staring at me with her steel-hard eyes and wagging her index finger in front of my nose. 'The Cross. There's no other way. These people don't know that and you're going to be held responsible.' Her hold on my hand became violent and crushing and her voice became increasingly harsh as she added: 'Don't think I'm a fanatic. I'm not.' Having spat out her disgust, she disappeared into the crowd. I can smile sadly about the incident now. At the time those comments threatened to crush me.

Expectations

John Sanford highlights another of the professional pressures with which the ordained person must live. 'The ministering person is dealing constantly with people's expectations. Perhaps in no other profession, except maybe that of the politician, is a person facing so many expectations from so many people, and, to make the situation more complicated, the expectations the people place upon the ministering person vary enormously.'[14]

Sarah Horsman lists some of these expectations:

'A minister may be called upon to be teacher, parish organiser, administrator, pastor (visiting and counselling) preacher, priest (leading worship and administering the sacraments), evangelist, theologian (studying and writing), spiritual director, and social reformer: not to mention youth group leader, carpenter, plumber, fund-raiser, reconciler, family man/woman, entertainer, and a fountain of unlimited goodness.'[15]

The expectations of a bishop are even more daunting as Bishop Michael Whinney reveals in his fascinating survey, *Episcopacy Today and Tomorrow*. Addressing the fictitious newly-appointed Bishop of Battlebridge, he writes:

> 'You will have read the somewhat daunting and yet inspiring words in our Ordinal where the Archbishop declares the work of a bishop. The list is not exhaustive, but covers the key roles as leader, servant, carer, over-seer, pastor, focus of unity, upholder of discipline, guard-ian of the faith, mission promoter, teacher, preacher and interpreter of the Gospel (prophetic role), ordainer and sender (apostolic role), president of the Sacraments of Christian Initiation (baptism and confirmation) and the Eucharist.'[16]

As for Archbishops, Lord Runcie summed up the situation succinctly when he wrote: they 'may regard themselves as experts in busyness and distractions'.[17]

Sarah Horsman's and Michael Whinney's lists leave me panting for breath. Unrealistic and impossible though they are, time after time it becomes evident that people in the pews hold these unreasonably high hopes of those who serve them.

A programme once transmitted by Central Television revealed that these were not so much expectations but demands. The presenter, Michelle Guinness, asked an elderly lady what she expected from her vicar and his family. The lady's reply sends a shiver down my spine every time I think of it. Between her tight, tense lips and with a tone of voice which seemed to say, 'Don't you dare contradict me', she said: 'Nothing but the highest.'[18] When being inter-viewed for the same programme a church-warden was asked if he thought people expect too much of the clergy. 'Yes, we do', he replied. 'We expect our clergy to have not only a dog collar round their necks but a halo round their heads.'[19]

This means, of course, that the person in full-time ministry, their spouse and their children, are placed on pedestals. A pedestal is a precarious place on which to live. Not only is it isolated, but it is a place from which you can do only one thing – fall off! When the fall comes, that person is met, not with kindness and compassion, but with a barrage of criticism. As John Sanford explains.

'For this reason, the ministering person pays a price in energy if he ignores these expectations just as he does in fulfilling them. It takes energy to contend with the rejection, criticism, or hostility of people, just as it does to please them by doing what they want us to do. Many ministering persons perform certain tasks in their work not because they want to, or even believe in their value or importance, but because it takes less energy to do the work than to struggle with people whose expectations have been disappointed.'[20]

Comparisons

As though the unachievable expectations placed on the clergy were not serious enough, the ministering person frequently faces an additional hazard – that of being compared unfavourably with the previous incumbent or curate or parish worker or with the pastor in the neighbouring parish. This means that the person concerned will be endlessly pouring out energy without ever receiving the affirmation every human being needs if he or she is to function effectively and well. Jack Dominian puts the position powerfully when he says:

'Of course it is easier to recognise the things which annoy us and to believe that we are helping [a person] to grow by pointing out their weaknesses. This in my view often achieves precisely the opposite result, by confirming the other person's sense of defect, weakness and badness. The proper balance is always to place affirmation as the principal means of communication.'[21]

Yet, as someone confessed to me recently, 'I don't know how

to affirm our Rector. My husband and I want to but somehow it seems rather presumptuous even to try.' 'The word affirmation', according to Jack Dominian, 'comes from the Latin "affirmare" and it means to make firm, to give strength to. To give strength to what? To the human personality.'[22] In the absence of such sustaining affirmation and in the wake of its antithesis, constant and carping criticism, the ministering person frequently falls prey to a debilitating feeling of failure: the major contributing factor to burnout.

This sense of failure might express itself in a crisis of faith, like the priest who once confided in me that he no longer believed the words he was praying Sunday by Sunday as he led his congregations through the Liturgy: or like the clergy wives who have revealed that they have long since ceased to believe in the God their husbands serve. Yet Mary Anne Coate reminds us in her sensitive book *Clergy Stress: The Hidden Conflicts in Ministry*, even when clergy find themselves suffering such crises of faith, they are still required to preach. The sense of failure then becomes self-perpetuating,

'If there emerges too great a discrepancy between what our being wants to say and what other people want to hear then something is likely to snap – either our health or the relationship between us and our congregation. . . . What we may notice is an ever-increasing sense of exhaustion. What others may notice is a certain staleness in the preaching that is offered and a readiness to do anything other than preach – read poetry, use the visual arts, have music or dancing instead of a sermon – anything rather than be exposed to the bankruptcy of no longer being able to preach and communicate creatively.'[23]

Family pressures

Clergy families find themselves under as much pressure as the ordained person, though for different reasons. One of the pressures for the clergy wife, for example, is that, whereas most professional men have a 'buffer' to protect them from interruptions and inessentials, very often it is the clergy wife who is expected to fulfil this role: to answer the stream of telephone calls, to deal with the tramps at the door, to handle the complaints whether they are reasonable or not. This can leave the wife of the clergyman feeling isolated and helpless, frightened and friendless. And trapped. Referring to the practice some parishioners have adopted of attacking the Christian leader through his or her spouse, one vicar's wife exposed the lack of logic in this way: 'If you employ a plumber to do a job and you're not satisfied with his workmanship, you wouldn't dream of ringing his wife to complain. But if my husband preaches a poor sermon or makes a mistake, disgruntled members of the congregation seem to feel that they have a right to get at him through me.' This pig-in-the-middle existence can put pressure on even the most resilient partner as well as putting pressure on the marriage.

Families also suffer because the vicarage continues to be the hub around which the parish revolves. In the absence of a parish office, as one wife put it, 'the family must put up with a constant stream of callers with the consequent lack of privacy'. This means that 'you can't let fly at the children or, if you do, you feel guilty that someone has heard. Vicar's wives aren't supposed to lose their tempers.' Another source of stress stems from the expectation imposed on many wives that their husband's secretary should work in their home. As one explained to me. 'It means that, from Monday to Friday, we enjoy no privacy in our own home. She answers my door bell. She answers the telephone. It's as though the home is not mine but hers. And the children hate coming in from school to find her here.'[24]

At the same time, a clergy wife might find herself feeling frustrated with a husband who works long hours and who appears to be 'married to the ministry'. The kind of questions I am frequently asked at conferences for clergy wives reflects this frustration and the sense of helplessness it evokes:

'Work seems to be his priority from 7.30 am–10.30 pm. How can I cope with so little quality time with my husband?'

'How can I learn not to resent the time he spends with others when I so long to share my thoughts with him?'

'What do you give up to make time for each other?'

'How do you find the time to develop a deeper relationship with your spouse in the midst of extreme time demands from people in the congregation who desperately need attention?'

Like their husbands most clergy wives find coping mechanisms to deal with these and other pressures unique to their vocation but everyone has a threshold of tolerance and when, because of illness, resources have dwindled from reservoir to puddle proportions, many find the stress intolerable. It is then that St Luke's, with its prayerful atmosphere and its peaceful surroundings, its private wards and its patient, competent, caring staff has a special part to play in caring for the carers: in nurturing the nurturers.

Inability to 'down tools'

St Luke's is able to offer its patients luxuries which most hospitals these days cannot afford: doctors and nurses who have time for their patients, an atmosphere which exudes calm and peace, surroundings which are in harmony with a clergyman's vocation. St Luke's also offers Christian leaders and their dependants a flexibility which makes it possible for the patient to choose the timing of an operation or period of hospitalisation. This is not a queue-jumping technique but rather a recognition on behalf of the medical profession that a parish needs its priest or its deacon and their family. They will therefore do everything within their power to ensure that the clergy can plan their hospitalisation round the pressing engagements in their diary.

Derek Nimmo summed up the situation well when, in 1973, he broadcast an appeal on behalf of St Luke's:

'I have been for several years Chaplain to the bishop of St Ogg's (in television's All Gas and Gaiters). This morning, however, I'm speaking on behalf of those whose dog collars do not come from the BBC's Wardrobe Department.

In this age – of rush and pressure and long hospital waiting lists – St Luke's has a rather special role to play.

Just as with doctors and nurses, our clergy, too are people we seem to expect should always be there when we want them. And, as far as possible of course, they like to be. But they're very human, like the rest of us (perhaps sometimes a little more so!) They can't avoid illnesses: they are not immune to stress: they need operations and treatment to restore their strength: and, of course, they want to get back to their work as soon as possible . . .

St Luke's is both Nursing Home and Hospital. It exists to help clergy back to fitness by every possible means, with the least delay and the least inconvenience to those they serve . . .

St Luke's looks after not only the clergy, but as often as possible their families, particularly the hard working wives who are so often known as "unpaid curates": also lay church workers, members of monastic and conventual Orders and Missionaries . . .

I don't want you to think that these patients are singled out for better or different treatment from other patients in other hospitals. It's really a question of their readiness at any time, for people who just cannot "down tools" when a National Health bed becomes free. This is just one of the reasons why St Luke's is outside the Health Service. Missionaries, for example, long overdue for a thorough check-up can book into St Luke's well in advance to be sure of every necessary care before going off again. . . . And St Luke's really does pride itself on the standard of care (if pride is the right word). For the whole atmosphere of this small nursing home, complete with chapel, offers peace and comfort as part of the healing process. Nurses and house staff see to this.'[25]

Spiritual problems

St Luke's is not only as necessary as it was when Canon Cooper caught the vision of rescuing destitute clergy and their families from the workhouse hospitals, but maybe, more necessary than ever. As Evelyn Underhill pointed out to the clergy who attended her retreats over fifty years ago:

'The very first requisite for a minister of religion is that his own inner life should be maintained in a healthy state: his own contact with God be steady and true. But just because you are ministers of religion, and therefore committed to perpetual external activities, this fostering and feeding of the inner life is often in some ways far more difficult for you than it is for those for whom you work and whom you teach. The time which you have at your disposal for the purpose is limited: and the rest of your time is more or less fully occupied with external religious and philanthropic activities, often of a most exacting kind. There is a constant drain on your spiritual resources, which you simply must make good: while the relief and change so necessary for all of us if our spiritual lives are to remain keen, vivid, real, is often lacking in your case, going incessantly as you do and must from one form of religious activity to another.

The priest . . . has spiritual problems which are special to himself. He is one of the assistant shepherds, not one of the sheep. He has got to stick it out in all weathers: to be always ready, always serving, always eager to feed and save. An unremitting, patient, fostering care, the willing endurance of exhaustion, hardship, and risk: all these things may be asked of him. He is constantly called upon to give out spiritual energy and sympathy. And he has got to maintain his own supplies, his own religious health and suppleness, in a manner adequate to that demand: so to deepen his own life, [so] that he is capable of deepening the lives of others. In the striking phrase of St Bernard, if he is adequately to fulfil all his obligations, he must be a reservoir not a canal.'[26]

In St Luke's Christian leaders find themselves on the receiving end rather than the giving end. They find themselves with time and space to relax and to reflect. Their inner life is fed and fostered so that they emerge from the hospital a different and deeper person. As Peter Nicholson puts it, they are often made aware that God, the Great Shepherd, made them lie down so that they might look up; that in the looking they might re-discover the truth that their lives and their ministry come constantly under the caring eye of God.

Tenderness Made Tangible

'Suffering honed me, moulded me and burned away the dross:
it changed me . . . into someone who has found peace and been
able to come to terms with life on earth.'[1]

When Christians in leadership who have been haemorrhaging emotionally and spiritually also face the prospect
of surgery, they need more than medical care. If they are
to emerge from the experience enriched rather than embit-
tered, equipped to go on caring rather than crushed, full of
shalom, rather than further fragmented by a fragmenting
world, attention must be given to their emotional and spiritual needs as well as to their physical symptoms. St Luke's,
I was to discover, not only acknowledges this but, through
its team-work achieves it.

But as I mounted the trolley which was to take me to
the operating theatre, my thoughts centred, not around St
Luke's, but around the hospital in Nottingham where I had
been a patient twelve years earlier. Dressed as I now was,
in the familiar starched, white, hospital gown, and ready,
as I was, for the nurse to come to give me my pre-med.
injection, perhaps it was inevitable that my mind should
take a trip down memory lane.

As my mind travelled back in time and place to The
Women's Hospital in Nottingham where I had previously
undergone surgery: to the moment when, as now, I had been
waiting for that injection which, I had been warned, would
leave me feeling deliciously 'woozy', I remembered how the
nurse had come, had drawn the curtains round my bed,

given me my injection, and, before drawing the curtains back, had told me that the next thing that would happen was that someone would come to wheel me to theatre. But she had been wrong. On drawing back the curtains, I found, not only the ward-full of fellow patients who would, I knew, be watching me and sympathising with me, but the hospital chaplain. He had taken the trouble to discover the time of my operation and had come to pray with me and hold my hand until the time came for me to be loaded onto the trolley which would trundle me to theatre. I remembered how I had been particularly touched by this generous gesture because at 10 pm on the previous night, this chaplain, the Rev. David Stoter, had called to see me and to pray with me. I had not expected that late-night visit. Neither had I expected this second, surprise but most welcome expression of support and care.

I thought of David Stoter now and recalled the circumstances under which we had first met. Two weeks before I was admitted to hospital he and I had both attended a Diocesan Day Seminar entitled 'Who Cares for the Carers?' We had been in the same small discussion group: a group which seemed to conclude, at the end of the day, that no one was caring adequately either for the caring professions in the diocese or for the clergy and their wives who were attempting to come alongside emotionally fragile members of their congregations.

During the months that preceded this seminar, I had been suffering from a prolonged and painful bout of depression. The day might well have added to my desolation had it not been for this small group. Here, as the day wore on, each person seemed to discover a safe place where they could share a little of the frustration they were facing and spell out some of the stress they were encountering. Little by little, we each expressed our sorrow that, by and large, we felt unsupported in the work we were doing. It was in this context that I explained that life for me had been tough of late and that a further pressure I faced was that of major surgery. David had asked when I was to be admitted to hospital but, now convinced that no one really cares for the carers, I had not expected him to note the date in his diary nor that he would follow up our casual conversation with caring visits. Yet that is precisely what he did.

David, I had discovered through that brief encounter in the group, is a skilled and sensitive listener with a breadth of spirituality which I found most attractive and healing. He recognises that one of his roles as chaplain in a large teaching hospital is to minister to patients who have a very specific faith. Although these face the challenge of sickness with a number of ingrained, well-proven resources and coping mechanisms, they also have specific needs – for informal, extempore prayer, maybe, or for a more formal service of laying on of hands, anointing with oil or the sacrament of Holy Communion. He sees that one of his tasks is so to listen to the patient's words and mannerisms, eyes and face, body language and tone of voice that he can assess their needs quickly and accurately. This paves the way for one of his other roles – to forge a trustful rapport that, should the patient choose to do so, he or she might ask questions or express fears, hopes and uncertainties.

As I looked back now on his ministry to me, I realised that his carefully-learned listening skills had never been offered to me in a cold, clinical way. Neither had he ever attempted to hide behind his professionalism, though his professionalism had always impressed me. In David, I had sensed someone who had so submitted his ability to listen and care to God's Spirit, that his many natural and God-given gifts had been honed before being offered to patients. David was therefore free to offer non-judgemental kindness communicated through the tenderness of touch, the warmth of facial expression and this uncanny ability to appear at the bedside of the right person at precisely the right time.

For a few seconds I experienced pangs of home-sickness. I would have liked to have had David by my side now. In the twelve years since I had been a patient in the hospital of which he had been a chaplain, I had come to know him better and had heard endless appreciative comments about the effectiveness of his ministry from other patients, members of staff at the hospital, colleagues and theological students who work with him. David believes, as I do, that people are on a journey: that part of his role when they come into hospital, is to establish where they are in their pilgrimage.

Removed as they are from their normal circumstances, dependent as they are on others, the scene is set for them either to regress or to take great strides forward. He sets himself the task of hearing what the patient says, conveying understanding, acceptance and affirmation so that, if they choose to do so, patients can take strides forward. Even if they do not make this calculated choice he frequently finds that when a patient discovers that they are being held in a tenderness made tangible, they are put in touch with that inner energy which motivates them to reach a different place from the one they had reached before they were hospitalised.

I so longed that this period of hospitalisation would take me further along the pathway to God, that any suffering which should be entrusted to me should not be wasted, that I longed for the ministry which had worked for me in the past: for that familiar face. But I was to discover that, through St Luke's there were new lessons to be learned about ways of making headway.

The nursing staff

The arrival of the Sister on duty broke in on my reveries. She was to be married the following Saturday and the whole of the Third Floor staff seemed to be involved in the wedding. We talked about her hopes and plans for the wedding day before she gave me my injection. Within a few minutes, it seemed, I was woozy – a feeling which held no fear for me having experienced it before.

As my trolley was pointed in the direction of the lift which would take me to the operating theatre, again my mind took me back twelve years to the Nottingham hospital. There, when my trolley had been wheeled to the threshold of the theatre, I had been greeted by another surprise. Instead of meeting just an unknown anaesthetist, I had been met by Vicky, a member of our congregation who happened to be doing part of her training in this particular hospital. She, too, had taken the trouble to discover the time of my operation and had gained permission to stay with me until I was anaesthetised. Vicky's smiling face was the last thing I saw as I passed from consciousness. It was also the first thing I saw when I came round from the anaesthetic. Although by this time she was off duty, she had stayed at the hospital until my operation was completed, had met me as I emerged from the operating theatre, and had stayed by my bed until it became clear that I was as comfortable as could be for the night.

These memories filled me with gratitude but, as the trolley reached the theatre, despite my wooziness, I was jolted back into the genius of St Luke's. Whereas, in Nottingham, when I had been greeted by Vicky, I had been met by one of the few members of staff who had time to give me the personal touch which means so much to a patient, now I was greeted by the anaesthetist who was one of a whole network of staff members who made time to communicate to each patient the basic message, 'You matter'.

The anaesthetist had conveyed this message to me the previous day when she had visited me in my room and explained step-by-step what would happen prior to my operation: after my bath, I was to expect the pre-med, just before the operation my consultant would pay me a short visit and that she would be there to meet me at the door of the operating theatre. This preparatory visit, laced as it was with affirmation of the surgeon and kindness for me, helped us to establish a rapport which meant that when, eventually, we did meet on the threshold of the operating theatre, I felt I was meeting, not a stranger, but a friend. The anaesthetist had been correct. While I was lying on my trolley in my room, poised and prepared for surgery, my consultant had popped his head round the door, waved and called out with a friendly grin, 'See you in a few minutes!' It was a brief but important encounter. It brought back memories of the trusting relationship which had been established between the two of us several weeks earlier in his consulting room and helped me to feel that, here in St Luke's, I was cocooned with kindness. This helped me to feel supported, understood, even contented as I drifted into unconsciousness.

I have no idea how long my operation lasted. What I do know is that, later that evening, as I regained consciousness, I heard someone groaning. I also remember feeling shocked when I discovered that the person was me. I was still lying on the trolley and two nurses were with me saying, soothingly, 'It's all right. It's all over. It's all over now.' I remember the tenderness of their touch as they lifted me from the trolley to my bed. And I remember the gentleness and understanding tone of their voice. But apart from recalling the frightening feeling of thirst, I can recall nothing more of Thursday – the night of the operation – nor even which of the nurses treated me in this tender way.

But I remember Friday.

Throughout Thursday night, so I was told, I was given pain-killing injections so I experienced little discomfort and by six o'clock on Friday morning, I was wide awake. The night sister, Lucy Wong, and Dolly, her colleague, had clearly been keeping an eye on me all night because, as soon as they saw that I was awake, they helped me out of bed, and though mobility proved a problem (I had a bottle attached to one side of me and a drip attached to the other), they helped me reach the wash-basin in my room where I was able to refresh myself by washing my face. Painstakingly, and taking care not to touch the sensitive area around my wound, they then washed my entire body, discarded the blood-stained hospital gown and invited me to choose which of my clean night-dresses I would most like to wear. They then helped me back into bed where, lying back on the freshly plumped-up pillows I registered, with amazement, that I felt remarkably well: that it had felt so good to be invited to choose what to wear. As I recorded in my Prayer Journal later that day: 'I don't recall feeling like this after my hysterectomy!'

To prevent me experiencing the nausea which can be so distressing to patients who are recovering from a general anaesthetic I had been warned that I would be given no food or drink until Sunday. This posed only one problem: 'My throat feels so dry and my lips are parched,' I complained to Lucy. 'Have you any lip lotion?' she asked. It had not occurred to me to bring any with me so Lucy disappeared and returned a few minutes later clutching a small jar of her own lip balm. 'From the Body Shop', she explained, grinning broadly. 'Try spreading some on your lips'. The lotion was balm indeed: soothing and effective. Almost

Detail from Fildes: Awaiting admission to the casual ward *(c.1880)*

The reredos

Holy Communic

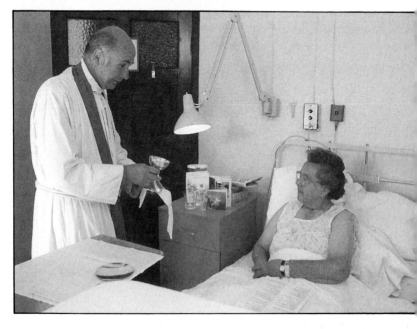

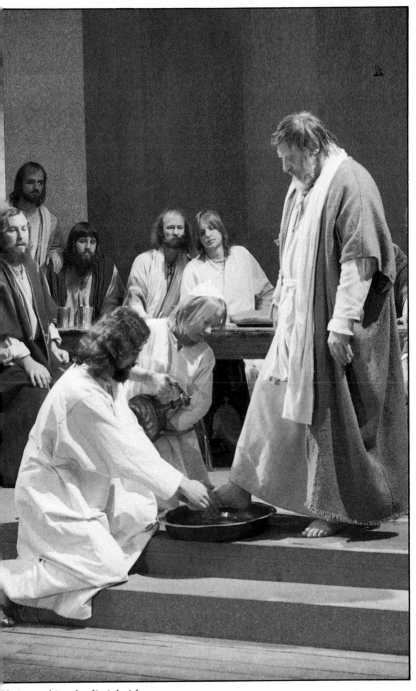

Christ washing the disciples' feet

Praying in the Chapel

The kitche

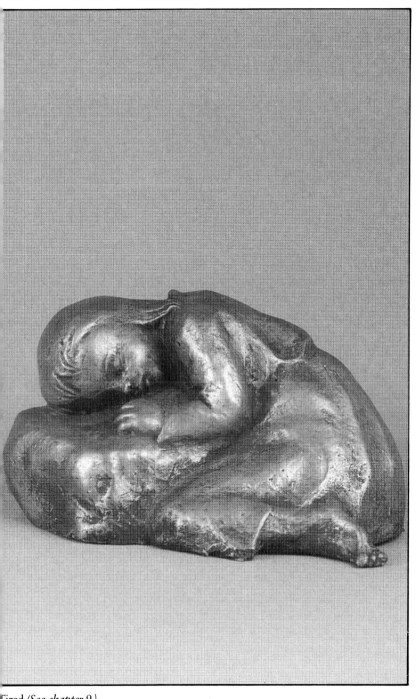

Tired *(See chapter 9)*

Peter Nicholson with squirrel board *(See chapter 11)*

Praying together

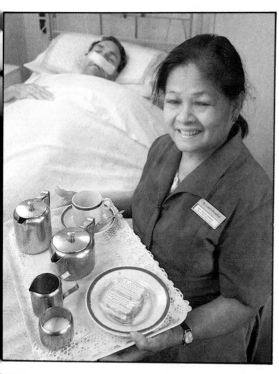

(Top) Lita at work
(See chapter 9)

(Bottom) The operating
theatre

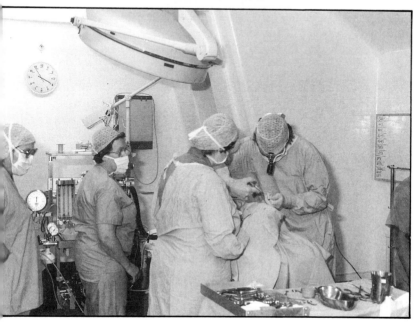

St Luke's Hospital: a view from the Garden

immediately, the dryness disappeared from my lips. I was not only relieved but deeply touched by Lucy's generosity and thoughtfulness. She need not have gone this extra mile but I was to discover that this was typical of her. She then gave me a small bell which, she said, I was to ring whenever I wanted anything. Whether I needed help to use the commode or another pain-killing injection, a mouth wash or help to pick up a book or tape which was out of reach, nothing seemed too much trouble for any of the nurses. Indeed, very frequently, my needs were anticipated before I could express them – gestures which contributed to the feeling that I was being cossetted by kindness.

As I have reflected on the quality of care I received that day and on subsequent days, I have frequently likened it to the kind of love Jesus gave to his disciples: the kind of love which he expressed, in particular, during the Last Supper when he washed his disciples dirty, sweaty feet. On this occasion, Jesus was assuming the role of a slave. Commenting on this moving piece of the Master's ministry, Sheila Cassidy observes that it was on this occasion supremely that Jesus demonstrated the fact that 'the love of God must be cashed out in love of neighbour'[2]; that life and love are about service and sacrifice; that love pours out its life for another. 'And life is not just blood given once and for all, it is time and energy, tears and laughter, poured out hourly, daily, over a lifetime.'[3] She goes on to tell of an occasion when she visited the l'Arche Community in the French village of Trosly Breuil on the edge of the forest outside Compiegne. This community is now home to more than two hundred men and women. Some are mentally handicapped, some are helpers. Her visit coincided with Holy Week and on Maundy Thursday, as is the custom in many churches, a re-enactment of the foot washing was to take place. To prepare themselves for this part of the liturgy, the entire congregation sat in a huge circle in the centre of which sat Patrick, one of the helpers, and Michel, one of the handicapped members of community. Beside them lay a towel and basin, their tools for the foot-washing task.

During the sermon, Sheila observed Michel poised, impatiently waiting for the moment when he would be permitted to wash Patrick's feet.

'His eyes were fixed on the water and he held the towel in readiness. At last he was allowed to begin. No silver jug and basin here. . . . This was the real thing: a washing up bowl, full of warm soapy water with Patrick's foot plunged firmly in. Lovingly, Michel soaped it, up and down, round the heel and then gently between each toe. At last, he was satisfied, and lifted it out onto his lap to dry. Gently he patted the clean skin and separated the toes, drying each one individually. Then the other foot was soaped, rinsed and dried with equal care. I sat fascinated. Here was the carer being tended by his charge. Here was Michel, the simpleton, showing us how to love. It was not just the gentleness, but the rapt concentration and attention to detail. He was showing us in his own way that people are precious, that the human body is wondrously beautiful, to be honoured and handled with care. I was reminded of times I had seen nurses at the hospice, washing an unconscious patient with such infinite tenderness that it breaks my heart. This manner of handling the body is for some an instinctive thing, an expression of a love that possesses the carer, driving out natural squeamishness or distaste and replacing it with an innate sense of the holiness of people, of their infinite worth. I find in this unselfconscious love a very special revelation of God.'[4]

What Michel had done for Patrick, Sister Lucy and Dolly were doing for me. It was as though they were reverencing my body as well as treating me with respect. Whereas in Nottingham, in the context of a busy NHS hospital where the nurses are so busy that patients hesitate to bother them with small requests, I had been dependent on David and Vicky for emotional and spiritual support, here in St Luke's, support was being lavished on me by each member of a most impressive team which included the nursing staff. Each one was busy, but not so busy that they had neither time, energy or inclination to give personal care to the patients.

What I did not recognise fully at the time but what impresses me as I reflect on the situation is that, while I was a patient in St Luke's, I was benefiting from a generous dose of the Benedictine spirituality which had proved so attractive to me when I had studied its theory as a student, and which had made a fresh impact on me more recently when I had revised its principles with the help of Esther de Waal's illuminating commentary on The Rule of St Benedict, *Seeking God*. In St Luke's, it was as though I witnessed this spirituality being lived out by people who will almost certainly be surprised to learn that they were incarnating a way of life which had been inspired, first by Jesus, and perpetuated by a sixth-century monk who wanted to show his followers how the Kingdom of Christ could be lived in community.

Fun

As I recorded my impressions in my Journal while I was a patient: 'I cannot recall ever before being on the receiving end of a *team* of inter-dependent people who seek, through their professional skills, to communicate the message which lies at the heart of Benedictine spirituality: "that body, mind and spirit together make up the whole person"[5]; that "all of the elements of our make-up are God-given and are equally worthy of respect."[6] Watching the way they transmitted this message was both liberating and illuminating.'

The message was never conveyed in a sanctimonious, pious or overtly spiritual way. On the contrary. As I also recorded in my Prayer Journal two days after my operation, the staff were such fun to be with – especially the night staff.

I think of Sister Lucy, for example. Coming, as she does, from Singapore, I had felt an instant rapport with her because as I have mentioned in chapter two I have visited her homeland several times, love it and cherish the friendships I still have with several people in that country. Lucy is not only a most skilled and sensitive nurse, she is also a bundle of energy and fun and a most creative person. A delight to be with.

At the time of my operation, her creativity was being expressed by attending cookery classes and, typical, I imagine, of her generosity, she had offered to make and decorate the wedding cake of the Sister who was so soon to be married.

During her cookery class two days after my operation, Lucy had been making from icing sugar, sprays of roses, arum lilies, little leaves, and delicate traceries of gypsophila. These had been carefully stored in an air-tight tin which she had brought into my room to show me. They were exquisite and she was justifiably proud of her handiwork. I watched, enthralled, as she showed me how to make them. During the long night hours, when we patients were all asleep, she told me, she hoped for a few quiet moments to continue the task of making more of these tiny flowers which were to cover the celebration cake.

Lucy's excitement about the wedding, her tales of time spent at her cookery classes and her description of her recent pilgrimage to Medugorje in Yugoslavia acted as a bridge between the outside world and the hospital. Apart from the other things she gave me, this brought me a necessary sense of balance. Lucy and Dolly, whose graciousness I also valued, showed me, too, how special it is to be on the receiving end of a relationship where two people enjoy a rapport which benefits others and is laced with humour. This sense of humour is so important. Without it, as Esther de Waal rightly points out in her interpretation of The Rule of St Benedict, we may never sense the presence of Christ residing in certain people: 'To see the face of Christ in all those whom we meet day in day out is never easy. It often asks from us patience, imagination, good humour.'[7]

Lucy, like many of the other members of the nursing staff, taught me, by example, another lesson which is central to Benedictine spirituality, one which I trust I shall never forget, and which is key to this decade of evangelism: that our goal is Christ, that 'we get there by deeds not words'.[8]

Practicalities

When Lucy went off duty early on Sunday morning, I was introduced to a day Sister I had not met before, Sister Thomas. Whereas Lucy was bright and brought to me the fun of a fulfilled life, Sister Thomas brought to me another ingredient which was essential to my sense of well-being, especially on this, the third day after my operation when I was tempted to feel that I was stronger than I really was: a sense of stillness and calm: a sense of timelessness.

Sister Thomas has worked at St Luke's for over twenty years, joining the staff in 1967 when she found within herself a longing to give to patients more time than proved possible within the hectic routine of a normal NHS ward. While I sat in my chair, she made my bed. I watched her. She, too, was giving me a practical expression of spirituality which I so much need to learn; that Benedictine maxim highlighted by Thomas Merton soon after he entered the Cistercian abbey of Gethsemani: 'that concern with doing ordinary things quietly and perfectly for the glory of God which is the beauty of the pure Benedictine life.'[9] The ideal which Esther de Waal also underlines: that we should move easily 'between praying and studying and working with [the] hands',[10] that we should move equally easily from the chapel to the library, from the library to the kitchen.

Although she was many years younger than Sister Thomas, probably young enough to be my own daughter, Stephanie became my teacher in another aspect of spirituality which I also associate with The Rule of St Benedict: that of doing ordinary tasks extraordinary well.

Sunday was special, not only because of the extra sense of quietness which seemed to pervade the entire hospital but, because I was allowed to eat again. The hot water (my choice of drink), and two slices of bread, butter and marmite which Lucy brought me for breakfast tasted like nectar and the smell of marmite still brings back the gratitude I felt for that meagre but welcome breaking of my post-operative fast. Similarly my lunch of tomato soup, brown bread and fruit in jelly brought me special joy. I savoured the reds of the soup and the jelly, marvelled at the texture of the bread and relished every morsel giving thanks to God, not only for the food, but for the kitchen staff who had prepared it and the domestic staff who had laid my tray so tastefully turning the frugal meal into a feast.

After lunch, I tried to sleep but almost as soon as I nodded off, I was awakened by a ticklish cough which was reminiscent of the cough which had troubled me while I was leading the Retreat before my operation. The problem this time was that, because of the position of the incision made by the surgeon's scalpel, I had discovered, to my cost, that to laugh proved painful. This, I knew, was a temporary inconvenience, that all patients who have their gall-bladders removed experience it and that it would quickly heal so I simply begged people not to make me laugh too much. But now that I felt the need to give a good hard cough to clear the tickle, I was frightened. Such coughing would, I felt sure, result in more pain than I was ready to cope with. When the tickle turned into a spasm of coughing, I discovered that these fears were not unfounded; that the act of coughing did tear at my wound and that this caused excruciating pain. I then became obsessed with the irrational fear that I might cough so hard that I would burst my wound and this fear added to my distress in rather the same way as the attempt to stop coughing in church often seems to make the situation worse. I rang my small bell in panic. Stephanie came. I don't know what I expected her to do but I was grateful that she was there. I felt the need of support. Sensing my distress, Stephanie at first simply stayed with me. Then, suggesting that ice might help, she left me for a few fleeting moments before returning with some iced water. This seemed to help. Stephanie left me but almost as soon as she had gone, I had a second spasm. This time, not wanting to be a nuisance, I decided not to ring the bell but to try to be courageous and to cope on my own, so I ignored my little bell. But Stephanie, ever-attentive, heard me coughing again and came to my side at once bringing more ice with her. Again, I felt grateful for her tenderness and concern because suddenly I felt very fragile and vulnerable, helpless and weary – in need of the kind of support and strength which, at that precise moment, I felt incapable of finding within myself.

When Stephanie left me, I fell asleep again, only to be woken up by a fresh attack of coughing. This time, I wept tears of fear and frustration before discovering that one way of relieving the pain was to sip iced water and to walk around the room. Having done that for a few minutes, I climbed back into bed and was about to doze again when

Stephanie popped her head round the door to make sure I was all right before she went off duty.

Stephanie never ever spoke to me about God. What she did was to embody a vital strand of Benedictine spirituality which Jean Vanier the founder of the l'Arche communities expressed so well when he said that love is not doing the extraordinary but knowing how to do the ordinary things in life 'tenderly and competently'.[11] When a person offers another such tenderness and competence, they may never speak of God but, as Teresa of Avila reminded her novices, they allow Christ to touch through their hands, love through their face and speak through their lips. To be on the receiving end of such tenderness and competence, I found, is both humbling and healing: humbling in the sense that such love handles the lowly, hidden parts of ourselves and healing in the sense that, despite continued pain and frustration, it fills the sufferer with a sense of well-being.

When Stephanie left for a well-earned weekend off, I felt in no sense bereft. There was no sense in St Luke's that when one of the nursing staff went off duty, the patients would be abandoned and neglected. The level of nursing competence and care was so consistently high that where one nurse or Sister left, the next took up the threads with the smoothness and skill with which athletes pass a baton to each other. Each person brought their own unique expression of concern. They so co-operated with each other and respected each other that they appeared to overlap with ease and this inter-dependence seemed to form a comforting chain of concern and caring. With the nursing staff I felt I was benefiting from what Sheila Cassidy calls 'a team which functions as a single person'.[12] This, in itself, became a healing experience.

Spiritual sustenance

Eventually, I did manage to have an afternoon sleep. I woke up feeling refreshed and admitted to my husband on the telephone that I was looking forward to attending the service of Holy Communion in the chapel at 5.15 pm. When I mentioned this longing to Sister Thomas, she simply asked:

'Do you think it's really wise to go down to the chapel, dear? It's not yet three full days since your operation. Why not let me arrange for you to receive the sacrament in the quietness of your own room?'

My initial reaction was one of disappointment. I had so looked forward to drinking in the stillness of the chapel. But when I reflected on the questions I had been asked, I sensed the wisdom which lay behind them. I had only just started to eat again and so far had walked no further than the toilet which was situated within a few yards of my room. To reach the chapel would necessitate a journey in the lift and a much longer walk along the length of the ground floor. By the time I reached the chapel, I would probably feel so exhausted that I would scarcely benefit from the liturgy or the spiritual feast concealed in the bread and the wine. Instead, I settled myself in my prayer corner grateful that it would be possible to listen to the entire service on the hospital radio and that, eventually, the sacrament would be brought to me by the chaplain.

As I listened to the readings and liturgy being relayed from the chapel, I was shocked to discover that today was Trinity Sunday: this fact had completely escaped my attention. Since my operation, I had found it impossible to concentrate on prayer or serious reading. Until this moment, this had not worried me. I had expected my prayer to go through a period of seeming paralysis. I knew that this happens to most post-operative patients and, as I recorded in my Prayer Journal, 'I feel content simply "to be" and not "to do".' It was not that there was a complete absence of prayer. I was discovering great comfort from listening to my tape of the monks of Mount St Bernard Abbey chanting the Daily Office. That morning, too, I had noted in my Journal, 'Television has been a very real blessing to me today. The visual is so powerful.' I had been watching the quiet, contemplative act of worship, *This is the Day*, which is transmitted at 9.15 am each Sunday. What had touched me most powerfully was the music: John Rutter's version of the hymn: 'For the beauty of the earth' and the lovely Taizé chant, 'O Lord hear my prayer . . .': music which I often play to retreatants on Quiet Days or during retreats. The music today had been enhanced by such superb photography that it seemed as though the beauty of God and the wonder of his creation was permeating every corner of my room among the chimney stacks. But when a patient is recovering from an anaesthetic, their emotions are notoriously mercurial and now, waiting as I was for the chaplain to bring the bread and wine, I felt far from God. So much so that I burst into tears.

Again, it was quiet music and a picture rather than words which touched me where I appeared to be hurting. While I waited for the chaplain, I pictured him standing outside the chapel greeting, in turn, each of the patients who had attended the service. And I listened to two tapes: a song which had been given to me in New Zealand and another of those plaintive Taizé chants which I find draw me most easily into the felt presence of God.

The song is called 'Come as you are'. Sung by a Carmelite monk, through it God always seems to say personally to me what the monk is singing:

> 'Come as you are
> That's how I love you
> Come as you are
> Feel quite at home
> Nothing can change the love that I bear you
> All will be well, just come as you are.'[13]

Those words triggered off more tears but this time they were healing tears rather than bitter ones and as I played the Taizé chant: 'Stay with me and keep watch with me', I noticed that a new sense of perspective and peace was stealing over me in rather the same way as the sun sometimes burns its way through seemingly solid thunder clouds and then spreads its light and warmth over everything in sight.

By the time the chaplain came, a sense of inner calm had been restored. Still sitting in my armchair, I had found the place in the book of icons my husband had bought for me on the day of my operation, the picture I love: Rublev's *Icon of the Holy Trinity*.

This is a picture which I often use when I pray. Rublev, the Russian iconographer, painted it in an attempt to bring before his needy countrymen, the good news that God, the

Father, the Son and the Holy Spirit so indwell us that we can always encounter the Godhead. The icon is sometimes called A Circle of Love because the three persons of the Godhead are sitting in a circle. On the right hand side of the circle sits God the Holy Spirit. His head has been painted in such a way that it points the person of prayer to Jesus who is sitting in the centre of the circle. Jesus, in turn, gazes at his Father as though he is saying, 'Let me take you into his presence.' I prayed now, wordlessly, that the Holy Spirit would take me to God's Son and that, in turn, the Son would take me to the Father. I gazed at the empty place at the table which Rublev has painted and longed that I might take my place at that table where a chalice reminds us that the Son sacrificed his life on the Cross of Calvary such was his love for the world.

As the chaplain placed into my hands first the wafer and then the silver chalice which contained the wine, I ate and drank with gratitude. Because of the place I have reached on my own spiritual journey, the service of Holy Communion is of vital importance to me and though I doubt that I shall ever fully understand precisely what Jesus meant when he told us that the bread we receive is his body and the wine his blood, what I do know is that, in some mysterious, mystical way, these elements are nutritious; as essential to my spiritual well-being as food and drink are to my body.

What I also discovered, as this short, powerful service progressed, was that, though my ability to concentrate on words was severely limited, prayers like the prayer of absolution seemed wonderfully liberating, prayed, as they so obviously were by this chaplain, with deep conviction and sincerity.

When the chaplain left me, I lingered in my prayer corner where I continued to gaze at the icon and where I once again tuned into the powerful sense of Christ's presence which had so often seemed to fill this room.

Even when Sister Thomas came to take my temperature and check my pulse, the silence was not broken. It was as profound as ever. Because she knows how to be, not only active in contemplation but contemplative in action, her presence never felt intrusive. On the contrary, her presence always seemed to embody a little of the sheltering love of the God who cares.

The domestic staff

Even when supper was brought in, the sense of peace which now pervaded my room was not destroyed. The person who carried my tray, a person with a deep personal faith of her own, saw where I was sitting, seemed to sense the powerful, prayerful atmosphere and tip-toed in and out of the room stopping only to enquire how I was and to admire, with reverence, the icon of the Holy Trinity.

That evening, as I lay in bed, a member of staff I had not met before came to visit me. She entered my room very quietly and asked how I was feeling. Having had no visitors other than the chaplain that day, I was glad of her company. As we talked, our minds and spirits seemed to meet in the richness of a real and rare encounter. Our conversation changed from its starting point – the horrors of the bomb blast which had wrecked buildings in the centre of London during the night to the personal pain with which we are sometimes entrusted. She asked me whether I was finding my faith a help or a hindrance as I struggled to recover from the anaesthetic and she confessed that when she had been through a prolonged and painful bereavement, her own faith had appeared to fail her. Such sharing, because it was mutual, seemed strengthening rather than draining and by the time she left my bedside, I sensed that we had both been enriched by the conversation which had centred so much around the God who moves in mysterious ways to assure us that we come constantly under his caring eye.

When my friend, for that is how I thought of her, had left, I made certain entries in my Prayer Journal – a discipline I tried to keep up most days. In this Journal there is a section for recording the good things which have happened over the past twenty-four hours. On any given day, I find it challenging and helpful to discover the variety of ways in which God has expressed his love. On this occasion, I looked back, not only over a period of twenty-four hours, but over the whole of Friday, Saturday and Sunday – the days since my operation. It was then that I discovered that, whereas in Nottingham, God had appeared to come to me supremely through the attentiveness and expressed concern of two people: David Stoter, the chaplain, and Vicky, the junior doctor, here in St Luke's, he had come through a network of caring people: through the fun-filled, generous, sensitive, extrovert night-staff: Sister Lucy and Dolly; through the quieter, equally sensitive, wise and caring day-staff: Sister Thomas and Stephanie. He had also come to me through the ministry of the chaplain who, by the way he serves the patients, makes it so clear that, like the nursing staff, he counts it a privilege to care for the carers. He respects those who work alongside him: the Matron and her team, the consultants and Canon Nicholson, the domestic and kitchen staff who each channel in their own way, God's love to each patient; that he values the quiet, friendly, family atmosphere which has been generated at St Luke's and which seems to be unique to it. I had been fed, too, by thoughtfully-prepared and beautifully-presented light meals and by the spiritual banquet of the sacrament of bread and wine. But I had also been helped by the privacy and prayerful atmosphere of my room and by the television.

My mind went back again to the time when I had been a patient in Nottingham. The atmosphere there had been so different. There had been a television – one in each of the four corners of the large ward. How different today's experience had been from the daily dose of *Dallas*, *Dynasty* and other soap operas which had been our fare in that particular ward. I thought, too, of the patients with whom I had shared my time in the Nottingham hospital: the elderly lady who, discovering that I was married to a clergyman, felt that I was someone with whom she could share her innermost secrets and problems – even someone to whom she could make her confession: the patients who showed, by their embarrassment, that they were not quite sure how one is supposed to talk to a vicar's wife; the very sick patient for whom I had felt a special concern because she was so much more needy than I was, but whom I felt too weak really to support in the way I longed to.

As the chaplain of St Luke's rightly puts it, the quieter atmosphere and the privacy which St Luke's offers to its patients makes a vital contribution to their sense of well-being and to the speed with which they recover. For people who, because of the nature of their work, need and have grown accustomed to a degree of peace and quiet, the average ward in the average hospital comes as a culture shock. They are not only faced with this pressure, in a general ward, there is the additional pressure of being faced with a sea of need when, what they so desperately need is not to feel that they must continue to give out to others, nor to feel that, because of their vocation, they should summon supernatural courage, but rather that they should be given the freedom, like all other patients, simply to receive in a way which is most meaningful for them.

Through the whole team which operates as a single, competent but tender person; through the privacy of my own room where I could spread my own belongings at will; through the television whose volume I could control and whose programmes I could choose and through the sensitive atmosphere which embraced both stillness and laughter, a healing environment has been created. Many members of the St Luke's family frequently refer to it, and Jimmy, the porter, described it as: 'that special something – that marvellous feeling, which, when analysed, boils down to the fact that St Luke's has discovered a whole variety of ways of expressing care to the carers and in so doing explodes the myth that, to be prayerful, a person must be inactive. In St Luke's I was witnessing true prayer: the prayer which results in a life concerned for the well-being of others: a life which does not seek the limelight but which is content to serve as and when opportunities arise.

8

More Members of the Family

'We are in community for each other, so that all of us can
grow . . . so that Jesus can manifest himself through it.'[1]

Christian communities can be like the little girl in the
Nursery Rhyme. When they are good, they are very, very
good. When they are bad, they are horrid. When they are
good, as Jean Vanier, himself the founder of some of the
most impressive communities in the world stresses, they
contribute to the growth of each member of the group who
have chosen to live or work together. St Luke's, I sensed, is
such a community. That is what makes it, in the words of
a clergy wife who was a patient there recently, 'a place of
healing rather than a place of sickness'. That is what makes
it a place where the staff themselves change and mature.
That is what makes it a place to which some nurses are
attracted. As one nurse expressed it, 'The reason why I
applied for a post at St Luke's was because I really wanted
to grow in my spiritual life.'

But what, I asked myself, are the ingredients which go
into making up such a welcoming, Christ-like, healing
place? Again, I found my answer in Benedictine spirituality
and was moved to discover that, whether intentionally or
unintentionally, St Luke's operates on Benedictine lines.
According to Esther de Waal, St Benedict insists that 'no
single monastic work is more important than any other; all
things should be done equally well. So the sacristan preparing the altar, the cook preparing the food, the kitchen
workers who serve at table, the attendants on the sick, are

equally engaged in the work of God'.[2] As she points out, it
follows that if we respect the work a person does, we shall
respect the person themselves. 'If the Rule says that the
gardening tools are as worthy of attention as the altar vessels, then it should follow that those who deal with them
are also worthy of equal respect.'[3]

This Benedictine principle was demonstrated throughout
my stay at St Luke's. Take Monday morning, for example.
The day started early with the arrival, among other members of staff, of Jimmy, the porter. Jimmy, an Irish Roman
Catholic, had worked at St Luke's for over eight years. He
described himself as 'the odd-job man'. 'I do just anything',
he said. On Monday morning, as on every other morning he
knocked gently on my door and brought me my newspaper.
While he waited for me to pay for the paper, he looked
appreciatively round the room. His face alight with joy, he
exclaimed, 'Your room looks wonderful – just like a rose-
garden, really it does. All your lovely flowers and plants.'
He stopped to admire the white hibiscus my husband had
given me on the day of my operation and asked me what
kind of plant it was, touching it in a way which clearly
reflected the reverence he has for created things – especially
flowers and plants.

Jimmy loved working at St Luke's. 'I've never been as
happy in any job', he told me. 'There's something about this
place. . . . It's a good feeling to be able to help somebody
who at this moment just can't help themselves. That's the
way I look at it. . . . It doesn't matter what time I finish
work. The job must come first. It's a marvellous place to
work . . . Anything I can do. I'm only too glad to do it. I'm
only happy when I'm busy. It's the attitude the workers
have that makes the atmosphere of this place. All they want
for you is that you should get better.'

Jimmy has a wonderful way with people which is a God-
given gift. He received the respect and love, not only of the
patients, but of every member of staff. So much so that,
when he fell prey to pneumonia and was amazed to find
himself a patient at St Luke's, he received VIP treatment
from the staff as well as cards and greetings from countless
others. 'People I don't even know', he said, 'but they all
seem to know me and seem to think of me as a friend. It

was wonderful.' And when Jimmy travelled to Australia to attend the wedding of one of his daughters, the entire St Luke's community seemed to enter into the joy and jubilation of the occasion: when his family prevailed upon him to retire, he was presented with a most generous cheque – a further sign of the high esteem in which he was held by everyone.

On that Monday morning, after I had glanced at the headlines of the paper Jimmy brought me, I settled down to pray for him and the other members of the hospital family. At this stage of my recovery, my brain still seemed anaesthetised and I wrote my prayers rather than just saying them. That morning, in my Journal, I held into the caring love of God:

'• the domestic staff who work long hours and whose ministry can be so vital to the patient. They need sensitivity, compassion, a sense of humour, tenderness.
• the night staff as they go home to sleep after, maybe, a boring night when not much has happened, or a busy night attending to patients in pain or riddled with anxiety or a frustrating night punctuated by obscene phone calls which were a problem at that time.
• the Matron with heavy responsibilities for the running of the hospital, and working very long hours.
• the consultants: for skill, understanding, discernment, good rapport with patients, God-dependence.
• the nurses: for the ability to treat each patient as though they were the wounded Christ; for friendship, the freedom to smile, a compassion which communicates through the eyes, the face, the touch
• the physiotherapist and anaesthetist: for skill, discernment and a sense of humour.'

I was in the middle of recording these prayers when there was a gentle knock on the door. In response to my invitation to 'Come in', the patient who had been admitted to the room next to mine on the Sunday afternoon entered. Although we had never met before, we found a great deal in common. Elizabeth said that she felt she knew me because she had read most of my books and had attended the London launch of my latest publication, *Open to God*. She told me that she was a deacon from a church which has been discovering that God does not always heal through medicine but that he was showing them that he sometimes touches and heals a sick person in direct response to the prayers of his people. Elizabeth told me of the prayer group in her church which had received seemingly miraculous answers to their prayers. I identified with much of this as I, too, come from a church which, over the past sixteen years, has witnessed many startling answers to prayer: a person healed of crippling arthritis,[4] someone healed of potentially paralysing burns,[5] the rapid recovery of a tiny baby whose condition, at birth, was causing grave concern, to mention but a few. We also shared that, belonging to a church of this nature can prove to be as much a problem as a blessing when God chooses to use the skill of the surgeon and his team as instruments of his healing; how we had both been on the receiving end of unwise, uninformed, even cruel comments when members of our congregations discovered that we were opting for surgery plus prayer; how, in some instances, this had been interpreted as surgery instead of prayer. I sensed that we were both helped by such sharing; that it paved the way for Elizabeth to share some of the fears she had been harbouring about the forthcoming surgery; fears I understood and identified with in the light of my own pre-operative terror. By the time she left me, Elizabeth and I had become firm friends and as I returned to my prayer time, I added to my requests, 'patients facing surgery that the Lord will penetrate their fears and anxieties, hold them in his peace and assure them that they come under his ever-caring, ever-watchful eye.'

Patients

Patients are members of the community of St Luke's although they are there only temporarily. This is manifest in the respect with which they are treated by the staff and the way in which they respect and minister to each other.

Two days after my operation I faced a long day without the prospect of visitors but the priest who had visited me on my first day had told me that another friend of his, a vicar called Charles, was a patient on the floor above. He had suggested to Charles, that at some stage, he should come down to visit me.

Charles chose this Saturday morning to take a trip in the lift and discover where I was. We spent a delightful half-hour together talking about the conference where we hoped to meet again and going on from there to share ways in which hospitalisation, with its enforced rest and time to think, was changing our attitudes and shaping our vision for our future ministries. Then Charles suggested that we might pray together which we did. After he had returned to his room, I realised that this was the first time that part of my spiritual make-up had been touched. I had been on the receiving end of formal prayer: services of Holy Communion and Anointing – all of which I had valued more than words can express. But this was the first time anyone had prayed with me in an informal way using the extempore, spontaneous kind of prayer which forms an important and vital part of the prayer life of the evangelical tradition from which I come.

On Monday evening, I had the privilege of praying in this way for my neighbour Elizabeth. I had been wondering, in the light of the things she had shared that morning, whether to offer to support her in this way when, once again, there was a knock on the door and Elizabeth entered. We talked again about the kind of fears, irrational and realistic, which face the patient undergoing major surgery and, at the end of the conversation, as she was about to leave, she simply asked: 'Joyce, I wondered whether you would pray for me before I go?' I used no oil, no laying on of hands, just words, love and silence to hold the little I knew of Elizabeth into the hands of the all-powerful God. I knew that, despite the feebleness and inadequacy of my words, I was sharing with Christ, the great Intercessor in holding this servant of the Gospel into the caring presence of the Father. I recognised that despite my own fragility, I was being given the joy of becoming one of the bridges on which God and Elizabeth met.

Next day, while I lay in bed I followed Elizabeth in my imagination and with my prayers as she was wheeled from her room into the lift which would take her to theatre. I found it most moving to picture her in the operating theatre being on the receiving end of the generosity and skill of the surgeon who was performing her operation. In a way I had never before experienced, I felt deeply involved in all that was going on. When Phyllis, the clergy wife who was sharing a room with Elizabeth, came to tell me that Elizabeth was back from theatre, I was filled with joy and sensed that the presence of God which had seemed to surround and enfold her while she was in theatre would continue to permeate her as she recovered from the anaesthetic.

Others have told me how important fellow patients have proved to be in the healing process. Peter Nicholson, for example, recalls an occasion when he was a patient at St Luke's: a clergyman knocked on the door and explained that he was a patient in the room above. 'I always carry holy oil with me', he said. 'This morning, I had the distinct impression that I should go to the person in the room below, and offer to anoint them.' Peter accepted the offer with alacrity and gratitude admitting that this prayer, for him, had proved to be the turning point in his recovery. Peter Nicholson also marvels as he recalls how, when patients minister to each other in this way, 'friendships are formed which then last for years afterwards'.[6]

I have found this claim to be true. I am not only still in touch with Elizabeth, the deacon. I am also in touch with Brian, the priest who was in the room round the corner.

I first visited Brian soon after he was admitted as a patient. I learned from one of the nurses that he had travelled a long distance to reach St Luke's so I imagined that he would not be besieged with visitors. When Brian invited me into his room, I could tell that he was about to pray the Daily Office so I apologised for interrupting him. He dismissed the apology and asked whether I would like to say the Office with him. I welcomed this opportunity to pray with someone, so accepted the invitation. Since I had not long had my operation, we returned to my room where I could sit up in bed while Brian prayed the liturgy.

This brief encounter formed the beginning of a bond between us. After his operation, the proverbial flaming June lived up to its name and wooed us out of our wards and onto the roof-top where we could sit, and chat and soak up the sun to our heart's content. I found in Brian a soul friend. He was not from the same spiritual stable but he clearly understood and identified with my spiritual journey with its quest for stillness, Quiet Days, retreats and contemplation. I found it refreshing to talk with someone who finds renewal in silence and aloneness. Brian recalls that he found our friendship enriching for different reasons. 'Although we never discussed the matter, the conversations I had with you seemed to suggest that I should look for new horizons. I do hope that I will be "open to God" and that when the "right" thing appears, I will be sensitive enough to recognise it and have the courage to move on.' In a letter written some months after we had both been discharged from St Luke's, he took up the theme of the mutual ministry between patients: 'I think as patients we all ministered to one another and I was particularly struck by how sensitive people were to others' needs. They didn't invade their privacy if they felt people wanted to be left alone or were not feeling too well at that time. The privacy of a room also meant that patients could share thoughts quietly with one another and in a sense minister to each other more intimately than in a noisy crowded ward.'

Elizabeth said something similar in one of her letters: The support and friendship of fellow patients 'was tremendous . . . I asked to be in a twin room and I think that this helped initially. It was lovely to have someone who knew the ropes and was able to help me settle in. She was also there when I went for my op. and was very sensitive to this as she was when I returned. For the two other days we were together, because I was in bed Phyllis was my feet and hands when necessary. By the time I had been there for 24 hours she had introduced me to most mobile folk on the same floor. We freely visited one another and sat and chatted together. One had the feeling that many of the folk needed an ear. This is probably the result of being in ministry. I found it a tremendous strength to be free to ask another to pray with me when I needed this before the operation. . . . I also appreciated the visits of others when I was confined to bed. This was never without sensitivity ie knocking at the door etc but oh! so welcome to see a face round the door enquiring if it was "all right" to come in.'

Support of patients for one another is a recurring theme in the hundreds of thank you letters written to Peter Nicholson, the Matron and the staff of St. Luke's and also in the letters which some past patients have written to me. One patient recalls, 'the good company of my room-mate'. Another, a monk from Mirfield, admits, 'I have been in hospital a number of times in the past 50 years: this was the only time I have positively enjoyed the experience! I was in a ward for two initially with a priest somewhat older than myself, who went out halfway through my stay: thereafter I was on my own. He and I got on well and were able to say the Offices of Morning and Evening Prayer together.' Mrs Bardsley, Bishop Cuthbert Bardsley's widow, recollects how, on one occasion, when her husband was a patient in St Luke's, 'four Bishops were there . . . and they were able to minister to each other.'

But, as Peter Nicholson recalls with relish, 'very often you will find a new, young curate ministering to a bishop'. This is part of the ongoing genius of St Luke's. Very often, too, it is in St Luke's that Christian leaders from different traditions learn to understand each other. I remember visiting a certain ward where a friend of mine was a patient. She is from an evangelical background and has been greatly influenced by the charismatic movement. I chuckled to myself when I discovered that she was sharing a room with a nun from a contemplative order and discovered, without surprise, that they appeared to have little in common.

It was without surprise, too, that I later received a letter from my friend. 'At first,' she wrote, 'my room-mate and I seemed rather distant from one another but as time wore on, we found ourselves sharing quite deeply and learning to understand, appreciate and respect one another's spiritualities.'

Consultants

Patients are not only treated with respect by the staff and each other, in turn, they feel a great deal of respect and express endless affirmation for the more permanent community of St Luke's. This became clear to me, first as I talked with fellow patients and then, later, as I read those thank you letters which patients have written over the years.

As we sat out on our make-shift patio, the roof-top of Floor Three, Brian, Elizabeth and I talked frequently and appreciatively of the staff. Not one word of criticism crossed our lips. In particular, we talked about the consultants.

Each of us was being treated by a different consultant and none of us could find words to express the gratitude we felt for the attention we were receiving. It was not just that we were benefitting from the skill of eminent physicians, though we were all being cared for by men and women who have reached the top of the professional ladder. What impressed and puzzled us was that these people, alongside nearly one hundred and fifty others, give their time and skills year in and year out to patients at St Luke's. 'Why', we would ask ourselves, 'do they do it?' All of them work long hours in the big teaching hospitals in London. All of them could be using the time they spend at St Luke's either earning money by seeing private patients, relaxing or being with their wives and children. Yet they donate this time to church workers.

We gave up trying to discover why, between them, the consultants who serve St Luke's should donate, in effect, more than a quarter of a million pounds to the hospital each year; indirectly, contributing this money to the church. Instead, we spent our time marvelling that these doctors came to see us so regularly – usually either early in the morning on their way to their National Health hospitals or late at night on their way home.

My consultant had performed my operation at 6 pm on Thursday evening having had a busy day at the hospital where he sees NHS patients. Before 8 am on Friday morning, to my great surprise, there was a gentle tap on the door of my room and in response to my 'Come in', I discovered that he had come to see how I was.

He seemed genuinely pleased to see me lying back on my pillows looking and feeling so well. He assured me that the operation had been a success, informed me that the gall bladder had been very 'gunged up' and that the operation had certainly been necessary, and then, with the usual twinkle in his eye, he produced from the pocket of his pin-striped jacket, a small jar. 'I brought you a present', he said with an impish smile. 'I thought you might like to see what I took from you.' Laughing, he added, 'These are a few of the gall stones. I thought you might like to see what they look like. They're yours. You can keep them if you like.' I chuckled and determined to keep my souvenir at least until I could show it to my husband even though he might not appreciate the thought of examining my trophy!

The consultant's 7.45 am routine 'ward visit' was as different from a typical ward visit as the warm, Mediterranean Sea is to the Atlantic Ocean. On this first morning, for example, I was lying back on my pillows listening, through my personal stereo, to the Monks of Mount St Bernard Abbey chant chunks of Scripture from the Morning Office when he arrived. Still recovering, as I was, from the anaesthetic and the effect of a series of pain-killing injections, I was finding it impossible to pray in a spontaneous way, to use my imagination in prayer or even simply to be still – well-tried methods of prayer which normally form a part of my prayer diet. What I was finding, however, was that, the Daily Office was doing for me what it did for the monk Thomas Merton: 'through my constant immersion in this tremendous, unending cycle of prayer, ever renewing in its vitality, its inexhaustible, sweet energies ... drawn into that atmosphere, into that deep, vast universal movement of vitalising prayer, which is Christ praying in men to His Father, ... from the secret places of His essence, God began to fill my soul with grace ... grace that sprung from deep within me, I could not know how or where.'[7]

My surgeon's arrival in no way interrupted or disrupted this prayer. In some strange, almost inexplicable way, it seemed to be a part of it. I could not understand this at the time but having reflected on the situation since, and knowing as I now do that, for this particular physician, his work is an expression of his spirituality, I recognise that, just as God was coming to me through the liturgy, so he was coming to me through the laughing, compassionate eyes of the surgeon. Just as God had appeared to Abraham in the guise of three visitors, so, through this godly man, who never mentioned the word 'God' to me, he was incarnating the fact that he is a God who keeps his children constantly under his all-caring eye. My surgeon was making real for me an observation made by a biographer of William Wilberforce about the members of the nineteenth-century Clapham Sect who sacrificed so much to bring about social change in the name of Christ: 'These wise men never endeavored to mould our unformed opinions into any particular mold. Indeed it was needless for them to preach to us. Their lives spoke far more plainly and convincingly than any words. We saw their patience, cheerfulness, generosity, wisdom and activity daily before us, and we knew and felt that all this was only a natural expression of hearts given to the service of God.'[8]

Since I was the patient of one consultant only, my experience of the surgeons who donate their time, energy and skills to St Luke's was severely limited, I therefore asked the present Chairman of the Medical Staff Committee, who had been associated with St Luke's since 1975, to do the impossible and speak for the rest of this team. 'Do all the consultants profess to be Christians?', I asked. 'A number do but not all.' 'Then why do they give their services to Christian workers in this way?', I persisted. 'It's a recognition of what the clergy stand for. Lay people can acknowledge God without actually adhering to the formularies of the church. They feel this is a good thing to do. The type of person who works here would give you a good deal wherever you encountered them. But I think people still do look up to the clergy – they recognise what they stand for: God, the Christian Church. After all, many people will call upon their services – marriage, funerals and so on.' Speaking more personally, he went on, 'I've always respected the clergy greatly. We're not good, in the church, at expressing such affirmation.' Working at St Luke's is an expression of 'a desire to use one's skills, or to use the ecclesiastical term "talents", for the church which one values. It's one's gifts to the church – from the medical profession and others. I sometimes feel I don't do much in the home parish. I'm not on the PCC and I don't attend many mid-week meetings but this is something I can do which seems to be of value.

It is spare time work which one is happy to do. One is fortunate to have time to do it. Nobody has to work here. They do it because they enjoy it. My wife and I (she's in medicine too) have had some very happy experiences of working here. The consultants and I enjoy looking after this particular group of patients.'

'Does it ever occur to you to think that what you are doing is giving expression to Matthew 25?' I asked, 'that parable where Jesus tells us that when he returns "in all his glory" he will affirm the kind of work you are doing: "I was sick and you looked after me . . ." '[9]

Having talked for some while to this eminent, though modest man, I might have anticipated his response: 'One is very reluctant to equate with these ideals which one recognises as being right. I can't honestly say I'm conscious of that but if others choose to see it that way, I'd be very happy.'

Had I quoted to him a portion of the Rule of St Benedict which both he and his colleague and friend, my own consultant, embodied so humbly yet powerfully, I feel sure that he would have expressed further surprise. Yet if I had read to either of them Esther de Waal's paraphrase of the Rule which says, 'The expert is so to exercise his skill that he benefits the whole; he must work in the spirit of respect both for his material and for his fellow men. The satisfaction lies in the work itself and not in the personal recognition that it brings . . .'[10] I would simply have been holding before them a mirror in which they could see a reflection of themselves. In similar vein, I could have added: 'The vital thing is that we approach our work in the same way that we approach our possessions. We are stewards and not slaves, what we have and what we do belong to the life on loan from God, and it is through that life in its entirety, with all its unspectacular strands, that we shall make our way to him. . . . so that in all things God may be glorified.'[11]

Just as we patients respected and valued Jimmy the porter, the nursing staff, the chaplain and the help we were able to give to each other, so we valued highly each of the consultants with whom we came in contact. Patients' letters reflect this. An eighty-three-year-old patient recalls; 'I had a good surgeon who inspired confidence and trust from the start and all went well with the operation. I sent him a Christmas card thanking him for his success in my running repairs.'

Another, a bishop, told me in a letter,

'I was extremely impressed by everything at St Luke's Hospital during both my visits there. What impressed me particularly, however, was the amazing amount of care and concern shown by the consultants in the midst of their extremely busy lives. I recall that, on my first visit, I had scarcely settled into my room when the consultant came round to see me, and told me what I could expect when I visited a particular clinic in the City the following day. I had scarcely returned from the clinic when he turned up to see how I had got on and to interpret the documents which I had been given at the clinic . . .

In the same way, a different consultant was looking after me during my second visit and he, too, showed the same degree of attention and concern throughout my visit.

I need hardly say that the level of skill, both pastoral and medical, which the consultants, and indeed the staff in general, exhibited was of the highest possible standard. . . . I have nothing but good to say of St Luke's.'

A vicar who was a patient three times over a period of five years remembers how, on each occasion he was 'overwhelmed by the kindness and generosity on the part of the consultants and others who give their service to St Luke's' and in particular recalls, with gratitude 'the charming and talented specialist' who treated him.

One patient's letter assured me that the co-operation which so clearly exists between my own consultant and his supportive wife exists with others as well.

'I think I need to give a bit of background to my short stay in St Luke's', wrote one clergy wife. 'I was in the Royal Free X Ray department having an annual screening for breast cancer due to a family history of this disease. "By mistake" the temporary secretary had put me down for an ultra sound scan instead of the usual mammogram. With this scan's precision a lump was clearly visible which had not been picked up on two previous mammograms. When the geneticist in charge of the screening programme came down to talk with me about this shattering evidence, I asked her about St Luke's as a possible venue for surgery. She said something like, "Oh my husband gives some of his free/spare time to St Luke's, would you like him to do the operation?" By the afternoon of that day I had met her husband in his consulting rooms and all was fixed for my admittance to St Luke's and surgery.... I am just so grateful to the consultant who gave his time and talents to me and for me so that I had the minimum time to wait before the operation.'

The letters from which I have quoted were all written within the last decade. But the respect for the consultants which they reflect has a long history. In 1904, for example, in his address at the Annual Meeting at St Luke's, the Bishop of St Albans told a moving story of a clergyman

'actively and usefully engaged in the diocese of Winchester. He came up to London suffering from a terrible complaint. He had a wife and family dependent upon him, and so was only able to afford a poor and most insufficient lodging in which to wait for the possible operation. His wife came and told me his story. He was taken in by the Hostel of St Luke as a free patient; he was to pay nothing. He had only to move from his lodging with its insufficient treatment, and improper diet, and was placed in your blessed home, for it is indeed a very House of Mercy. What was the result? In a very short time he was not only restored to health, but had sufficient strength to go for a change of air with the confident hope that he would be able to resume his work in the Church of Christ after no considerable lapse of time. And this was due entirely to the treatment he received when at the Hostel of St Luke. I have in my pocket a letter which his wife wrote to me the other day. She speaks in the warmest terms of gratitude of the staff and of all connected with the Hostel of St Luke. She alludes to the skilful medical attention which her husband had, and not only to that, but to the extreme sympathy and marvellous care and love with which they had treated his complaint. She went on to speak of the nurses in the same terms.'

Going further back in time, in 1896, also at the Annual Meeting, the Rev. Dr Belcher also testified to the high esteem in which the consultants were held:

'I feel that the one great charm in a movement like this is the brotherly love and charity which animates the whole of it. When I went to the Hostel this morning I met two clergymen whom I knew. I told them that I was coming here this afternoon and they desired me to let you know how deeply grateful they are for the experience, attention, and medical skill expended upon them and how thankful they are for the kindness they receive from everybody at the Hostel.'

And, as Dr de Havilland Hall observed in that same year:

'We must remember also, what a glance at the list of the medical staff will show us, that they are not those junior members of the profession who have yet a fame to make, and have plenty of time at their disposal, but men of skill and experience, men who have reached the very top of their profession, and whose time is of great value. They cheerfully sacrifice not only time and money, but rest and recreation, and no doubt very often sleep also. And I can assure you that the skill, science and kind hearts which they place at the service of the Hostel, are a very valuable contribution to the Institution.'

The General Secretary

To return to the present, Peter Nicholson, the General Secretary of St Luke's, writes equally warmly of the current consultants:

'133 leading London consultants, all Christian men and women, very busy people – the top in their specialities, give their services gladly and willingly at St Luke's without taking a penny piece and in their own time, too, so that the Church's full-time ministering servants can be treated at once and returned with all speed to the many who rely on them just to be there. I am constantly amazed by the cheerful self-giving, especially when they must be absolutely exhausted. . . . What an example to other Church people in the exercise of time and talent!'[12]

The Matron of the Hospital also spoke warmly and appreciatively of the consultants who serve St Luke's. Asked by an interviewer on Radio Essex whether, like the Matron portrayed by Hattie Jacques in the *Carry On* films, she had any trouble with the consultants who serve St Luke's, her response was witty, warm and enthusiastic. 'No trouble at all. . . . They do an excellent job. We never have any problems with our consultants. They follow up their patients. We don't have to call them back. They come and visit. It is a special place, St Luke's.'

In that same interview, Matron was asked: 'What of the nurses?' With equal warmth and appreciation, Matron responded: 'There's a serenity about my nurses. There's a calmness. They love their patients here. They just settle in and get on with it. Because of the family atmosphere of St Luke's, they just love it here.'

Peter Nicholson not only speaks highly of the consultants, he seems to know personally each member of staff and clearly cares for each one. Similarly, the staff hold him in high esteem. 'He's like the father of the hospital', someone told me as they struggled to express their appreciation. This readily-voiced mutuality and support is one of the ingredients which goes into making St Luke's such a healing place for the patient. Behind the scenes, as Peter Nicholson readily admits, tensions do arise, as in any 'close-knit community'. 'People don't always see eye to eye. But because we try to listen to one another, because we try to lift one another up and not put one another down, we seem to grow best when conflicts arise and we try to solve them together.'[13]

I first met Peter, as I have explained in an earlier chapter, a few seconds after I had registered as a patient. He had spotted my heavy case and come to carry it for me. I met him again next morning after the service of Holy Communion when he invited me into his office for a chat. I remember being amazed, as I approached his office, not only that it was almost opposite the reception desk where there is so much activity, but that he chose to work with his door open, a gesture which communicated the non-verbal message: 'I am available.' And he is available: to anyone at almost any time. He also has his finger on the pulse of everything. This availability and shouldering of a huge responsibility contributes to a busyness which many people would find burdensome. But Peter seems to thrive on it. Before I met him and watched him at work, a saying of the Principal of the Theological College where my husband trained had dogged me: 'Beware the barrenness of a busy life.' Peter illustrated a different maxim: that a busy life can be both beautiful and balanced. The busy day, when approached with a positive, prayerful attitude and the sense of purpose Peter brings to it can become fulfilling, rewarding and immensely fruitful. Just as a seemingly-barren Mediterranean beach can produce carpets of blue and white statis flowers, so the potential barrenness of busyness can give birth to the fruit of the Spirit: the expression of love and joy, peace and patience, long-suffering and kindness.[14] If this is to happen, of course, there is the need for a balance between work and play. Despite his heavy and relentless workload, Peter is unafraid to relax; unashamed that others should see him relaxing. I recall, with gratitude, the frequency with which he has turned from his word processor to talk with me and regale me with tales which testify to God's goodness to St Luke's; the times when he has told me of adventures in the Holy Land where he loves to lead pilgrimages or to show me photographs of his family.

Peter illustrated what is, perhaps, the best-known maxim of Benedictine spirituality: *laborare et orare*, to work and to pray. Prayer, for him, is a priority. But his prayer is not compartmentalised. It permeates everything he says and does. His is a spirituality which is lived out in the mundane moments of his strenuous vocation; a spirituality which sustains and supports him through crises as well as one which fills him with awe and thanksgiving. Such a robust, vibrant, practical spirituality would surely have rejoiced the heart of St Benedict as much as it rejoices the heart of God himself for Benedict believed in balance, harmony and integration.

As Esther de Waal interprets The Rule,

'Neither the Benedictine community as a whole nor its individual members are expected to be working feverishly, consumed with a restless energy which damages health and strength, the phenomenon known in management circles as burn-out, the result of working too hard with no rhythm or relaxation. This is not a Benedictine virtue! Instead there is contentment with the familiar, the ordinary, the monotonous.... There is no differentiation between things that matter and things that do not. Instead all activities are seen as significant.... St Benedict tells the cellarer that the humble equipment which he handles deserves the same reverence as the altar vessels ... all belongings are to be treated as if they were sacred. There is no room for any area of life untouched by God. For God is present and accessible in every moment and in every activity.'[15]

At the same time, 'prayer lies at the very heart of the Benedictine life'.[16] As in the life of Christ, 'it holds everything together, it sustains every other activity.... Praying can never be set apart from the rest of life, it is the life itself.'[17] Therefore time must be made for prayer and nothing must be preferred to personal and corporate prayer. In other words, 'the whole Christ is seeking the whole person'.[18]

With a father-figure like Peter keeping a watchful eye on the staff family, it was hardly surprising that, in St Luke's, the carers felt cared for; they were constantly assured that their person, their ministry and their future came constantly under the caring eye of God.

The quality of a community like St Luke's reflects the character of the individuals who make it up and the relationships between the individuals who live and work together. What the caring community of St Luke's offers to the carer is not just medical expertise and tenderness, but the opportunity to witness first hand how effective a community can be when it recognises itself for what it is: in the language of St Paul, 'the body of Christ'.[19] The St Luke's community embodies the Biblical insight that this body is 'not made up of one part but of many'.[20] That it would be a nonsense for one part, like the foot, to claim 'because I am not a hand, I do not belong to the body'.[21] The St Luke's community appears to have so assimilated the importance of each part of the body expressing concern and care for the other parts that it is a joy to watch and a pleasure to be with.

As such it is a parable of the Kingdom. Embedded within its philosophy and lifestyle I was finding yet more clues to help me answer my questions: What are these Kingdom virtues we pray for? What are the standards of this Kingdom we sing about with such verve? The community life of St Luke's was demonstrating for me what I have witnessed in the best of Benedictine communities: the hidden power of a corporate life based on Biblical principles including respect for all people, contentment, joy in serving, the enjoyment of creation, a balance between working and praying. Did I hear God say what Jesus said to the lawyer after he had told the parable of the Good Samaritan: 'You go, then, and do the same'?[22]

Hearing is Healing

'To listen totally means that one takes another's whole life into one's being and cares for it'[1]

A grateful patient once made a splendid gift for St Luke's: a quilted tapestry which now hangs in the entrance hall of the hospital. In the centre of the quilt stands a church. This church is encircled first by a ring of leaves and then by a glut of strawberries, cherries and other fruits. The church symbolises the clergy and other Christian workers who come as patients to St Luke's. The leaves and the fruit represent the staff of the hospital who enfold these carers with the superlative kind of love and care I have been describing.

One of the ways in which the staff convey this care is through the seemingly-simple medium of listening: that art-form Gerard Hughes calls 'the most healing gift anyone can possess'.[2]

The staff at St Luke's recognise that hearing is healing. Many of them work in this particular hospital because here, they know that, however busy they are, time to listen to their patients will not be elbowed out. As one of the night nurses put it to me, 'It's wonderful to have time to nurse properly – time for the patients.' And Matron spoke of 'the joy of having the time to listen to patients'.

But, as I have attempted to spell out in my book, *Listening to Others*,[3] the art-form of listening requires, not only time, but certain skills. The staff I encountered at St Luke's laid these skills at my disposal and, in doing so, reminded me just how healing it is to be heard.

On the Monday after my operation, my consultant arrived as usual at 7.45 am and, as usual, expressed his delight at the progress I appeared to be making. And he gave me two pieces of good news. One was that I could now eat whatever I liked. The other was that, since I was so well, I could choose either to stay at St Luke's until my stitches were removed the following Sunday, or I could go home within a few days and ask my own doctor to remove the stitches.

However happy a patient is in hospital, news of going home usually sounds like music in their ears. I was no exception to this norm. Even so, I was glad that no pressure was being exerted at that moment. My consultant advised me to make my choice at my leisure. So when he left me, I simply recorded in my Journal, 'I am tempted to stay: to be nursed and gentled along. Lord, may my decision be made on the basis of "What's best for the Kingdom"' and my mind turned to other thoughts. Several cards had arrived in the post that morning. Among them a humorous one. I recorded in my Journal, 'I must be very tired today ... I can see that the card was meant to be fun but it feels as though the senders are not taking seriously the nature of my operation nor the uphill task of convalescence. Perhaps we need to pray for sensitivity to send just the right card to the right person?'

If I had stopped to analyse what was going on inside me, I could have read the language of my own distress and discovered from this over-reaction that I was not yet ready to be discharged from the cocoon of St Luke's and to be thrust back into the maelstrom of parish life once more. But I thought no more about the card after I had placed it alongside the others which now lined my room.

Days after my operation my Journal reads:

'So many things to record!'

Among the 'so many things' I mention that, for the first half of the night, I was sleeping without a sleeping tablet and that seemed a mark of progress. I also mentioned that my consultant had not visited me that morning – the first time he had not appeared since my operation:

'I've just been down to Communion. I was glad that Brian was travelling in the lift. This was my first venture away from the third floor since the operation. As I sat in that chapel I had learned to love before the op., I realised how much I have been re-shaped by this week. My world has shrunk from the size of the globe (this time last month I was working at a cracking pace 12,000 miles away in New Zealand), to the size of one of the rooms in St Luke's. I've had the challenge of transforming it into something lovely and felt touched today when Jimmy described it as "a rose garden" and when the physio exclaimed the other day, "Oh! You have made it look pretty" but I feel a different person from this time last week.'

Just how different I felt from 'this time last week' became evident later that day when my husband came to visit me for the first time since the operation.

David came carrying grape juice, various books I had asked for, more cards and my mail, which I had also asked him to bring. He looked exhausted. From the trip? From looking after himself? From coping with the parish? I wasn't sure. Nevertheless, he was bright and bubbling over with news. When I asked what he had been doing since we last met, he told me. Because the work of the parish is also a major part of his life, he inevitably started to talk about the various meetings he had attended and the various people he had seen and, as he did so, I listened, not only to his words and enthusiasm but to my own emotions and reactions. I watched myself nose-dive. As David talked about some of the people and situations which continued to put pressure on him although he was, at that moment, already over-stretched, I felt both angry and helpless. Angry because it felt as though the entire parish with all its needs and demands was invading my safe, private world; helpless because I knew that there was nothing I could do to help; that I would be unable to be of much use for weeks to come.

My cough was still proving troublesome and, while David and another visitor were with me, I started to cough uncontrollably. This tore at my stitches and when the time came for David to leave, I was sobbing helplessly. The proverbial penny had dropped. I knew I was not yet fit to cope even with the thought of returning to the pressures of a home which, in so many ways, is the hub of the parish yet I wanted, more than anything to be with my husband and not to appear to be rejecting him.

When David left, I wept again. It had been a bitter-sweet reunion. Eventually, my tears disappeared and I decided to attempt to deal with my tear-stained face. I was still at the wash basin trying to wash away all evidence of my distress, when Stephanie popped her head round the door. 'Nice to have people from home, isn't it?', she said and to her amazement, I burst into tears again. After I had calmed down, I explained the whole sad saga: that though I had been excited when the consultant first mentioned the word 'home', the visit had shown me that I was not yet ready to cope either with the return journey or with living 'over the job'.

'She was wonderful,' I recorded in my Journal. 'Just what I needed. A typical kiwi! She held me. Let me talk. Understood. Cared. Then gave me space.'

Stephanie's style of listening was indeed, superb. Young though she was, at that precise moment, she was the adult and I was more like a troubled child. Apparently unperturbed by this, she opened her arms, allowed me to be enfolded by them and held me while I sobbed again. Her empathy and understanding were like balm to my battered emotions. So much so that, within a few minutes, I had calmed down whereupon she helped me into bed, sat in silence holding my hand until I assured her with a watery smile to prove my point, 'I'm all right now', and then she left me sensing, correctly, that what I now needed was space to think things through for myself.

Did Stephanie warn Lita, the Filipino domestic to treat me as though I was fragile, I wonder? I shall never know. What I do know is that, when Lita brought in my supper she could not have been more sensitive. I might have been wearing that label which hangs around the neck of Paddington Bear, 'Fragile! Handle with care!' Her obvious, though unexpressed concern and love so touched me that I sobbed my way through my cod mornay, ravioli and cheesecake and then asked whether I might go by myself to the chapel.

That morning a beautiful card had come from a concerned

friend. I took it with me now. The photograph of one of Dorothea Steigerwald's statuettes seemed to encapsulate the way I felt – exhausted, forlorn, lonely. 'Only this figure is at peace and I'm not', I thought.

For twenty minutes or so, I knelt in 'my' place in the chapel. For much of that time, I sobbed quietly. A young man was cleaning the chapel. But his presence was not intrusive. In some ways it helped to have him there. Gradually, peace seeped into me.

Picking up my picture, I wandered into the vestry, reluctant to leave the calm of this 'safe place'. For several minutes more, I stood gazing at the picture of the thorn-crowned Christ which hangs there. 'His face is full of pain, but he is looking to his Father', I thought. And I found coming from somewhere deep within myself, an echo of a resolve once made by the Psalmist: 'I will lift up *my* eyes to the hills, to Father, that's where my help comes from.'[4]

At peace again, I returned to my room. On my return, Stephanie came to check that I was in one piece and, again, I valued her non-intrusive, sensitive care. I re-read the letters David had brought me, wrote up my Prayer Journal and was surprised to hear a knock at the door. By this time it was past visiting time and I wondered who could be coming to see me. To my amazement, my 'Come in' heralded the arrival of my consultant. This was the first time he had paid me an evening visit so I had not expected to see him at that hour of night. Had Stephanie told him about my mini-set-back? Again, I shall never know. What I do know is that, when he asked me how I was, to my embarrassment and annoyance, the tears began to flow again. But I need neither have been embarrassed nor annoyed for the consultant showed no signs of either reaction. On the contrary, I was touched when I saw that, in response to my tears, his own eyes filled with tears and his face was full of compassion and concern. Before checking my wound, he took the time to sit down, to listen to my turmoil, to empathise and to explore with me the options. Removing from me the choice he had given me two days earlier, he decided that I should stay in St Luke's until the stitches were removed. He decided that, instead of staying at home to convalesce, I should go to a quieter place where I could 'queen it', to quote his own words. Putting the problem in perspective, he reminded me of something I was well aware of but of which I needed to be reminded: that most patients suffer post-operative blues at some stage of their recovery. And, having examined my wound, he offered sensitive reassurance that physically, all was well.

After he had left I felt exhausted. My stitches were pulling and I was wrung out. But as I wrote in my Journal: 'I see there's healing to be received . . .' and I began to recall the healing which had already come to me that day through people, through pictures and through the peaceful chapel.

Healing first trickled into my grazed spirit when Stephanie displayed understanding and compassion instead of surprise or condemnation at my distress. This assured me that she felt that I was of sufficient worth to involve herself in my trauma; and of itself this is a healing message.

Next, healing came through the spontaneous, non-possessive embrace in which she enfolded and held me. This deepened within me the sense that, vulnerable though I was, I was accepted and valued with that vulnerability. It also assured me that there was at least one person in my world who was prepared to share my burden with me. Healing also came through that sensitivity which seemed to discern with absolute accuracy when I needed presence with its unspoken message of solidarity in my pain and when I needed solitude. This assured me that Stephanie had accurately discerned the kind of person I am. Fragile, yes. Quick to accept appropriate help when it is offered, yes. And yet, essentially a very private person with inner resources on which I have learned to draw in solitude so I need space.

Healing had come through pictures: through the postcard which a friend had felt prompted to send from Germany; through the picture which hung in the vestry of the chapel reminding me again of the power of the visual which can wing the grace of God into our grazed areas with a power which words do not possess. And more healing came simply through being in that powerful but safe place, the chapel.

Other post-operative patients have described memories which are not dissimilar to my own; occasions when the chapel became much more than an oasis; when it became a house of healing. I think, for example, of the bishop's wife who told me how much it meant to her to be able to go to the chapel. 'It was so special to know it was always open, that I could lie on the floor before the altar (the only relatively comfortable position!) and be sustained.'

In his book *Restoring Your Spiritual Passion*, Gordon MacDonald points out that

> 'we need safe places in our worlds. Not merely when we are in trouble but when we need to rest a bit, to regain our measure of spiritual passion and composure for the continuing challenges of the cue balls that constantly come at us . . .
>
> Those of us who have lived in the freer Protestant traditions have not been adequately taught of the value of the holy places: sites exclusively reserved for worship and spiritual listening. Hearing only of the dangers of excessive emphasis upon religious architecture, we have denied ourselves the peaceful atmospheres of altars, shrines, and chapels. However legitimate the reasons for concerns about these things, insufficient thought has been given to what takes their place as an alternative.
>
> How important it is to understand that safe places can be those where all the senses are involved in lifting us to heaven and into the presence of the waiting Father. A safe place is a place of silence where the inward ear can hear, a place of beauty where the eyes can take in color, form, and order (the symbols of God's being and actions), and a place of peace where the body can relax as the inward person reaches upward to hear the Spirit speak . . . We must come to see that genius is involved in setting aside on the maps of our lives places reserved only for the restoration of our spiritual passion.'[5]

Not surprisingly, perhaps, healing had also come that day through one of God's instruments of healing, my surgeon. And yet such gifted physicians are not always best remembered for their listening skills. As I recalled the way my consultant had heard my tale of woe, I marvelled. That evening, in my room, in the presence of Stephanie, an Agency nurse, he had made himself vulnerable by incarnating the injunction of St Paul, to weep with those who weep. Building on the rapport and trust which he had already taken the trouble to establish, he also took upon himself another Pauline principle: that of bearing my burden. Sensing, correctly, that, left to make the decision for myself, I might decide to go home prematurely, having heard that I felt incapable of coping with being catapulted back to the parish, he suggested, instead, that I should stay at St Luke's until the stitches were removed. We then explored together whether there was an option open to me other than remaining at home to convalesce. Was he consciously taking Jesus as his model, I wonder? Or did it just happen that what he offered me was the kind of counsel Jesus offered his distraught disciples as they walked from Jerusalem to Emmaus on the first Easter Sunday evening? As Dr Gary Collins, Professor of Psychology at Trinity Divinity School, Illinois, points out, on that occasion Jesus, the apparent 'stranger', first established a relationship of trust with the two people he met. He then explored with them their problem before disentangling their confused thoughts and feelings. Whereupon he left them but not before he had stimulated them into action and given them the strength to negotiate life on a new set of terms.

What Jesus did for those disciples on that never-to-be-forgotten night, my consultant did for me. His concern and care underlined the message he had communicated consistently from the moment of my first consultation, 'You matter'. In this, too, whether he recognised it or not and whether he intended it or not, he was communicating through his own person, the words of St Peter, 'It matters to [God] about you'[6]; underlining the title of this book that, through his listening and the care of the entire family of St Luke's, I was continually being cherished, continually kept under the caring eye of God.

Lucy, as always, underlined this message when she came on duty that night. When she first arrived, I warned her that I had had a weepy day and that there was a particular programme I wanted to watch on television. She left me to watch a most moving documentary about the divided island of Cyprus. The film showed how the Greek Cypriots had been forced to leave their homes on the Northern side of the island as a result of the Turkish invasion of 1974 still live with the deeply-felt longing to return to the villages they love. The television presenter and his crew visited the occupied territories of Famagusta and Kyrenia and filmed derelict houses and damaged churches; villages which had been so tragically abandoned. They then went back to the Cypriots and, in one of the coffee houses which are still the central meeting places for men on the island, they showed the film. Loving Cyprus and the Cypriots as I do, I was deeply touched by the childlike look of joy and recognition as the cameras homed in on the leathery, weather-beaten faces of refugees who were catching a glimpse of their own homes for the first time in fourteen years. Peering at the screen, as many of them were, they would, from time to time point, exclaim as though with ecstasy, 'there's the church', 'that's the casino', 'there's my house'; then, with a sigh of relief laced with pain, 'it's still there'. Feeling afresh their pain as I have done so often when I have been in Cyprus restored a sense of perspective about my own troubles. When Lucy reappeared, I told her about the programme before noticing that she had handed me a gift which set the seal on the healing experiences of the day. My eyes opened wide when I peeped into the paper bag she gave me. Inside lay a generous helping of huge, mouth-watering prawn crackers she had made. She and I shared them before she handed me some sleeping pills which she advised me to take to ensure that I slept soundly. I accepted gratefully. The day had left me exhausted.

My Journal reminds me that next morning, although I had slept until 7.45 am, I was still weary. Unable to concentrate on any of the books which lay, invitingly, by my bedside, I turned to something else Lucy had brought me, a series of tapes about the Medugorje phenomenon.

Two-way listening

Like many of my friends and acquaintances, Lucy had recently visited this Yugoslavian village where, many believe, Mary, the mother of Jesus has appeared repeatedly to some of the children who live there.

For some time I had been intending to explore these claims. To my ultra Protestant ears, they posed more questions than answers. Yet, as one trusted friend put it, 'If you take the Biblical injunction "by their fruits ye shall know them", it is clear that our Lord lies behind this. In Medugorje, rifts between individuals and communities have been healed by reconciliation, many miraculous healings have happened, "the blind see, the lame walk" and the fruits of the Spirit: love and joy, peace and long-suffering, gentleness and goodness abound.' Lucy testified to the same good news. She had obviously been deeply touched by her pilgrimage there and because of the relationship which now existed between the two of us, I was anxious to understand her journey and had therefore asked if I might borrow the tapes which she had bought and which contain the kernel of the Medugorje message. That morning, as I listened to one of these tapes, I found that what was being said about the sufferings of Christ spoke to my own condition. Speaking of the Cross, the voice on the tape simply said: 'it is the source, the origin of our salvation.' And of Jesus' sufferings on the cross, he made this startling observation, which, though obvious I had not seen with such vividness before: 'Jesus was *nailed alive* to his Cross.' 'Suffering is not a mystery, it is a revelation,' he went on quoting Oscar Wilde. 'Divine suffering reveals how much God loves our sinful selves. Jesus did not come to explain suffering or to take it away but to fill it with his presence. As Therese of Lisieux put it, "It is our love Jesus thirsts for." ' To bring the comfort and healing of Christ's passion into our life, the speaker suggested that, among other things, we should read about it, pray the Stations of the Cross (a method of meditating on the events leading to the crucifixion) gaze at the figure of Christ on the Cross, let him speak to us and attend the Eucharist regularly: methods of prayer which were meaningful to me and not beyond my capabilities even though I was just beginning my convalescence.

The tape had touched me in my tiredness. In particular, the words 'Jesus was *nailed alive* to his Cross' had lodged in my heart and the suggestion that, in prayer, we should gaze at that figure on the Cross and let him speak to us. My mind went back to those words of St Paul: 'becoming like him in his death.' Perhaps in the gazing I would understand what the apostle meant?

I was grateful for the loan of the tapes; grateful that Lucy had talked to me about her pilgrimage. I became conscious that talking to Lucy had fanned a flame which had been flickering in me with increasing strength for fifteen years: the flame of longing that we, in the Church, might enjoy a greater degree of unity than we have yet achieved.

If I interpret the Gospels correctly, this desire is but a pale reflection of Christ's own longing. I think, in particular, of that most moving prayer which seemed to come from deep within his innermost being which he uttered within the context of the Last Supper:

> 'My prayer is not for [these my disciples] alone. I pray also for those who will believe in me through their message, that all of them may be one, Father, just as you are in me and I am in you. May they also be in us so that the world may believe that you have sent me. I have given them the glory that you gave me, that they may be one as we are one: I in them and you in me. May they be brought to complete unity to let the world know that you sent me and have loved them even as you have loved me.'[7]

Such oneness comes, I have been discovering, not through attempting to dot all the theological i's or cross all the theological t's nor through playing an ecclesiastical game of 'let's pretend': let's pretend that the gulf created by the Reformation ceases to exist. Rather, such unity comes to those who, recognising that there are significant barriers to unity, recognise, too, that oneness comes first through closeness with people rather than through theories and theology. As Christians of different denominations draw alongside each other and concentrate on the things that unite them like the Lordship of Christ and prayer rather than magnifying the points of division, unity does take shape. This unity deepens when Christians listen to one another with the desire to learn from the other rather than listening with the intention of criticising the other or setting out to prove where the other is theologically 'unsound'. The oneness increases when Christians of all persuasions acknowledge that they are not custodians of the whole truth but that they have been given Biblical insights which, when pieced together with insights entrusted to those whose journey into God through Christ has taken them along a different route, can create a detailed map complete with contours rather than a mere sketch map. The togetherness grows, when, to use a phrase coined by the Anglican Bishop and the Roman Catholic Archbishop of Liverpool, David Sheppard and Derek Worlock, Christians from different denominations discover that they are 'better together' – more complete, more rounded, more effective in heralding the Kingdom of Christ, more likely to impress on the watching world the reality of the Lordship of Christ.

Lita

Fuel was added to this flickering flame by Lita who used to bring me my meals. Lita is even smaller than I imagine the Zacchaeus mentioned in the Gospels would have been. More importantly, she not only shares Zacchaeus' size but also his determination to encounter Christ.

One day, when Lita came into my room with a jug of water, she asked me a question which, I sensed, she had been longing to ask for some days. 'Mrs Huggett, are you a Roman Catholic?' Puzzled, I explained that though I have many Roman Catholic friends and though I count it a privilege to lead retreats and Quiet Days with Roman Catholics, I am, in fact, an Anglican. She seemed satisfied with this reply and went on to explain that the reason she had asked the question was that, in my prayer corner, I not only had a candle and a cross but an icon and she thought that Anglicans were not permitted to use such aids to worship. This led on to a series of brief conversations which further convinced me that Christian unity cements people in an unbreakable bond of love even though they retain certain theological differences. I was able to explain to Lita why I found the visual so powerful and meaningful, not only when I was ill but in the normal course of my prayer. Little by little, as she gained confidence in talking to me in a language which is not her mother tongue, she told me her story.

Lita used to work for an English family in Hong Kong. It was they who brought her to England. Having worked with them in this country for six years, they then decided to return to Hong Kong. Lita, however, preferred to stay in England as she wanted to see the pilgrimage places in Europe: Fatima in Portugal, Rome, Lourdes and the Holy Land (the latter a dream which remains, as yet unfulfilled). That is when she took up her post at St Luke's where she has worked for the past ten years. Life for a Filipino living in Central London, can, she told me, prove very lonely at times. Loneliness, at one stage of her life, led to depression and it was at this point that the Roman Catholics in Westminster came to her aid. They befriended her and, as a result, she became one of their enquirers exploring the faith with them. With shining eyes and a smile which spoke quite as eloquently as her words, she told me how, week by week, she had received from this church, not only the warmth of the kind of fellowship which helped her to feel as though she had, to use her own words, 'lots of brothers and sisters in Jesus Christ', but such faithful, consecutive Bible teaching that she discovered a firm faith of her own. So much so that now, although she finds the work at St Luke's tiring and demanding, she loves it – particularly the opportunity it gives her to talk to the patients about her faith. 'I like to talk with them,' she confessed, 'because I learn more with them especially when they're talking about the Bible. Sometimes at the church, they give me a Bible passage to read and then say: "Tell the community what the reading means to you." Sometimes I ask the patients to help me because I think that I cannot express what I want to say and the patient helps me. When I ask the patient to help me about the Bible, they always tell me: "If ever you have a problem about the Bible, just ask me." And I feel happy.'

If my own experience was anything to go by, Lita gives quite as much happiness as she receives. Her presence, her sensitivity and her smile were like the proverbial ray of sunshine even though, at times, it was clear that she was working under pressure. She said to me: 'Two years ago there was a Bishop here – a patient. At this time I was having difficulties. He asked me, "Do you trust in Jesus?" I said, "Yes." He said to me, "Listen to God. Trust God's Word." He told me that I'm very close to God and this gave me peace of mind. Sometimes I still feel lonely in this country on my own but I feel happy when I am talking to the patients.' I wondered if the Bishop felt about Lita as I did. Every evening, I learned that Lita goes to the chapel to pray. 'I like it there. It's very peaceful. I pray before the crucifix. I pray the rosary and say my own prayers.' And her prayer not only spills over into her work, if I observed her correctly, her life is a prayer. Watching the way she has learned to integrate work and prayer, openness to God and faithfulness to duty was one of God's gifts to me during my stay at St Luke's.

Being with Lita gave me an injection of joy as I realised that, here in St Luke's, true ecumenism was being experienced. For true ecumenism happens when Christians realise that God is not confined to work within the narrow, blinkered limits of any one denomination or school of Christian thought. Rather, he is at work in everyone. True unity comes when we detect the tell-tale signs of the Holy Spirit's activity and allow this to draw us to those whose doctrinal beliefs and prayer practices may differ from our own.

Listening to Lita also reminded me that actions speak louder than words; a truism I needed to have underlined at the beginning of this decade of evangelism. One of the things that impressed me about Lita's story was that the members of her church first heard her loneliness and did what they could to alleviate that before introducing to her the notion of Bible Study and conversion to the Christian faith. Friendship evangelism, I have observed over the years, is the most effective form of spreading the Good News. Lita and her Roman Catholic friends have reminded me that the most effective way to begin to spread this Good News is first to listen to a person's story, next to seek to identify where they are on their journey into God, then to affirm their God-implanted yearning for him rather than presenting him with a pre-determined set of beliefs to which we require them to adhere.

Such hearing is also deeply healing, because it takes a

person deeper and deeper into God which is, at root, what each person desires. As St Augustine put it in those often-quoted words: 'Our hearts are restless 'til they find their rest in you.' Hearing also heals in that when we listen to another person's prayer pilgrimage with an openness and desire to learn, we are helping to heal the hurts and misunderstandings which have divided the church for years. When we do this we are playing a small part in bringing to pass that heart-felt prayer of Christ, that they may be one.

The most powerful form of listening, I was discovering is listening laced, not merely with professional empathy (valuable though this craft of viewing life through the other's eyes is), but listening laced with the more costly gift of the compassion which clearly suffers with the sufferer. Listening born of the brokenness and vulnerability which hears and touches the brokenness and vulnerability in the other. In this two-way listening, had I stumbled on something of what lay behind Paul's phrase: 'becoming like him in death' and that other curious claim of Christ which he had impressed upon St Paul: 'My strength is made perfect in weakness.'[8]

10

The Value of Visiting

'The way to "God alone" is seldom travelled alone.'[1]

No one enjoys being weak. Weakness frequently gives rise to frustration. Those of us who complain most persistently that 'time flies', that there are not enough hours in a day or days in a week to do all that needs to be done are often the first to complain that, in hospital, time drags. We find ourselves caught in the cleft-stick situation Henri Nouwen describes so well from the irony of his own experience. Henri Nouwen, a much-sought-after teacher, lecturer and writer confesses in his book, *The Genesee Diary*, that the day came when:

'while teaching, lecturing, and writing about the importance of solitude, inner freedom, and peace of mind, I kept stumbling over my own compulsions and illusions. What was driving me from one book to another, one place to another, one project to another ... What was turning my vocation to be a witness to God's love into a tiring job? ... Maybe I spoke more about God than with him. Maybe my writing about prayer kept me from a prayerful life. Maybe I was more concerned about the praise of men and women than the love of God. Maybe I was slowly becoming a prisoner of people's expectations instead of a man liberated by divine promises.'[2]

He realised that he would discover answers to these questions only as he stepped off the treadmill of his hectic schedule. Side-stepping for him did not involve hospitalisation. Rather, it involved a calculated choice. He would clear his diary and enter a monastery where he would live for seven months, not as a privileged guest but as a monk.

Even while he was busily putting this plan into operation, he found that he was caught in 'a web of strange paradoxes', that he was not as strong as he thought. 'While complaining about too many demands, I felt uneasy when none were made. While speaking about the burden of letter writing, an empty mailbox made me sad. While fretting about tiring lecture tours, I felt disappointed when there were no invitations. While speaking nostalgically about an empty desk, I feared the day on which that would come true. In short: while desiring to be alone, I was frightened of being left alone.'[3]

Clergy and other Christian workers can similarly suffer from withdrawal symptoms when they are stripped of all their roles and required to rest, particularly in hospital. Hospitalisation poses particular problems. The hospital day can seem long. Patients are often roused from sleep well before 7 am but may not finally turn their lights out until after 11 pm. This means that they have a great deal of time to think. Without the distraction of work and family, hobbies and relationships, coffee breaks and tea breaks, meetings and telephone calls, they cannot escape the powerful emotions which clamour for attention: the fear and the grief, the restlessness and the loneliness, the preoccupation with self and the spiritual lethargy which seem to be the companions of many sick people at some stage of their hospitalisation and convalescence.

Courage for those who are afraid

Roger Hurding, a psychiatrist who has encountered much personal suffering as well as listening to the struggles of hundreds of others, describes the fear which intimidates many patients facing surgery. For some 'the worst pain is the pain anticipated. It is the fear that discomfort might be too much to cope with that particularly undermines. It is this apprehension that is often behind anxiety about operations and other surgical procedures. Will it hurt? Will it be more than I can bear? Will they realise I'm in pain? Will I be able to call for help? These fears are deep seated.'[4] They bring with them a sense of helplessness and powerlessness.

Norman Autton, in his book *Touch: An Exploration* sheds further light on the subject when he claims that 'when illness becomes a traumatic event in one's life the individual experiences anxiety, insecurity and low self-esteem. The more serious and prolonged the illness, the greater are the opportunities for anxiety to threaten the patient.'[5] Quoting the psychiatrist Jack Dominian, he underlines the fact that 'the experience of illness is a complex psychological situation. Anxiety, depression, denial and regression are some of the common psychological responses. In sickness and in hospital care a patient experiences the anxiety of disintegration.'[6]

In his searingly-honest book, *Fear No Evil*, David Watson explained how succumbing to such fears left him experiencing an unprecedented sense of powerlessness:

'When I first heard . . . that I had cancer, the news hit me like a thunderbolt. All human hopes and securities were suddenly shattered. "it *can't* be true," I said to myself foolishly and anxiously. "That sort of thing doesn't happen to me!" But it did, and my deepest fears were realised . . . The worst times for me were at two or three o'clock in the morning. I had preached the gospel all over the world with ringing conviction. I had told countless thousands of people that I was not afraid of death since through Christ I had already received God's gift of eternal life. For years I had not doubted these truths at all. But now the most fundamental questions were nagging away insistently, especially in those long hours of the night. If I was soon on my way to heaven, how real was heaven? Was it anything more than a beautiful idea? What honestly would happen when I died? Did God himself really exist after all? How could I be sure? Indeed, how could I be certain of anything apart from cancer and death? I literally sweated over these questions, and on many occasions woke up with my pyjamas bathed in cold sweat! Never before had my faith been so ferociously attacked.'[7]

Fear, as Sheila Cassidy reminds us, weakens every part of our anatomy: it attacks the knees turning them to jelly so that we wonder whether we shall be able to walk. It attacks the mind, paralysing thought and clouding vision like a blindfold so that familiar landscapes disappear and we are left disoriented and alone. It might make us want to scream out in terror, or 'cower like an animal, teeth bared, quivering.'[8]

In chapter two of this book, I described how fear demolished my defences. While I was a patient in St Luke's, I detected similar signs of terror holding fellow patients in their deathly grip. As I wrote in my Journal one evening: 'I've just been talking to the new patient next door. She's obviously very frightened about her forthcoming operation.' And as I write this chapter, I recall the look of terror in the eyes of the clergyman who had been flown into London from overseas. Suffering as he seemed to be from some as yet undiagnosed tropical disease and accompanying signs of nervous exhaustion, he was clearly struggling to keep feelings of panic under control. We patients were like people who have been ship-wrecked. We used the little energy we had to send out distress signals to the selected few: those we sensed would understand and care; those who, though they might be able to do nothing to rescue us from our plight would at least stay alongside us and show by their love and their presence that they cared. Many of us fellow patients threw lifelines to each other.

Some of us were fortunate. We also had visitors whose physical presence communicated that life-saving message that it mattered to them what happened to us and who, by sacrificing time and energy to be with us, showed their willingness to stretch out a helping hand. I found it fascinating to discover how healing these messages are to the person who is paralysed by powerlessness; how, quite literally, at such times, people seem to possess the ability to pour courage into the patient.

My first visitor encouraged me in this way. This visitor, the priest I mentioned in an earlier chapter, so radiated calm and peace and the presence of Christ that, when I reflected on the visit after he had gone I concluded that, instead of rushing from the Underground station into my room, as I would have been tempted to do, he must have prepared himself prayerfully for this visit. I learned later that he had, indeed, slipped into the chapel for a few minutes of quiet before visiting a patient on the Fourth Floor and then me.

In her helpful book *Listening*, Anne Long explains very movingly how she prepares herself to listen to another person:

'If someone has asked me for listening time I try to build in personal preparation, however short. I need to be open to God both for myself and for the person coming. . . . Quite often the last thing I feel like doing is to listen to someone and it is helpful to acknowledge this and realise that my own resources *are* inadequate. Sometimes I uncurl my fingers and simply hold out empty hands to God. I seek to be still in God's presence and not to fear my own emptiness or distractedness or inadequacy. [I take comfort from Maria Boulding's reminder that]: "Provided only that you consent . . . the work of grace is going on in you through the whole business of living, to hollow you out, to make you capax Dei . . . able to receive God."⁹ And this receiving of God is important if we are to be available to him for the person. I also hold the person by name into the love and light of God, asking that what we need will be given.'¹⁰

In the solitude of the chapel, had my friend prepared himself in a similar way? Was this the reason why everything he said and did seemed to be shot through with the strengthening love of Christ? Is there a lesson here for me to learn? These were some of the questions I asked myself later that day.

My next visitor, my daughter, similarly strengthened me but the methods she used were quite different. She simply shared my helplessness. I am not saying she invited me to share my feelings. She had no need to do that. She sensed them and was sensitive to them. Perhaps, more than anyone, she was best equipped to do this. She had been with me when the second gall-bladder attack knocked me sideways. She has also seen me struggle with depression in the past. And, good friend that she is, she has the strength of character to sit with me, in silence when necessary, communicating through touch or an understanding smile or her willingness to be helpless alongside me that she is prepared to stay with me for as long as it takes. Such costly self-giving is strangely liberating. It makes no attempt to eliminate fear or apprehension and it makes no attempt to pray away symptoms or signs of stress or distress. Yet it communicates the solidarity with the weak which, of itself, is immensely healing and supportive.

Friendship for the lonely

My visitors not only gave me courage, support and the sense of well-being we call peace, many of them proved to me that they wanted to accompany me through this enforced period of hiddenness. This was an assurance I needed to have underlined time and time again because, as I was to discover to my cost, patients may not only be assaulted by fears (rational and irrational), they may also suffer a deep, existential loneliness.

In *Just Good Friends?* I have described loneliness from my own experience:

'Loneliness is a feeling: or, more accurately, a jumble of feelings. It is the feeling that you matter to people, not for who you are, but for what you can do. For some, it goes deeper than that: it is the anxiety that you do not matter at all. If you died tomorrow, no-one would even notice, let alone care. It is a feeling of alienation. . . . a feeling of being cut off by others. It is feeling that no-one is even aware of your heart-hunger, *Your* need for care, love and support. . . . the feeling that you have ceased to be important to a particular person or body of people. Loneliness attacks the senses so that you feel isolated from your peers. You seem to be rejected, estranged, abandoned, you believe that nowhere are you fully understood.'[11]

Most people spend most of their lives avoiding listening to the language of this most basic human loneliness which is common to single people and married people alike. In hospital, we cannot do that. There, all our escape routes are blocked: we have no meetings to attend, no sermons to prepare, no stream of urgent telephone calls to make or receive, instead we have plenty of that elusive commodity we call time. And in the long, sometimes sleepless hours of the night as well as in the uninterrupted moments of the day, while we are alone with our thoughts, our loneliness stares us in the face and either leers or smiles at us.

Clergy and Christian workers can take out no insurance policy against this sense of isolation and separation, this fear of being rejected and estranged, this dread of being abandoned, this hunger for caring and support. On the contrary, many of them seem particularly prone to such loneliness. Someone has painted the picture powerfully:

'Mountain climbers say it often: "The higher up you go the lonelier it gets." The same experience applies to leaders who, in their climb to the top, have found that the oxygen gets thin, the available companionship increasingly sparse. The plains and mountains and valleys of human intercourse where a man or woman must maintain some vestige of the general can provide territory for acute isolation and loneliness.'[12]

In hospital, visiting times more than any other time can trigger off such loneliness. That, at least, was my experience. My Journal reminds me that I first felt the pangs of such pain on the Saturday after my operation. I had had no visitors on the Friday but that had not mattered because I spent most of the day dozing. Talking to visitors would have required more energy than I would have been able to muster. But Saturday was different. I had woken at 5.45 am and, having been helped to use the commode and to wash, had enjoyed the luxury of a lazy morning. But at this stage of my recovery, my brain still felt anaesthetised so I had inclination neither to pray nor read and since I was still on a drip, there were no meals to punctuate the day. When visiting time began, sounds of laughter and hilarity from the next room brought me face to face with reality: although I had told my daughter on the telephone that I was not expecting visitors but that that would be all right, I suddenly realised that it was not all right. I was, in fact, feeling bereft. Lonely. My husband telephoned and that helped me to feel in touch with the outside world and, more importantly, with home. Even so, I was becoming increasingly conscious that, despite the marvellous care being lavished on me by the staff of St Luke's, dark and menacing clouds of loneliness were thickening fast.

I watched these clouds with fascination when the unexpected happened. The Sister on duty had hardly wheeled away the trolley phone, when I heard a gentle knock on my door. In response to my invitation to 'Come in', to my amazement and delight, in walked John, a member of our congregation. In response to my squeals of surprise, 'What are you doing here?', he explained that he happened to be in London where he was speaking at a weekend conference. That morning he had had a strong sense that he should come to visit me during his free afternoon. I was not only tremendously touched that he had used up his free time to visit me, but grateful to God that he had alleviated my loneliness with a friend I had known for many years. As I expressed my reaction in my Journal, 'It was such a joy to see him. We chatted. He prayed. And the storm clouds disappeared.'

I knew, of course, that John and his wife Killy would be praying for me. But as Sheila Cassidy rightly reminds us, when we are ill, because we are particularly fragile, we need tangible reminders of this prayer and care. 'If people do not know themselves cared for, they will be prey to a thousand fears of being misunderstood or rejected. Having experienced this kind of care myself ... I know that the feeling of security and affirmation engendered is enormously healing. I believe it is one of the most important ways we can experience and mediate Christ's love.'[13]

John's visit had certainly restored within me that much-needed sense of security. Although his visit was short (and rightly so because it would have drained me to have a long conversation so soon after surgery), it had left me peaceful. Prayerful. It was as though when John peeped round the door, God had slipped in with him. And maybe he had. As the late R. A. Lambourne expressed it, in every encounter between the sick person and the visitor Christ is both the sufferer and the visitor. 'He is the sick man [or woman], the prisoner, the child, the stranger. He is the giver of the cup of water . . .'[14] He is the *visitor*.

A few days later, I was again assailed by loneliness. So much so that in my Journal I described visiting time as a 'bitter-sweet occasion'. 'Again, it's visiting time and I'm poised between trying to be patient, accepting, recognising that nobody may come and yet so much hoping for at least one visitor. At the same time, I am desperately tired and know I need to rest so too much excitement from too many visitors wouldn't be a good idea. I also long for time to think and pray.'

On this occasion, my loneliness was not alleviated by the appearance of a person. Something much more significant happened. It was as though I was given the courage so to listen to the language of my inner longings that, instead of running from my apparent inner emptiness, I could face it and even make a descent into the eerie chasm. As I did so, a miracle seemed to take place. I realised that loneliness is a mirage. Deep within myself is not emptiness but fullness: the presence of the indwelling Holy Trinity – Father, Son and Holy Spirit. Whereas I had been pining for people, God was wanting to draw me into a deeper intimacy than any person could give: the intimacy of the love which flows so freely between the three members of the Godhead: Father, Son and Holy Spirit.

As I made my descent, I found myself drawn into that circle of love where I felt held in an almost tangible, over-powering peace; overwhelmed with the realisation that I was being enfolded in a love which was more pure, more kind, more caring, more tender than the deepest of human love.

Was it coincidence that the following day I stumbled upon the following in Jean Vanier's little book *Treasures of the Heart?* I think not. 'Even the most beautiful community can never heal the wound of loneliness that we carry' writes Jean Vanier.

'It is only when we discover that this loneliness can become sacrament that we touch wisdom, for this sacrament is purification and presence of God. If we stop fleeing from the solitude, and if we accept our wound, we will discover that this is the way to meet Jesus Christ. It is when we stop fleeing into work and activity, noise and illusion, when we remain conscious of our wound, that we will meet God. He is the Paraclete, the One who responds to our cry, which comes from the darkness of our loneliness ... Community life is there to help us not to flee from our deep wound, but to remain with the reality of love. ... We are in community for each other, so that all of us can grow and uncover our wound before the infinite, so that Jesus can manifest himself through it.'[15]

Near the cottage in Derbyshire where I sometimes retreat to write, a certain garden reminds me of what happened to me that day. From April to June this garden is filled with the hymn of all creation as the fragrance of daffodils and narcissi and later of bluebells and azaleas mingles with the call of the cuckoo and the soothing sound of bird-song. It merges with the feast of the colour: the pinks and purples, yellows and creams, whites and reds of the rhododendrons, the blues of the gentians, the silver of the birches, the browns of the maples and the flaming oranges of the azaleas. Yet, as a plaque peeping from the azaleas reminds the visitor, the site of this garden was once a scourge on the landscape. It was a disused quarry until an elderly man contemplated its corners, seeing not ugliness but the potential beauty with which the place could be transformed if rhododendrons were planted. Loneliness, I discovered that day, need not be a blight to the soul. Like that disused quarry loneliness is full of potential beauty. If we will explore its nooks and crannies and work in them rather than running from them, we can create a garden within which is full of the fragrance of Christ; a place where his whisper can be heard and his presence most keenly felt. The entrance to this garden is concealed in the centre of our weakness. If we would find it, we must not run away from our pain but enter into it. This is one of the ways in which God's strength is perfected in our weakness. This is also one of the ways of becoming like Christ in his death. He did not run from the pain, he embraced it. For him, this was the road to his Resurrection.

While I was still reeling from this encounter with the God within, a visitor did arrive. I appreciated and enjoyed our time together, particularly as this was a friend in the publishing world and we were able to spend some time dreaming about this book – conceiving its shape and exploring its contents. Making friends with our loneliness does not result in a self-sufficiency which strips us of the need for people. Rather, it sets us free to enjoy friendship to the full because we no longer impose on our friends the expectation that they will deal a death-blow to our loneliness – an expectation which, to quote Henri Nouwen, results in relationships which are 'needy and greedy, sticky and clinging, dependent and sentimental, exploitative and parasitic;'[16] relationships which do not promote growth but restrict it. Instead, we hold our friends on an open palm, offering them the gentle and 'fearless space in which we can move to and from each other'.[17] We allow our weakness so to draw compassion from others that it and our friendships are transformed.

After my visitor had gone, I felt so nourished and energised by the God who had walked with me in my inner garden and who had then come to me in the person of a caring friend that I wanted to become nourishment for others. So I decided to do a spot of visiting myself. First, I went to the patient in the room next to mine and then visited Brian who, I suspected, had had few visitors that day because, like me, he did not live near London. I smile as I recall those visits. I had nothing to offer these fellow-patients except myself. Similarly, they had nothing to offer me except themselves – their innate 'I am'. Yet we found that, in effect, saying to one another, 'Here I am', we were enjoying a growing intimacy which, of itself, brought an inner, ongoing healing.

Support in loss

I would like to be able to make the claim that, having re-discovered the elixir of that solitude with God which transfigures loneliness and having been supported by so many people, I never felt abandoned again. Alas! That was not my experience. As I grew stronger and prepared to leave hospital and, in particular, during my first week at home, I often became more conscious of what I had lost than of the riches I had gained. Many people suffer similarly after an operation. Even though I steeled myself for a painful transition from hospital to home, I did not prepare sufficiently. Perhaps it is impossible to expect a patient to do so?

I was to leave St Luke's after lunch on Sunday. My Journal reminds me that Saturday and Sunday were bittersweet days. Saturday dawned bright and warm so I sat out on the roof-top soaking up the sun. It was there that my consultant found me when he came to examine the wound for the last time. He was delighted with the way my wound was healing, confirmed that my stitches could be removed the following morning and that I could then go home. After we had chatted for a few minutes, he shook my hand and said that he had enjoyed looking after me and I struggled to find words to express my thanks. As I confided to my Journal after he had gone, 'Verbal thanks seemed so feeble; so inadequate somehow. The debt of gratitude I owe him for his time and skill is immeasurable and there are no words to express my thanks for his felt care and concern for me as a whole person. I'd so like to give him something which would express my gratitude. But what?'

I spent the rest of the morning on the roof-top listening to Lucy's Medugorje tapes and talking to Brian and Elizabeth. While I was there, Katherine came to say goodbye before she went off duty. As we talked, she took from her pocket a pair of scissors with which she cut off the plastic label I had worn round my wrist for the past two weeks. As I told my Journal a little later, my name, date of birth and the name of my consultant had appeared on that label. Cutting it off had seemed symbolic. 'Within 24 hours, I shall leave this place which has become so very special to me: an oasis.

I'm sad but excited, quietly slipping into gear for whatever comes next, restless, in one sense longing now for a bigger world, for beauty, for the company of my choice and yet, in another sense, aware that I leave a part of me behind: in the chapel, with Lita, Lucy, with my consultant and Stephanie and the other members of staff. I've depended on them. They have propped me up and they will always have a special place in my heart.'

I enjoyed lunch on the roof-top. Then Brian came to join me. We chatted about Quiet Days and Retreat Houses, bats and vicars with seventeen parishes – and constipation! When clouds covered the sun, I returned an unread book to the library and, finding Matron in her office, attempted to say goodbye to her before she went off duty. Tears filled her eyes and mine as I expressed my gratitude as warmly as possible.

For the remainder of the day, I felt as restless as the weather. 'I long to go for a walk but am rather frightened of walking round the square on my own', I told my Journal. 'I want to pack but it's too early. I feel very betwixt and between.' I tried to imagine how it would feel to go home. Was I ready: physically? Emotionally?

I wrote thank you letters to people who had been praying for me, dressed, went for a walk and started to take down my cards, conscious as I did so, that I lurched from excitement to heaviness at the thought of leaving.

On Sunday morning, I packed early. The room looked very bare stripped of my books and prayer corner and my bright cards and flowers. When Sister Thomas came to make my bed, I realised that someone else would be sleeping between those starched, white sheets and I confessed: 'I really don't want to leave.' She chuckled. 'I never thought I'd hear a patient complain about *leaving* hospital', she said.

I asked if I could spend some time in the chapel. Sister Thomas agreed. My intention had been to re-dedicate myself to God and to give thanks for all I had received from St Luke's. I found I could do neither – at least, not verbally. Instead, I wept. Tears are a language. These tears were expressing the inexpressible: that mixture of gratitude, awe, longing and excitement which I was experiencing in such quick succession.

I took a last look at the chapel before visiting Elizabeth. I was still chatting to her when my husband arrived. He had come earlier than expected. When I saw him, sorrow was replaced with joyful anticipation of home and time together. At my request, he had brought with him gifts for various people. As we took these to the people concerned, joy and thankfulness seemed to percolate round the Third Floor. Elizabeth insisted on coming to the front door with us when, eventually, we tore ourselves away. I left St Luke's in a blaze of glorious sunshine while Elizabeth stood on the doorstep in her dressing gown and waved goodbye.

'I'm ready to leave', I thought happily as David drove out of Fitzroy Square.

But the drive through London on a hot, humid June afternoon soon taxed my strength and the drive up the motorway to Nottingham quickly reminded me that a patient remains in a state of shock for several weeks after surgery. The noise and the speed bewildered me, making me tense and acutely conscious that my back was hurting. At the same time, I found myself marvelling at the freshness of the countryside: the green fields and the trees.

Whenever I have been away from home, I love driving through the familiar streets of Nottingham. That Sunday was no exception. Even more, I enjoyed exploring home. It was tidy, neat and clean. Welcoming. In that sense, it felt good to be back and to be surrounded by our much-loved belongings. 'And yet it's so big', I wrote in my Journal, 'And there are the stairs.' I had forgotten about stairs; the time and effort it takes a convalescing person to climb them. I had forgotten, too, about carpeted floors. I found myself longing for the hospital's parquet floors which did not mask the sound of approaching feet and I pined for the familiar people around me: 'the kiwi nurses, the friendly Sisters, Matron, Elizabeth, Brian.'

We arrived home at 4.30 pm. I went to bed for a rest. David needed to attend the Evening Service at our Church. By the time I woke up, he had gone. Suddenly, a terrible and terrifying wave of loneliness swept over me. 'I was hungry', I complained in my Journal. 'There was no one to prepare my supper. I wanted to know what the time was, but I hadn't unpacked my case and couldn't lift it so everything had to be tipped out in the hall. The battery of my watch had run out while I was in St Luke's and, since the kitchen clock had also stopped I was dependent on my alarm clock to tell me the time. I watched the news and pined for the smallness of the hospital room where everything was to hand: bed, chair, TV, cards, books, tapes – all in one room, everything in its place, no demands, no stairs, no responsibilities, lots of props. Suddenly all these things have been shifted from under my feet and I'm finding it hard to keep my balance.'

This acute sense of loss and bewilderment persisted for days. And the dependence on David distressed me: 'I'm struggling to keep my head above water . . . The transition from a hospital where I was treated as someone special, cherished, to home where I'm expected to be able to cope with the demands of people on the phone is phenomenal. And when David disappears for any reason, I collapse.'

And there were other problems: I found it impossible to gauge my own strength so David and I would attempt walks which would leave me exhausted. I found it irksome to wear clothes which touched my wound because it was still very sensitive, and, hardest of all, people seemed to assume that, now that I was at home, I was well. As one person expressed it in a letter: 'With the operation now behind you, it must feel good to enjoy energy and vitality again.' As I confessed to my Journal, 'I can't even imagine what energy feels like. I can't imagine how it feels to warm to the love of God. Everything seems dead – all my senses seem numb in this minute-by-minute struggle to survive. And yet, I am better than I was yesterday. A lot better. I can see that.' Several people helped. David, my husband, was rock-like: immovable in his determination to serve me and love me back to wholeness. In addition to running the parish, he prepared my meals, washed up, stayed with me as much as he could. The people from the parish who brought us ready-made meals helped too. In fact, they seemed like gifts from God. Our need for such practical help was urgent.

Spiritually, a letter and a book came to my rescue. The letter was from Ian, the monk I had met and spent the day with before being admitted to hospital. The letter was short, supportive and contained a single piece of advice: 'Look at light and shade'. The book was the unpublished manuscript of Paul Wallis', *Rough Ways in Prayer*. The author had invited me to write a Foreword so I had read the manuscript while I was preparing to go to hospital. I had found it helpful then and turned to it now in the hope that it would keep me spiritually afloat. It did. As I told my Journal: 'I'm finding *Rough Ways in Prayer* helpful . . . particularly what he has to say about the prayer of attention.' He suggests finding or writing a prayer and praying it from conviction rather than from feeling. I turned to George Appleton's *Prayers From a Troubled Heart* and read and prayed: 'There have been times, O Lord, when I have walked the hill tops with You, when I have felt You near, and my heart has been warm in the remembrance of blessings in the past. But now . . . my heart is dry and cold, moods of depression come over me, prayer seems unreal. You seem hidden, dark clouds descend upon my spirit . . . let me hear You whisper, "Keep steady, if you cannot give warmth of feeling, give your desire for Me, your hunger for Me, your emptiness . . ." '18

That strengthening whisper came to me, time and again, as I heeded Ian's advice to look at light and shade. As I wrote in my Journal one day, 'I realised, as I gazed at the sycamore tree this morning, that some of the leaves were being bathed in bright sun-light while others were in the shade and yet others were being dappled by light even though they were mainly in shadow. Yet all were equally alive and all were contributing to the nurture and beauty of the tree. . . . I watched light and shade in the sky too. As clouds scudded across the sky concealing the sun and then revealing it again, this created such a wonderful combination of light and shade, shapes and glory. Somewhere deep down that's speaking to me about praying from the pit. It's actually creating something rather lovely.' It was to my Journal that I confessed my many ups and downs: 'I watched TV this evening. That was the best part of the day . . . I don't think I've ever felt so incapable of reading before. . . . I feel really bored. There are so many books I'd hoped to read but I can't concentrate on any of them. . . . I did not write anything yesterday because I felt very much better. In fact, I spent most of the day working on *The Smile of Love* . . . But today I feel *so* different.'

It was in my Journal that I would sometimes record my complaints to God: 'O God! How long will this convalescence last?' I was grateful that my Journal listened because, when I first returned from hospital, there was no one else to hear me. David was forced to immerse himself in domestic chores as well as being steeped in parish responsibilities. And for a week no visitors came.

At first, the absence of visitors simply left me a little sad and bereft. But when day after day no one came and people only telephoned if they wanted advice or even counselling, I found it hard to understand the seeming conspiracy of silence. Were the members of our church, which prides itself in being a caring church, suffering from compassion fatigue or had I done something radically wrong? I discovered subsequently that people had decided among themselves that, on arriving home from hospital, I would need to be left alone and I can understand why. I am normally a person who craves privacy and I have made similar deductions about home-coming patients myself. But on this occasion I needed companionship and felt too fragile to take the initiative and risk telephoning to ask someone to come. Consequently, until my children came to the rescue, feelings of rejection compounded the problem.

Other clergy couples and Christian leaders have confessed to the same experience. 'No one has thought of ministering to me since I came out of hospital', blurted one ex-patient of St Luke's several months after being discharged.

Nicky Cruz, too, exposes the problem in his moving book, *Lonely But Never Alone:*

'A minister friend of mine who pastored a church for several years, faithfully seeing it through ups and downs and in betweens, confided in me recently . . . I gave everything I had to that church during those years . . . I neglected my family, but what do you do with the multiplied demands constantly pressing you? There were always sick people, my appointment book bulged with troubled souls needing counseling, and my phone rang incessantly so that I could hardly give myself to prayer and the study of God's Word. If I took a day off, there was no rest unless I left town. Then I was often criticized if someone happened to die or needed me on that day.

But I accepted all of this as part of what I signed up for when I gave my life to God's service. I did not complain. Neither did my family . . . A funny thing happened, though. When it came my turn, and I had to resign because of illness, the sick and troubled hands I held during those years did not reach out for mine. I faced my trial all alone. Where were all those people who gratefully said, "I couldn't have made it without you, Pastor?" Do they suppose I don't need a loving touch, an encouraging word, concrete evidence that somebody cares? Maybe they think I am so spiritual that they could offer little comfort at a time like this.'[19]

Christian leaders, of course, need just as much 'concrete evidence' that people care as anyone else who is vulnerable and sick. Roger Hurding explains why. Drawing once more on his own experience of vulnerability he observes:

'When I first became blind it was my situation of extreme dependency that was specially hard to adjust to . . . Behind the frustrations of these practical matters, was the deeper pain of a basic loss of adult freedom . . . it was a "back to childhood" experience.'[20]

He goes on to explain that other patients feel keenly this sense of loss:

'Whether being ill leads to the loss of employment, status, usefulness, acceptability, mobility, sight, hearing or other bodily functions, it is important to see that such deprivation can result in a form of grief or bereavement. These specific losses are often undergirded by a loss of independence . . . and, paradoxically, a loss of contact with others. In the first, there can be a sensation of being "taken over", however lovingly, and the second, a feeling of being "left out".'[21]

'That's it in a nutshell', I said to myself suddenly loathing the lack of independence in particular. While listening to the language of my own loss I realised that even the most resourceful patient needs and longs for people more than ever before. Deep down I yearned for people who would do for me what the Good Samaritan did for the man who was mugged while travelling from Jerusalem to Jericho; people who would be for me what the Good Samaritan was for this man left battered and bleeding by the wayside; people who would provide a human crutch on which I, the bewildered victim, could temporarily lean. For like that victim, I was conscious that, for several weeks after surgery, my entire being remained in a state of shock. Inwardly I cried out for people who, like that Good Samaritan would see and be sensitive to my plight – who would come to me, carry me emotionally and spiritually for a while, provide me with the mobility whose loss I felt so keenly and take me to a safe place where I could rest; those who would be willing to abandon their own plans to express practically what they were saying so eloquently in letters and on cards: that they were concerned for my welfare.

Some did. My husband, my son and my daughter gave me endless support. The memory of their love-in-action lingers on. I know from sitting on the other side of the fence that staying alongside a sick or convalescing person is a costly calling. Even so, 'bottomless pit' of need that I was, I longed for others who would give me the benefits of the kind of care Peter Speck describes so helpfully in his illuminating book, *Being There: Pastoral Care in Time of Illness*[22]: the kind of care which seems essential to the sick person's survival.

Peter Speck suggests that the sick or convalescing person needs someone willing to share their experience of becoming ill and being ill; someone who will make known to them, not necessarily with words, that they are loved by God; someone who will represent the whole, caring Body of Christ and assure them that they are being prayed for.

He goes on to suggest helpful ways of communicating this care and points out pitfalls to avoid. Remember that the patient is in a state of shock, he advises. So be gentle and genuine. Where necessary, communicate your care non-verbally: through touch and silence; by doing little practical tasks which the patient cannot do for themselves; by bringing a well-chosen gift which expresses the inexpressible in a tangible way and will remind the patient of your care after you have returned to your own home, by determining to listen rather than to talk, aware that the patient may want to share with you their own feelings of fear or hope, faith or despair. He quotes, helpfully, from the writing of Jo Anne Kelly Smith who, when dying of cancer spelled out the patient's need in this moving way:

> 'When *anyone* comes to visit me, I don't want him to come with his own agenda . . . I often get the feeling that before people enter my room, they try to decide what to say. I don't want to hear their concerns. I want them to empty their heads of their own ideas. When you visit a sick person, fill your head with thoughts about that person, your care for him. . . . If you just go in and listen, they'll do all the "saying" because they really want to talk about themselves. They need to get in touch with their feelings and they need to tell it to another human.'[23]

Among the pitfalls Peter Speck mentions are the following two. Don't feel you have to stay for the entire visiting time. Prolonging your stay can be counter-productive. It can result in patient fatigue. And don't try to cheer the patient up. In underlining this second principle, he quotes from Charles Causley's poem: *Ten Types of Hospital Visitor:*

> 'The fourth attempts to cheer
> His aged mother with light jokes
> Menacing as shell-splinters.
> "They'll soon have you jumping round
> Like a gazelle," he says.
> "Playing in the football team."
> Quite undeterred by the sight of kilos of plaster, chains, lifting-gear,
> A pair of lethally designed crutches,
> "You'll be leap-frogging soon," he says.
> "Swimming ten lengths of the baths."
>
> At these unlikely prophecies
> The old lady stares fearfully

> At her sick, sick offspring
> Thinking he has lost his reason –
> Which, alas, seems to be the case.'[24]

As I read that poem, I was reminded of the occasions when I had to beg visitors and patients not to make me laugh. Laughing tore at the wound in my side causing discomfort and pain. But as I reflect on this list of do's and dont's, I think, with gratitude, of those who obeyed them. Like one of my earliest visitors, a friend who lured me back into the world of books by bringing me the story of a missionary to China who happened to be the father of someone I had worked with and grown fond of in New Zealand. Or the timely arrival of flowers sent to me by my friends in the Women's Fellowship; and the spray of freesias which, arriving as it did from someone who wished to remain anonymous, gave me such pleasure not only because of the richness of their colour and the fragrance with which they filled my room but because, when they arrived without a card, I imagined the card had been lost in transit. Since the name of the florist appeared on the wrapping paper, I telephoned to see if I could trace the sender. It was then I was told that someone had gone into this shop near the hospital, purchased the freesias with cash, asked that they should be delivered and said he wished to remain anonymous. The staff had great fun speculating with me about the reasons for the anonymity.

I think, too, of the visitor who kindly accompanied me round Fitzroy Square a few days before I was discharged. The day before, Stephanie had walked round the Square with me and, having coped with the excursion in her company, I had been told that, if I wanted to, I could now go out alone as long as I told someone on duty where I was going. Full of excitement, I dressed and prepared myself for this second adventure only to discover that, as I stood by the lift which would take me to the ground floor, confidence ebbed away. Suddenly Fitzroy Square seemed so big. Supposing I couldn't make it? Or suppose the drunk who had been there the day before was loitering outside the hospital, how would I cope? I was about to go back into my room where, doubtless, I would have been filled with regret, when

Elizabeth emerged from her room with one of her visitors. I explained my dilemma and asked Elizabeth if she would watch me from her window whereupon her visitor kindly offered to walk with me.

And that is what makes St Luke's so special. It so cradles the clergy that the place and the team are rather like another of those visitors described in Causley's poem:

> 'The sixth visitor says little,
> Breathes reassurance,
> Smiles securely.
> Carries no black passport of grapes
> And visa of chocolate. Has a clutch
> Of clean washing.
>
> Unobtrusively stows it
> In the locker; searches out more . . .
>
> Even when she has gone
> The patient seems to sense her there:
> An upholding
> Presence.'[25]

My pain and loneliness, loss of independence and temporary loss of abilities I normally take for granted (like reading and praying, driving and lifting) brought me face to face with those questions which had seemed so pressing before I was admitted to St Luke's: Who are the poor? What did Christ come on earth to do? What are Kingdom values and standards?

Lying in the ditch, as it were, of my convalescence, I contemplated the parable of the Good Samaritan from the vantage point of the vulnerable one, the victim, rather than through the eyes of the lawyer who asked: 'Who is my neighbour?' Like the lawyer, before I was admitted to St Luke's, from a position of strength and vitality, I was wanting to set goals and define boundaries. Now I viewed the question differently. The poor, I realised, cannot be classified. We are everywhere. I say 'we' because I now recognise that I am one of them. When people touch us in the pit of our need, we are assured that we come constantly under the caring eye of God. When people stay away, for whatever reason: we lie in danger of reading into this absence, not simply the neglect of humankind but the absence of God. Caring for the poor is Kingdom activity, even if it simply means drawing alongside one person and sharing nothing more than vulnerability, as Elizabeth, Brian and I had done in St Luke's. It was one reason Christ came to earth; it was his way of demonstrating to the world what God is like.

\

A Heart-Warming Gift

'The work began in Faith and Prayer'[1]

'Be objective. Think of St Luke's', I said to myself whenever post-operative blues persuaded me that nobody cared. 'Think of the care of the staff. Think of the self-sacrificial giving which is represented in the £2,000 per day needed to keep the hospital ticking over.' And I would re-live my second day in St Luke's when Peter Nicholson, the General Secretary had invited me into his office for a chat. I recalled how, for nearly three-quarters of an hour, Peter had regaled me with story after story which had thrilled me to the core because they had pointed me to two certainties: that the hospital had always been under the caring eye of God and that its ministry was living proof that the people in the pews really do care for the clergy and other carers.

Peter began his saga by being utterly vulnerable. This part of his story was prompted by my question: 'What brought you here to do this particular job?'

'I was a patient here for three weeks', he said. 'Three long weeks it seemed. I had suffered an exhaustion breakdown in a parish. All the check-ups revealed that there was nothing radically wrong although, when I first arrived, I slept for about three days straight off. A very wise matron stumbled upon the cure. I was to walk, she said, from here to St Paul's Cathedral every day and let the music of Evensong wash over me and then walk all the way back. So there was the spiritual in-take and there was the exercise, which was all I really needed.

'However, the consultant who saw me said, "If you don't change your job and come out of what you're doing, you'll be back here in six months." As it so happened, I was invited by one of the consultants who had known me for many years to come back to do this job and, almost six months to the day of my admission as a patient, I found myself sitting in the General Secretary's chair.'

Having been a patient on other occasions also, Peter recalled, with gratitude, all that he had received from the staff and the atmosphere of the place: 'It was a wonderful experience being a patient here. I wrote home to my wife every day – reams of it. It was something quite unusual and unique. It's to do with a combination of many things including the prayerful atmosphere and the surrounding of the love of the staff.'

By this time, Peter was warming to his subject and, with relish, he recalled how, as chief fund-raiser for the hospital over the past eleven years, he had revelled in 'God's surprises'.

The first surprise came in 1980. At that time, there was 'no anaesthetic and recovery room on the theatre floor. We needed to put this in. The cost was £48,000. We launched an appeal fund which seemed to stop dead at about £12,000. We were very concerned and wondered where we were going to find the rest of the money. We had decided we would go forward in faith because we felt sure we should raise the money. Thank God. When the work was finished and we received the first bill of £14,000, the first interim payment request, we also had in the same post, a gift from a Convent for £20,000. I went by train at once to the South Coast to St Saviour's, Hythe, and I learned from the nuns that they had had to sell their hospital and their chapel because their numbers had dwindled so much that they could no longer carry on. Faced with the prospect of closing the Convent, they had remembered that, many years before, St Luke's had helped to train some of their nurses. So they sent us this cheque. As I thanked them, I was able to tell them, "You've saved this particular project so, in effect, you've given us an anaesthetic and recovery room."

'The next year, 1981, we decided we must do something for our devoted live-in staff. The staff quarters had been

built in the bad old days so the amount of room in each bed-
sit was miniscule. We decided we would have to knock down
walls, make rooms bigger, put in central heating and so on.
That project was to cost £22,000. I wrote to various Trusts
asking for help. We received a letter back from the very
first Trust I wrote to which said: "We know the hospital
well. My brother was a priest. He was a patient there five
years ago. We decided only yesterday among the trustees
that we should help two small hospitals and your letter
arrived this morning. So not only will we give you the
£20,000 for the work you have done in the staff quarters,
we will give you another £10,000 for the work you completed
in the theatre." So that was the second surprise, "out of the
blue – or out of heaven." '

It was at this point that Peter saw in the SPCK bookshop
a poster with a squirrel on it; a squirrel with all its nuts.
Underneath were the words, 'God will provide'. He bought
the poster and stuck two stickers on it giving the name of
the Trust and the amount they had donated and he decided
that whenever God gave surprises like this, he would record
the figure on the poster. Peter showed me the poster. It is
now covered with stickers. 'It's so full that I'm not able to
use it any more but it's a constant reminder that if we are
faithful, if we are working and praying, doing what we
believe God wants us to do, then he will never let us down.
The money will be provided without our having to beg for
it.'

Ex-patients and well-wishers

Having shown me his prized poster, Peter continued to
recall God's faithfulness. He remembered the old kitchens.
'They were not at all up to standard. They had an old Aga
stove and in the mornings, when the anthracite was carried
in and shot from its containers onto the fire, the dust would
fly everywhere.'

The inspector from the Department of the Environment
decided that they should 'start again'. 'Our hearts sank. We
knew that this would mean more fund-raising. However,
we drew up the necessary plans.' Everything had to be of

stainless steel: among other things, new sinks and new cookers, new fish-friers and new warming cupboards, new grills and new tables. New floors and a suspended ceiling would also be required. 'What is more, we were told that it would take three months to complete the work.

"Don't worry about the preparation of meals", our cooks said, "We can prepare one hot and one cold meal a day on a six burner cooker in the pantry." And this is what they did for three months. They never let us down over a single meal. Meanwhile, we set to and wrote to banks and insurance companies, Trusts and industry and, in addition to the contributions coming from these sources, some two hundred and eighty people sent gifts (little gifts from ordinary folk, larger gifts from those in a position to give more), enabling us to realise the necessary figure: £48,000.'

The next year, when no major project was anticipated a large piece of masonry fell from one of the main, large gables into the street – about a foot away from Peter's wife when she was going into the hospital to help one day. Investigations revealed that the rendering on the huge gables was about three or four inches away from the actual brickwork. It was cracked all over and in danger of falling down. Builders were called in and scaffolding erected so that the work of scraping and cutting off all the rendering from these two gables could begin. While faced with the task of raising the money to pay for this project, they were also re-furbishing the interior floor by floor. 'The first thing we needed to do was to replace all the beds', Peter confirmed. 'It so happened that the first Trust I wrote to about this were willing to pay for the replacement of the entire twenty-seven beds. The next task was to replace the lockers and, at that time, I stumbled upon an order from a Saudi Arabian hospital which had been cancelled. We were able to pick up twenty-seven lockers for only £10 each.

'The next problem on the floors was to replace the bed tables with modern, adjustable tables. We thought that some people might like to do this as a personal gift because each table was to cost £57, a sum many donors would be able to manage. One bishop who gave a table said, "I shall remember to pray for the person eating off my table every morning." Some people gave more than one table so we were able to replace all twenty-seven tables very quickly.'

Clergy and charitable trusts

'That year, an ex-patient's daughter made the beautiful green altar frontal for the chapel and another patient gave a pair of candlesticks. Six commode chairs came to us as a gift from a priest and his wife.

'We then had an extraordinary gift. The doctors asked for a piece of equipment for the theatre which would cost £2,000. That same week, I had a letter from a friend of the hospital who said, "I've just had my 69th birthday and I have a feeling that you may need something. So I sold some Chinese vases and I enclose a cheque for £2,000" – which was exactly what we needed.'

That year, not only was the sum of £50,000 raised for the essential repairs to the building but the interior was also re-furbished in a way which explains why the building feels so cared for; why such a prayerful atmosphere permeates the whole of it.

'In March, 1986', Peter went on, 'The British Heart Foundation gave us a cardiac recorder valued at £3,500 and the Ship and Shore Establishment of the Royal Navy, whose chaplains have come here over the years, sent us £1,000 towards the cost of new theatre instruments. The army, navy and air force have always given generous grants from the collections they take at their services.'

During the course of this conversation, Peter explained the history of the quilted tapestry which I described at the start of chapter nine. He told me that it was made by Mrs Hughes of Sidmouth; that it took her three months to make and that on the back it says that it was made in gratitude to the consultants and staff who cared for her while she was a patient. It was hung in the entrance hall on May 22nd, 1986.

Next, Peter talked about the library. He described the pleasure he had received when quite out of the blue the General Secretary of the SPCK, Mr Patrick Gilbert, sent a message to say that if Peter went to their London bookshop, he could choose £500 worth of books for the St Luke's library.

Gifts large and small

'And there have been other remarkable gifts too', Peter recalled. 'A dear old lady, an ex-patient, always paid for our annual black and white TV licence. When a royal wedding was announced, she felt that we would want to go over to colour TV so she sent the exact amount for a colour TV licence not knowing that a few weeks before we had, in fact, taken up an offer by the people who rent us our TV to go over to colour so that our patients could enjoy to the full that Royal Wedding. In August 1986, that kind donor reached the age of 100. On admission to a Nursing Home she was unable to pay for our licence any more but I find it moving to remember that she paid for it right into her 99th year.'

I found it moving to imagine this elderly ex-patient giving so sacrificially. I was also fascinated to discover how imaginative the committee are in their fund-raising. As Peter put it: 'We try to do something different every year so in 1986, we wrote to every clergyman's son or daughter we could find in *who's who?* All kinds of gifts came from this. One clergyman's daughter, an author, sent us £25,000 worth of shares. Another clergyman's daughter, whose husband was a member of the Cabinet, rang me up and said, "Would you come to the House of Lords, have tea with me, and bring with you twenty covenant forms and I will make sure that I collect covenants from all my friends", which is precisely what she proceeded to do.

'All kinds of gifts have come in over the years. People have been really generous. For example, last March (1990), I was in the Holy Land taking a party and as soon as I returned, I received the devastating news that our auto-clave, the machine we use for sterilising theatre equipment, had been condemned during my absence. Where would we find £25,000 to purchase immediately a new autoclave even if we could get one? I telephoned the company who services the autoclave and the people who had condemned it and asked where we could acquire a new one. (They have to be designed and made as well as installed). "Well! You're in luck", he said. "We are making an autoclave for a hospital in the North of England and we've discovered that the hospital has not yet been built. So you can have this one and we'll make another one for them." This autoclave was installed within weeks. Meanwhile, very kindly, the large hospitals around us dealt with all the work which our steriliser normally does and gave us this service free.

'When the time came to pay for the new autoclave we were sent a gift for £20,000 right out of the blue by members of a charitable trust who had read about our need in our Annual Handbook. The Central Church Fund provided another £5,000 so we were home and dry.'

'What inspires individuals to give so sacrificially and what prompts trustees of charitable trusts, livery companies and commercial undertakings to donate money to St Luke's?' I asked when Peter paused for breath.

'They realise the clergy are fairly poorly paid. They also realise that clergy have given up an awful lot to do what they're doing. They've probably had experience of the work which clergy have done, either for them or for their family in the past or they just appreciate the fact that we're there. I shall always remember an article once published in the *Church Times*. It asked the question, "What is a clergyman for?" And it gave the answer: "Just to be there." To be there for God and to be there for people. We are there day and night and we will never refuse a call. People are very grateful for this. When a priest and his family are living in their midst, they see the sacrifices that are being made: the Rectory is a home for everybody. Everybody comes. No one is ever turned away. There is no privacy. It is open house. They appreciate this and so they give. That is one reason. There must be so many more.'

While I was convalescing, Peter continued to send me the Staff Bulletin, the weekly newsletter which he produces for the members of staff of St Luke's. When I read news items like the following, I realised that the people in the pew do care about the clergy and other Christian leaders:

'John and Brenda Starkey never forget what St Luke's

did for them as patients. Each year they hold a fund-raising event for the Hospital. On Wednesday we received £114 from them up there in Doveridge, Derbyshire. They had held a Coffee Evening for us.'

'Mrs Judith Ruff of Bournemouth organised a Coffee Morning and with the assistance of other clergymen's wives in the Deanery she raised for us the grand sum of £816.'

'Mrs Ann Thompson was a patient in February 1965. She has never forgotten the help we gave her. This year she is Chairman of the local Inner Wheel District (Rotary Club). A Church Service preceded a Rally of members and the collection of £230 at the service was sent . . . to St Luke's.'

'The children from a Sunday School in a tiny village in Gloucestershire gave their savings and a Good Friday Service collection to the Hospital: £36.'

'On Tuesday afternoon I went by invitation to talk to a pensioners' group associated with St Albans Church in Holborn. Fourteen people were there and two of them were over 90! They all live alone in small bed-sits and they look after themselves wonderfully. The leader of the Group is a Church Army lady and she visits them and sees to their wants. After my talk about the Hospital they had a collection in a teacup and gave me £9.30. What generosity! Among them was Brenda. In 1982 she fell off a chair at home and broke both legs. She got better but couldn't find anyone who would employ her. So we took her on here for two months as a temp, and she stayed for eight. It was a great surprise and joy to see her again.'

Such people: well-wishers, trusts and livery companies help to raise the £2,000 per day which is needed to maintain the hospital.

Cathedrals and parish churches

The church also plays its part in helping to raise the money needed to ensure that the hospital continues to be run effectively and efficiently. In addition to the donations and gifts made by ex-patients and the funds raised by them, thousands of pounds each year come from the Diocesan Board of Finance and cathedrals and parish churches. These give grants which cover one-third of the total annual expenditure of the hospital. Over the years, these contributions have increased dramatically. Whereas in 1980, when Peter Nicholson was appointed as General Secretary, churches and cathedrals contributed £80,121, in 1990, they were giving £251,626 to St Luke's. While Peter Nicholson expressed gratitude for this 'huge leap' and noted with equal gratitude that support from the churches seems ever on the increase despite 'all the demands on parishes for quotas, church urban funds and the like', he also expresses sorrow that fifteen Diocesan Boards of Finance as yet make no contribution to the work of the hospital. Ironically, one of these dioceses sent thirty-nine patients to St Luke's in 1990 but have not yet recognised that they might have a responsibility to make a contribution to the work of the hospital so that it can continue to minister to the needs of their clergy.

Such seeming neglect on the part of potential beneficiaries of the unique ministry of this hospital for the clergy must seem bewildering to a man who lives and breathes and loves St Luke's; a man who, when he took over as General Secretary in 1980, inherited a deficit of many thousands of pounds. But he concentrates on the goodness and faithfulness of God rather than the disappointments. Looking back over his eleven years in the General Secretary's saddle, with the seemingly miraculous timing of the arrival of many of the generous gifts, he observed: 'Over everything we do there is God's oversight. he sees our needs before we ask so although, as it says in the prayer, "he knows our ignorance in asking", his love, his care and his genuineness takes care of everything.'[2]

When I wiled away the time contemplating God's goodness to St Luke's, I concentrated on the stories which spilled from Peter Nicholson's lips. I also pondered the fact that from the inception of the hospital its financial affairs have been under the caring eye of God with all other aspects of its ministry.

A question posed by Dr Tindal Hart in his memoir on Canon Cooper had stopped me in my tracks before persuading me to explore some of the reasons why Christians should have contributed to St Luke's from its infancy until now. 'How did Cooper, an ex-SPG missionary, succeed in inducing so many rich, titled and influential people, both clerical and lay, to help him in bringing [his] two ambitious projects to fruition?'[3] Dr Hart asks.

Influential clergy

As Dr Hart himself postulates, one possible reason is that since Canon Cooper was held in such high esteem by the Archbishops and bishops, the archdeacons and other clerics who sent him from their dioceses with the kind of string of impressive testimonials I referred to in chapters four and five of this book, that such church dignitaries would doubt-less have supported him. Unlike their impecunious col-leagues, many bishops earned handsome stipends, like a certain clergyman who protested that he could not accept the bishopric of Exeter with its revenue of £3,000 a year 'unless he was allowed to hold it in conjunction with the living of Stanhope-in-Weardale which was worth £4,000.'[4] Most bishops, and a growing number of parish priests also enjoyed private means. So much so that it was estimated that, in the mid-century years, the official incomes of the clergy were substantially less in total than their private incomes.

Many of the better-off clergy displayed an astonishing degree of generosity. They used their wealth to support impoverished parishes: building parsonages with their own money from which future incumbents would benefit as well as themselves, giving huge sums of money to restore crum-bling churches, building mission churches and attempting to alleviate the needs of poor parishioners.[5]

On his travels, Canon Cooper would almost certainly have come into contact with such wealthy clergy. Did he inspire them to give to the work of St Luke's? Probably. As we have already seen, he seems to have been an eloquent and persuasive preacher and in pleading the plight of impover-ished clergy, he would have merely been underlining the growing concern being expressed by the laity that greater assistance should be given to their leaders.

Were the early Vice-Presidents and Executive Committee members among these great-hearted, pioneering clerics? Men like the Bishop of London, the first President of the Hostel of St Luke, the Bishops of Bath and Wells, Carlisle, Chester, Ely and Exeter to mention a few whose names appear under the early lists of Vice-Presidents. Or Canon Utterton and Archdeacon Atlay who made such major contributions to the progress of the hospital's ministry after Canon Cooper's resignation as Secretary in 1895.

Influential lay people

Dr Hart suggests another, equally plausible reason why, from the very beginning, Canon Cooper's plans met, not only with acclaim but with financial support and backing. His work as an SPG deputation preacher took him the length and breadth of the country. In the course of these travels he would most certainly have encountered many influential lay men and women as well as clergy.

In 1898, for example, the Council's Report for the year reads:

'Very successful drawing-room meetings have been held at Norwich and Winchester, the former being due to the exertions of Miss Evans and Miss Bignold; the latter having been held at the Deanery, by the kind permission of the Dean and Mrs Wood Stephens; the result will no doubt be most valuable in bringing the Hostel to the notice of many who may not have known anything of its work before, and thus increasing both the interest and support of the Institution.'[6]

We have no information about 'Miss Evans' or 'Miss Bignold'. Neither are we given any clue concerning the identity of 'donors of articles to the Nursing Home and Chapel'[7]: people like Mrs Bealey, Mrs C. V. Chipp, Miss Griffin, Miss Gwyn, Mrs Vignoles.

Wealthy Women

We do know that charity work was one of the major growth industries of the time, particularly among women. As James Wolvin describes the trend:

'Victorians were generous and unstinting in their work for charity. There were few worthy causes which failed to attract the money, organisational skills or energies of Victorians. In fact, among the middle classes, charitable work became a way of life, soaking up surplus energies, especially of the womenfolk and salving their stricken consciences. . . . Charitable activity became a characteristic feature of propertied life: to be broadcast aloud, emblazoned in the press and chiselled onto the side of public places and monuments. Such publicity guaranteed public sanction for the do-gooders; it conferred on them the approval of their peers. Men of wealth displayed their largesse in generous benefactions to the needy. *Nouveau riche* businessmen were quick to publicise their gifts to local charities. It was almost as if the act of giving money had to be public to be effective.'[8]

In addition to these public gestures, thousands of hours of practical work were put in as Victorians endeavoured to put right the wrongs of the world around them. According to *The Times* newspaper, in 1885, in London alone, there were more than one thousand local charities which reaped an income of four-and-a-half million pounds. As one journalist of the time put it: 'London boasts something like a hundred hospitals, a hundred homes and refuges for the houseless, fifty orphan asylums, over twenty institutions for the blind and deaf and dumb, fourteen for the relief of discharged prisoners, eighteen penitentiaries for fallen women, five asylums for incurables, over forty homes and institutions for poor sailors, and nearly twenty for soldiers; twelve charitable institutions for the benefit of poor Jews and between thirty and forty relief societies for the clergy.'[9] 'Millions of pounds in charity were poured each year into the bottomless hole of urban poverty . . . As fast as the money and the activities were generated and dispensed, new ranks of the

poor shuffled forward for food, clothing, shelter and care. . . .
A sample of 446 wills bequesting £76 million in the 1890s
showed that £20 million went to charity.'[10]

Several reasons why this upsurge in charitable giving
benefited institutions like St Luke's present themselves.
Clearly, one reason was that women, in particular, were
bored. Florence Nightingale described the scene powerfully:
'I see so many of my kind who have gone mad for want of
something to do. People who might have been so
happy . . .'[11] She, herself, 'craved for some regular occu-
pation, for something worth doing instead of frittering time
away on useless trifles.'[12] Her sense of dissatisfaction deepened with the years: 'my mind is absorbed with the idea of
the sufferings of man, it besets me behind and before . . .
all that poets sing of the glories of this world seems to me
untrue. All the people I see are eaten up with care or poverty
or disease.'[13] Her discontent with her lot continued until
she was allowed to train to be a nurse in Kaisersworth in
Germany. When she left that hospital, she felt entirely
different: 'brave as if nothing could ever vex me again.'[14] In
fact, she felt so well, so brimming over with vitality that
she wrote a thirty-two page pamphlet instructing the
women kept in 'busy idleness' in England of work, happiness
and comradeship waiting for them in Kaisersworth. Not all
her many readers were free to leave the country to train in
Germany. What they could do was to immerse themselves
in the task of alleviating the needs of the poor in England.
As James Wolvin explains. 'For many activists, immersion
among the poor undoubtedly brought its inner pleasures.
This was especially true for large numbers of middle and
upper class women who were denied access to purposeful or
organised work. Many turned to the poor, or other charities,
as a surrogate career, of which their menfolk approved and
to which they gave in abundance.[15]

The press

Another reason why the upsurge in interest in charitable
organisations coincided with the founding of St Luke's was
the pressure being brought to bear on the public by the

press of the time. In 1889, for example, Charles Booth began to publish the results of his research into poverty in the East End of London. His central point was that close to one third of the capital's population lived on, or close to, 'the poverty line' while a similar study conducted in York revealed that: 'We are faced by the startling probability that from 25–30% of the town population of the United Kingdom are living in poverty.'[16]

For those with eyes to see it, The Great Depression of the 1870s showed that, 'after more than half a century of industrial growth, there were limits to what the economy could achieve'; that there were 'layers of the population which remained untouched by the material benefits of industrial growth.'[17]

Christian conscience

These frightening facts bored their way into the consciences of Christian people. So much so that Hannah More, described as the most influential female evangelical of the time wrote: 'It would be a noble employment and well becoming the tenderness of their sex, if ladies were to consider the superintendence of the poor as their immediate office and set apart a fixed portion of their time as sacred to the poor, whether in relieving, instructing or working with them.'[18]

Many Christians of the time viewed involvement with the sick and destitute, not as a duty, but as a vocation. Florence Nightingale, for example, claimed that, just as Joan of Arc heard an objective voice outside of herself speaking to her, so God had spoken to her: "On February 7, 1837, God spoke to me and called me to His service." [19] Later, Lord Shaftesbury made a similar claim which we observed in an earlier chapter: 'I was convinced that God had called me to devote whatever advantages He might have bestowed upon me in the cause of the weak, the helpless, both man and beast, and those who had none to help them.'[20]

Perhaps, then, 'Miss Evans' and 'Miss Bignold', and the other ladies mentioned were among the unsung heroines of the time? What is more certain is that, one of the ways in

which money for St Luke's would have been raised would
have been through the so-called 'charity dinner'.

The journalist Blanchard Jerrold describes this popular
form of alms-collecting:

'Beyond compare the oddest, and at the same time the
most popular form of alms-collecting known in London,
is that systematically adopted by the hospital, asylum,
and benevolent fund managers – viz. the charity
dinner . . . Twelve and fifteen hundred pounds are often
coaxed from the pockets of a hundred and fifty gentleman
after a dinner. . . . It would be absurd to ask a man for a
subscription while he is waiting for his dinner: but he
beams at the bare suggestion – his own inner man being
satisfied. You have feasted him – he is your slave, and he
becomes a free agent again only when he has completed
the process of digestion. . . . The wary hospital governors
bow to the diner, and lay before him the plight of the poor
sick, while he tastes his first olive, and catches the fire of
the ruby light of his wine. That the plan is broadly based
on human nature, the "thirty thousand dinners" which
have been eaten in the name of charity in Bishopsgate
Street and by Long Acre, are good evidence.

The why the diners give, let us not too narrowly seek
to know: above all, let us not inquire in a cynical mood.
An enormous sum of suffering is hereby relieved; thousands of children are housed, fed, and put out in the
world. The widow has a smart little cottage placed at her
disposal. To the artist whom misfortune has overtaken,
is given peace of mind. . . .'[21]

Jerrold describes Charles Dickens as 'the prince of charity
dinner speakers':

'On fifty occasions [he] spoke . . . tenderly and becom-
ingly. Moreover he had a witching tongue that struck
direct to men's hearts . . . How he pleaded the cause of
the poor actor, making the women's laughter ripple from
their lips while the tears streamed from their eyes; but
above all how he spoke for the sick poor children! . . . I
can still catch the echoes of those tremulous tones in

which he who created Tiny Tim, and melted the world's heart over the death of little Dombey, pleaded for the sick and destitute children – conuring the men at the tables round about him to think of the weeping mothers by the hospital cots: then of their own happy little ones at home; and then of the sick child fretting for lack of healing care and wholesome sustenance. Oratory was never sweeter nor more persuasive than this: and never fell from human lips pleading a holier cause.'[22]

Experienced orator that he was, did Canon Cooper similarly use the medium of the charity dinner to plead the plight of the poor clergy?

We do not know. What we do know is that, while the Hostel of St Luke was still in its infancy, Canon Cooper had enlisted the support of Her Royal Highness Princess Christian, the daughter of Queen Victoria who had become the Patron of the Hostel. This was a wise move because the Princess was well-known and well-loved for her philanthropic work and a cause to which she was espoused would, undoubtedly invoke the interest of her devotees. The list of other patrons is impressive and includes: the Duchess of Rutland, the Countess of Shaftesbury, the Dowager Marchioness of Conygham, the Dowager Duchess of Marlborough.

It would also appear, from snippets of letters to Canon Cooper which have survived, that he personally invited various dignitaries to support the work of the Hostel by agreeing to sit on the Council. Canon Fleming writes from St Michael's, Chester Square: 'I am much interested in reading of the proposed Hostel for poor clergy and Church workers. I shall be happy to join the General Council, and to render what help I can to so good an object.' The Dean of Chichester wrote in similar vein: 'My dear Canon Cooper, – It may interest you to know that the late Bishop Wilberforce had so much at heart a work similar to that you are taking in hand, that he wished the memorial to Mr Keble to take that shape ... Many a valuable life might be saved to the Church if such a home could be provided.' And Canon Body of The College, Durham wrote: 'most gladly do I consent to my name being added to the General Council of St

Luke's Hostel. I will also subscribe £1 a year when it is started; it is a movement to supply a real need. Would it be possible to include all licensed Church workers in its constituency? It would meet a need I am face to face with sometimes, in connection with our diocesan lady workers. If this were possible, I would gladly subscribe £5 a year.' With all this support behind him, Canon Cooper must have surely have been aware that his scheme came under the caring eye of God? And when, in 1892, a small house became available in Beaumont Street, he and his wife must have been delighted that, at last, their dream was to be realised. Accommodating just seven patients, this building was given the name The Hostel of St Luke. Impoverished clergy were soon valuing its work. Within weeks of its opening, the President of the Hostel, the Bishop of London, claimed that 'seven patients have been admitted from the following dioceses: Lincoln, Peterborough, Worcester, Exeter, Llandaff, Norwich, and Truro. Several out-patients have also been treated.'

So great was the need of the Hostel that, within two years, the Council were searching for new premises. 16, Nottingham Place seemed to be an ideal setting so the Hostel was moved to this building which the Bishop of London used to refer to as 'this dear little place'. Despite the Bishop's enthusiasm, the Nottingham Place hostel boasted only eight beds and other drawbacks soon became apparent. As one of the consultants, Dr de Havilland Hall explained at an Annual Meeting, one of the problems was the lack of single rooms: 'we sorely felt the need of single rooms which the majority of people in times of sickness require. A few people, it is true, prefer a double ward, but in very many cases patients like to have a room to themselves.' This was not the only need, however. As Viscount Middleton stressed at the Annual Meeting of 1902. 'The present Home is clearly too small ... It would probably be quite possible to fill twice as many beds as are occupied at present, and very possibly treble the number if the accommodation could be provided.' Sir Dyce Duckworth M.D. agreed.

'The increasing demand for accommodation in the Hostel

of St Luke calls for increased efforts on the part of the supporters, with a view to providing the much needed new premises', he said. 'When one thinks that it only provides eight beds for sick clergy from all the dioceses, for their wives and children, one sees at once that the mitigation of suffering which is attempted by this Institution is certainly very homoeopathic, and it does not commend my sympathy in that respect. I think that an Institution like this, in the metropolis of the Empire, ought to have at least 50 beds, and I think all interested in the work should aim at providing no fewer than that number. I can bear testimony to the excellent work done and to the eminence of the men who do it. But I must say, as my professional brethren tell me who work in this place, that the requirements of modern medicine and surgery call for something better than a converted ordinary dwelling house, in which to carry on such a work as this. It is quite impossible to have the requisite appliances, or to give the requisite treatment in cases of serious disease, or those requiring a serious operation, in an ordinary private house.'

This spirited resolution was seconded by the Headmaster of the St John's Foundation School.

The resolution was carried unanimously even before Canon Utterton read a letter from a patient expressing the hope that a larger and more convenient building might be found, not least because 'the nurses suffer much in the present premises, and are much hampered in their work on behalf of the patients' and before the Bishop of London added yet another reason why a move was now urgent: 'When I see the care, the love, the self-forgetfulness shown by the doctors . . . I trust we shall soon be able to give them better accommodation in which to carry on their devoted and self-sacrificing work.'

An appeal for the proposed new building had already been launched and in 1904 numbers 13 and 14 Fitzroy Square where acquired. At first, only one house was rebuilt. This new Hostel of St Luke was opened in 1907 by Her Majesty Queen Alexandra and the first patients were admitted in October of that year; on St Luke's Day. As the need for more accommodation continued to grow and as funds continued to come in, the second house was rebuilt. This was opened in 1923 by Her Majesty Queen Mary. As time wore on, the hospital continued to attract the interest of the Royal Family. In 1957, Her Majesty Queen Elizabeth The Queen Mother graced it with a visit and, on the occasion of the seventieth anniversary in Fitzroy Square in 1977, Her Royal Highness Princess Alexandra gave the hospital the honour of a visit.

The reminder of one hundred years of such interest and generosity on the part of people from all walks of life and representing every generation filled me with awe and reminded me that the laity do care. St Luke's, after all, is their gift to us.

It is a gift which points me in the direction of an answer to my question, 'What did Jesus mean when he said, "Blessed (blissfully happy) are the poor in spirit"?' As I think of Canon and Mrs Cooper, campaigning to establish St Luke's, sacrificing time and energy to set the ministry in motion, as I contemplate those wealthy men and women of the Victorian era working so hard to furnish the Beaumont Street building and as I recall the way in which gifts large and small have been donated to the clergy via the hospital for nearly one hundred years, I am reminded of the women on whose resources Jesus seemed to have relied when he praised those who are in this state of poverty of spirit. Poverty of spirit cannot therefore refer to those who have no possessions, riches or talents. Clearly, those women were wealthy and gifted. Poverty of spirit must mean the refusal to allow our possessions or talents to hold us in their stifling grip. As one Jesuit expresses it, the person who is poor in spirit does not 'have the mentality of ownership nor does he live under the delusion that a person *is* more when he *has* more. Paul's warning . . . is flesh and blood for him: "Warn those who are rich in this world's goods that they are not to look down on other people; and not to set their hopes on money, which is untrustworthy, but on God who, out of his riches, gives us all that we need for our happiness." '23 Or as Gerard Hughes conceptualises it:

'Spiritual poverty is an attitude of mind and heart, so

centred on God and reliant on him that nothing created can serve as a substitute. A person who has the virtue of spiritual poverty may, in fact, have riches, but is in no way possessed by them. The riches are accepted as a blessing, but like all blessings they are for sharing, not for hoarding, they are to bring life to others, not to stifle it. The closer we can come to spiritual poverty, the greater our enjoyment of the gifts of creation.'[24]

Have we in the church become wedded to our possessions and our rights, our traditions and our talents? Is that why, in today's church, there seems to be such a sad lack of this blissful happiness Jesus describes? I fear the answer might be 'yes' and, recognising in myself the ease with which I turn to these substitutes for God, I prayed that God himself would increase in me that attitude of mind and heart which centres on giving rather than getting, on sharing rather than hoarding, on relinquishing rather than accumulating. After all, I reasoned, I cannot change the church but God can change me.

Living Prayer

'I think I was, in reality, substituting talk about prayer for actual performance.'[1]

God is always changing us, challenging us, moving us on. One of Charles Wesley's hymns reminds of this: We are being 'changed from glory into glory', he claimed. The Archbishop of Canterbury implied something similar when, in his Enthronement sermon, he reminded us that, for each fresh step of the journey, fresh commitment is required. The poem with which I began this book also reminds us that, as Christians, we do not stagnate, we are pilgrim people; people on a journey into God:

'For your prayer
  your journey into God,
may you be given a small storm
  a little hurricane
  named after you,
persistent enough
  to get your attention
violent enough
  to awaken you to new depths
strong enough
  to shake you to the roots
majestic enough
  to remind you of your origin:
  made of the earth
  yet steeped in eternity

> frail human dust
> yet soaked in infinity.'[2]

Hurricane Huggett not only shook me to my roots and awakened me to new depths, it provided me with answers to the question which had been puzzling me before I became ill: 'How can I live my prayer more effectively?'

These answers clarified while I was discussing the unique ministry of St Luke's with another ex-patient of the hospital, a retired bishop.

'St Luke's has underlined that my prayer must be lived, fleshed out,' I admitted. 'Spirituality isn't just about luxuriating in the love of God, though it includes that. It's about taking that love to others albeit in *weakness*. St Luke's seems to have shown me how to do this. While I was there, I experienced how it feels to be one of the helpless ones, how it feels to have my needs met. Now I seem unable to escape the cry of the poor. I hear it everywhere and know that I must respond to it.'

Being vulnerable with the vulnerable

'It's as though you're standing with the weak and being weak?' reflected the bishop. 'That's so like Jesus isn't it? He was a broken man. His body was broken. When he appeared to his disciples on the first Easter Day, he showed them his wounds and could say, Receive Holy Spirit. From his brokenness flowed compassion, love and forgiveness. This is the deep secret of our spirituality and the deep secret of transforming the community in which we live.'

We went on to explore the beauty of brokenness as we had experienced it in St Luke's. We surmised that we had emerged from St Luke's 'deeply healed' because people as different as Peter Nicholson, the General Secretary and Lita, the Filipino domestic had been willing to give us glimpses of their vulnerability as well as their strengths. We reflected on the mystery and I recalled Alan Brown's moving testimony.

Alan is now the receptionist at St Luke's. He had not been on the staff while I was a patient but he told his story on one of my visits to the hospital while I was researching this book.

Alan had once seemed to thrive on working flat out for a flourishing international company. Then tragedy struck. His wife died. Instead of coping with the stress of his job, Alan found himself crumbling under the strain and came to the conclusion that he should resign. Today he sits at the reception desk just inside the front door of St Luke's, answering the telephone, welcoming incoming patients and visitors and spending hours stuffing thousands of letters into the envelopes which will carry news of the hospital to its supporters. Like many other members of staff, Alan is now one of God's 'wounded healers'. Wounded healers touch others, not simply with their hands or their eyes, but with the bonding which binds beggars together – the kind of bonding Dominique Lapierre describes in *The City of Joy*.

In this book the author describes a Calcutta slum which is inhabited exclusively by refugees from rural areas; a shanty town where everything militates against its inhabitants: chronic unemployment, appallingly low wages, child labour, debts which can never be redeemed, the total absence of privacy·with ten or twelve people forced to share a single room to mention but a few of the deprivations.

Yet the slum's name, City of Joy, is not a misnomer. The slum was transformed into a place of joy by its people. Somehow these refugees managed, not only to transcend their condition but to become models of humanity. They discovered how to give respect to a stranger, how to show charity to beggars, cripples, lepers and even the insane. The City of Joy was full of joy because, 'here, the weak were helped, not trampled upon. Orphans were instantly adopted by their neighbours and old people were cared for and revered by their children.'[3]

Such seemingly-strange bonding is not rare. I was on the receiving end of it in Poland on one occasion. My husband and I were guests in the home of an impecunious pastor, his wife and family. They had invited us to lead a series of seminars in their church.

The shortage of food was heart-breaking: shelves in the supermarkets carried, at best, inadequate and limited supplies of tinned food-stuffs; at worst the shelves stood silent and stark in their nakedness. Yet, day by day, we feasted with the family. The eyes of the pastor's wife sparkled as she served sumptuous traditional Polish dishes to the squeals of surprise from her children. While we ate, she would tell us how, knowing they had guests from England, one person after another would bring gifts: eggs, chicken, cheese, butter: luxuries the family had not seen for many long months.

Out of their poverty, these people gave – not only food but joy. Their generosity generated more generosity so that Christlikeness seemed to be contagious – the Christlikeness which is summed up in Michael Mayne's phrase, 'the power of powerlessness'.

In St Luke's, the bishop and I had felt that power. It had reminded me of the power we feel flowing from Jesus in the Garden of Gethsemane when he asks his captors: 'Who is it you want?' They respond with his name, 'Jesus of Nazareth' whereupon he surrenders with those words of utter abandonment: 'I am he'. Faced with such surrender, helplessness and vulnerability, the soldiers draw back and fall to the ground – overpowered by powerlessness.

The realisation helped me to see that one way of living my prayer is to be vulnerable with those who are vulnerable; to be broken with those who are broken. After all, I reasoned, Jesus begs us to remember, not so much his strength and his vitality as his brokenness and emptiness: the brokenness of his body represented in the broken bread of Holy Communion, his emptiness represented in the outpoured wine.

Climb down the ladder

To offer others our 'I am' takes courage. Pride persuades us to project power and seeming strength rather than helplessness. Yet, as Jean Vanier expresses it from the richness of his own demonstration of self-sacrificial love of the mentally handicapped:

> 'The poor and the weak have revealed to me
> the great secret of Jesus.
> If you wish to follow him

you must not try to climb the ladder of
    success and power,
becoming more and more important.
Instead you must walk *down* the ladder,
to meet and walk with people
who are broken and in pain. . . .'[4]

Alan Brown, I had discovered, had found happiness in delib-
erately walking down the professional ladder. 'From the
first day I came here, everyone was very friendly towards
me and everyone appreciated anything I did', he told me.
'This has never happened to me before – not as openly as
it does here. This place draws out the good in people.'

Walking down the ladder had not only resulted in a happiness Alan could not have foreseen, it has qualified him to
come alongside people in pain. He senses that, when
patients come to the reception desk to be admitted to hospital, they are 'keyed up and nervous'. His qualification in
dealing with this unspoken suffering lies, not in his Ph.D.
or his experience as a successful businessman, but rather
in the ongoing memory of his own pain and suffering. He
illustrates so well another observation of Jean Vanier's:

'It is this recognition of our brokenness and
    of our wounds
which takes us off our pedestal: . . .
we are no different from those we try to serve;
we too are broken and wounded like them;
in a way we had not realized before
we are truly together brothers and sisters.'[5]

Be compassionate

Just as compassion for people motivated Jesus to become
utterly vulnerable, so it will be compassion which motivates
us to be vulnerable with the vulnerable and to climb down
the ladder which others are busily climbing.

Both the bishop and I admitted that, in St Luke's, we had
been awakened to new depths of compassion. We compared
this compassion with the professional empathy we both seek

to practice and which is so powerful. Empathy seeks to 'walk a mile in the other person's moccasins', to quote the Indian proverb; to sense how the other person might be feeling. Powerful though this aspect of healing is, it encourages a certain sense of rightful detachment: a relationship between helper and helped, counsellor and counsellee. Compassion, on the other hand, is far more costly simply because it feels with the sufferer. Compassion, according to peace and justice activist Jim Wallis, is that quality which hears the cry of the poor or sees a person in need and which acts because it resolves, 'I can't allow that person to continue to live like that.'⁶ As the bishop and I had both discovered through the ministry of St Luke's, such care communicates support at a level which words cannot reach. Although such caring is costly, like every Christian, I realised afresh that I am called to exercise this healing gift: to be clothed with compassion.

Micah insists: 'This is what Yaweh asks of you, only this: That you act justly, love tenderly and walk humbly with your God'⁷ Or as Jesus crystallises this call: 'Be compassionate as your Father is compassionate'⁸ And James speaks scathingly of those who claim to have faith yet ignore the plight of the poor.⁹

In claiming that spirituality must be lived and not simply prayed, I am saying nothing new. This is the only kind of spirituality which comes anywhere near a biblical expression of spirituality. A biblical spirituality is a spirituality which is always authenticated in its application. A biblical spirituality always concerns itself with others. A biblical spirituality dares to admit to vulnerability as it takes the light and the compassion of Christ into the dark and hurting corners of the world at great cost.

As John Stott puts it in *Issues Facing Christians Today*, the only spirituality worthy of the name is one which involves itself with the needs of the world:

'In the end there are only two possible attitudes which Christians can adopt towards the world. One is escape and the other engagement. "Escape" means turning our backs on the world in rejection, washing our hands of it (though finding with Pontius Pilate that the responsibility does not come off in the wash) and steeling our hearts against its agonised cries for help. In contrast, "engagement" means turning our faces towards the world in compassion, getting our hands dirty, sore and worn in its service and feeling deep within us the stirring of the love of God which cannot be contained.'[10]

What he goes on to say of evangelicals may be applied to charismatics and contemplatives and Christians wearing other labels also:

'Too many of us evangelicals either have been, or maybe still are, irresponsible escapists. Fellowship with each other in the church is more congenial than service in an apathetic and even hostile environment outside. . . .

Instead of seeking to evade our social responsibility, we need to open our ears and listen to the voice of him who calls his people in every age to go out into the lost and lonely world (as he did), in order to live and love, to witness and serve, like him and for him. For that is "mission." Mission is our human response to the divine commission. It is a whole Christian lifestyle, including both evangelism and social responsibility. . . .'[11]

It is the 'mission of the market-place' George Carey referred to on the occasion of his Enthronement as Archbishop of Canterbury, a mission which is rooted both in the worship of Christ and a concern for others which 'places us alongside the oppressed, the dispossessed, the homeless, the poor and the starving millions of our planet.'[12]

The bishop and I were revelling in memories of the way the compassion of Christ had been expressed to us in our powerlessness. The conversation was reminding me of conversations I had had with my prayer guide in the months before I suspected that my gall bladder might prove troublesome. During these months, I had been praying that I would see Christ more clearly, love him more dearly and follow him more nearly. Contemplating him in the Gospel narratives was giving me a clearer picture of him than I had ever had before and stirring up within me a longing to serve him more faithfully than ever before. As I had observed to my prayer guide, the inescapable challenge which was coming to me was that the call of the King inevitably involved some kind of identification with the powerless – the people among whom Jesus was born and lived and died. This conviction had deepened during my stay in hospital. It was giving birth to a disturbing dissatisfaction with the middle-class interpretation of the Gospels which I had imbibed for most of my life: teaching which insists that Christians must feed their minds through study of the Scriptures yet remains strangely silent about the Bible's insistence that Christ's followers should, at the same time, be feeding the poor; teaching which emphasises the need Christians have to soak up the love of God yet says nothing about the parallel importance of expressing that love to those for whom the name of God means nothing – particularly those who have nothing to eat, nothing to wear; teaching which presents Jesus as the Saviour who will bless us abundantly, even guarantee that we get rich quickly, but fails to present him as the One who requires us to turn from our selfishness; to become like him – especially in his attitude to the poor and those who suffer unjustly. I was not only disturbed, I was puzzled; searching for an answer to the question: 'What are the implications for me?'

To keep in step with the poor

'Who are the poor?' I asked the bishop. This was a question I had first asked as I flew out of Poland. Then I was comparing Polish Christians with the spirituality I see in the West and I was wondering whether impoverished Poles did not enjoy more spiritual riches than those of us who have been seduced by the consumer society of which we are a part and which persuades us to believe that self-pleasing and self-fulfilment rather than self-giving paves the way to happiness. Now the question had a different thrust. I wanted to know whose cry it was to which I was to respond.

'Don't we discover the answer to the question "Who are the poor?" by asking ourselves "How am I poor?" ' the bishop said in response to my question.

Memories of the loneliness I have described in an earlier

chapter rose before my eyes as he said this. I thought, too, of the powerless and the dispossessed with whom I had identified when I first fell ill: people paralysed by any kind of pain; people who, for whatever reason have been required to hand over the reins of their lives to others. Perhaps, then, the poor for me, are those who suffer like this? People in the parish. People in the neighbourhood. People who read my books. People like Patrick?

I told the bishop about Patrick. I had met him in unusual circumstances three weeks earlier: in the house of another bishop. I had just arrived and been welcomed most warmly by the bishop's wife when there was a ring at the door bell. She left me to return a few moments later followed by Patrick: a young man in his early twenties who carried a tartan suit case in one hand and a black, dust-bin liner in the other. These, we discovered later, held all his possessions.

Patrick was sleeping rough. He had not eaten for days and had made his way to the bishop's residence where he had collapsed on the door step. While the bishop's wife fed him with tea and cheese sandwiches, we listened to his story: the loneliness, the rejection, the abuse, the hurt, the frustration, the anger. As I watched and listened to the bishop's wife, I sensed that she felt as helpless as I did. Even so, we were not only able to put Patrick in touch with his deep-down desire to be helped; a desire which had become heavily overlaid with helplessness and hunger, the bishop's wife put Patrick in touch with people in the diocese who could come alongside him and provide appropriate practical help. When Patrick left, I felt glad that we had been able to become links in the chain of compassion which, hopefully, one day, will result in his transformation.

The world is full of Patricks. For some of us, though not all, they are 'the poor'. As Jean Vanier puts it:

'The poor with whom you are called to share your life
are perhaps the sick and the old;
people out of work,
young people caught up in the world of drugs,
people angry because they were terribly hurt
when they were young,

people with disabilities or sick with Aids,
or just out of prison;
people in slums or ghettos,
people in far-off lands
where there is much hunger and suffering,
people who are oppressed
because of the colour of their skin,
people who are lonely in overcrowded cities,
people in pain.'[13]

Practise poverty of spirit

In responding to the cry of the poor, few of us will be called
to emulate Lord Shaftesbury or Florence Nightingale,
Canon Cooper or Mother Teresa of Calcutta. We may well
be called, instead, to draw alongside just one person or
group of people at a time.

'My danger will be that, in coming alongside broken
people, I will once again be tempted to offer them strength
rather than weakness,' I confessed to the bishop. 'Such
strength can seem very threatening.' 'It doesn't uncover the
wound in the other person', he agreed. 'Our *brokenness* is
the instrument of healing.'

What will be needed, I mused, will be that poverty of
spirit displayed by those who have supported St Luke's over
the years; that poverty of spirit Jesus praised in the women
who supported his mission so faithfully: by their gifts and
their availability. Poverty of spirit, I recalled, holds its possessions on an open palm. While enjoying them to the full
for what they are, gifts received from the hands of a generous God, poverty of spirit refuses to cling to them or
depend on them but shares them. Poverty of spirit is characterised by generosity and genuiness, availability and
involvement.

Also needed for the journey is the ability to listen to the
language of my own pain and brokenness. How else will I
learn its lessons?

The bishop and I talked of the way in which in Gethsemane Jesus demonstrates how to listen to the language of our
own inner pain and fear.

Just as, at his Baptism, Jesus descended into the green waters of the Jordan and was submerged by them, so in Gethsemane he descended into the depths of his own dread: the dread of being encrusted with the evil which pollutes the world; the deeper dread of being separated from his Father. As he makes his descent, a curious thing happens. Terror turns to trust. He drops, not into nothingness but into the arms of the indwelling Father who sustains him. From deep within himself he finds welling up the will to say 'Yes' to whatever his Father requires of him. His will becomes one with the Father's. In his weakness, he discovers the secret of strength: it lies within him in the person of his Father.

In the same way, as we listen to the language of our own pain, as we go further, and pluck up the courage to plumb its depths, we find that God's strength is, indeed, made perfect in our weakness. It brings us to the well-springs of life: that indwelling source of sustenance and renewal which always flows into us from the Father, the Son and the Holy Spirit and out of us to touch the world in the kind of way St Luke's had touched and healed us.

Balance 'being' and 'doing'

If we are to fathom these mysterious depths, we must recognise our need for stillness. As God insists through the Psalmist, it is in silence that we discover him. 'Be still', he invites. 'Know that I am God.'[14] This is the knowing of intimacy not the knowing of academic learning.

The centrality of this silence has been stressed by people of prayer in every age. Thomas à Kempis insists that: 'In silence and quietness the devout soul makes progress and learns the hidden mysteries of the Scriptures.'[15] Kenneth Leech makes a similar plea: 'Only through ... periods of concentrated and intense silence can [the] interior and continual sense of God's presence become a reality ... Silence nourishes and feeds silence: the concentrated periods spill over into, and feed, the short times we manage to salvage from our day.'[16]

Making such silence possible had been one of the memorable gifts St Luke's had given to me. The bishop put it differently, 'They invited me to rest', was the way he expressed it. 'They seemed to want me to rest: to enter into my rest', as the old prayer puts it; to relax. I saw the importance of it. It reminded me of an occasion when I once heard Michael Ramsay speak about heaven. He quoted some words of St Augustine:

> ' "We shall rest and we shall see.
> We shall see and we shall love.
> We shall love and we shall praise."

Until you rest, you don't see. Until you see, you don't love. If you don't love, you won't praise.'

Such resting and seeing, loving and praising is healing simply because it puts us in touch with the Healer. Yet, 'all our life we're so busy in the service of God and his church that we don't have time to rest', the bishop said sadly. 'In inviting us to rest, St Luke's invites us to enjoy renewal in the very essence of our being.'

We had been holding this conversation under a healthy vine. As I gazed at its branches coiling around its supportive frame I was transported back into the chapel at St Luke's where the symbolism of the vine had spoken so eloquently to me. This stillness and rest of which we were speaking nourishes us so that we, the branches, may bear fruit. We had almost come full circle in our conversation. Right at the beginning I had expressed my conviction that St Luke's had shown me that, a spirituality worthy of the name, must be lived out; the staff had shown me how this is possible.

I thought of a claim made by the fourteenth-century Flemish mystic Ruysbroeck who underlined that Christians must never resort to rest as a means of escape from the world. Such so-called 'rest . . . is unlawful, for it brings with it in men a blindness and ignorance and a sinking down into themselves without activity. Such a rest is nought else than an idleness into which the man has fallen, and in which he forgets himself and God and all . . . activity. The rest is wholly contrary to the supernatural rest which one possesses in God.'[17]

Resting in God, true oneness with God, on the other hand finds a balance between 'being' and 'doing'. The bishop and I talked of Florence Nightingale, someone special to both of us; someone for whom mysticism (closeness to God) and love-in-action overlapped and interacted; someone whose interface with the world of the suffering and the world of politicians made of her prayer 'a taste of heaven in daily life'.

This taste of heaven can be experienced by us all. It comes both for our own enjoyment and to be shared with others. Jean Vanier shows us how:

> 'The secret is to learn
> to be silent inwardly,
> to be full of gentle laughter and joyfulness,
> to be compassionate to all those who are in pain.
> This harmony is a gift of God to us humans,
> based on openness and welcome:
> to welcome Jesus,
> the tremendous Lover
> and the Lamb,
> in whom joy and pain are intermingled;
> to sing and laugh and rejoice
> in the beauty of God's creation.
> Yes, it is true that God wants a joyful people
> but with our hearts open and welcoming
> to those who are suffering.
> This is compassion. . . .'[18]

In leaving us with this legacy of harmony, the hospital had given us an example: a way of explaining what God is like to a world for whom his name means nothing. We would do this by involving ourselves in promoting that curious counter-culture of the Kingdom which is characterised by this recognition that brokenness can be beautiful, that compassion counts, that pain can set our feet on the pathway to wholeness.

Let life revolve around God

We would not become experts overnight. God would go on changing us, converting us, calling us to step out in faith. Conversion does not happen instantly. It takes time. It is a process which is ruthless and relentless. In Jim Wallis' words:

'There are no neutral zones or areas of life left untouched by biblical conversion. It is never solely confined to the inner self, religious consciousness, personal morality, intellectual belief, or political opinion. Conversion in Scripture was not a self-improvement course or a set of guidelines to help people progress down the same road they were already travelling. Conversion was not just added to the life they were already living. The whole of life underwent conversion in the biblical accounts. . . . Transformed by God's love, the converted experience a change in all their relationships: to God, to their neighbour, to the world, to their possessions, to the poor and dispossessed, to the violence around them, to the idols of their culture, to the false gods of the state, to their friends, and to their enemies.'[19]

The ongoing experience of turning from self to God becomes increasingly important to me with the years. When I first became ill, I had prayed that the God who transforms very ordinary things like water and bread into symbols of his grace would use my small crisis to turn me to him – to take me deeper into himself. In the chapel at St Luke's, during that restful period before my operation, I had prayed that I might learn the lessons of my illness. Gradually, as the bishop and I talked, I was becoming aware of the way in which these prayers were being answered.

During my time at St Luke's and the months of convalescence, I had travelled along the path of prayer. Like the ducks I sometimes watch diving under water then bobbing up in a different part of the pond, I had bobbed up at a different place on the prayer path. And I had bobbed up with a burden. God's burden. We, in the churches should offer the poor and the marginalised the same kind of vulnerability compassion and poverty of spirit with which the staff at St Luke's draws alongside its patients: that 'foot of the cross' ministry which, according to Sheila Cassidy, 'demands not just that we do things for people but that we be with them', that 'ministry of presence' which simply involves us drawing alongside the needy, 'impotent as they are impotent, mute as they are mute, sharing their darkness'.[20]

'This kind of contemplative caring seems all too rare these days', I thought. But that's hardly surprising. After all, to stay alongside someone who does *not* respond to prayer for healing or whose problems cannot be ironed out overnight lacks glamour and is enormously draining. Yet such is the plight of millions of people in our world today that this is precisely the kind of help which they need – like the elderly people in Manchester I had read about who 'are so desperately lonely that they join a bus queue for the sake of companionship, not to catch a bus'.[21] Or like some of the citizens of Birmingham.

Statistics suggest that around the average inner city church there are 2,000 houses with 10,000 people who could walk to the church within ten or fifteen minutes. Commenting on these figures, Michael Griffiths, former Principal of the London Bible College points out that, almost certainly these will represent:

'500   households needing a neighbourly hand of friendship;
 20   unmarried mothers;
100   elderly, housebound people, living alone;
 10   discharged prisoners;
100   deprived children;
 10   homeless;
100   broken marriages;
 20   families in debt trouble;
100   juvenile delinquents who have been before the courts in the last three years
 80   persons in hospital
 80   alcoholics'[22]

and vast numbers of unemployed people.

The word 'God' will convey nothing to the majority of

these people. For some, the word is synonymous with a spoil-sport, a tyrant, an ogre. Or it is simply a form of abuse. If we are to convey to them 'that God is not a distant God, a God to be feared and avoided, a God of revenge, but a God who is moved by our pain and participates in the fullness of the human struggle',[23] it is vital that we embody these characteristics. This may mean that we are given the costly role of staying alongside the broken and the powerless, supporting them with our presence as well as our presents for as long as it takes, trusting that through our support they will find Emmanuel, God with us, in the same way as I found him in those who drew alongside me before and after surgery. We shall be called to spend less time in the cosy corners of our Christian fellowships. Instead, compassion may ask us 'to go where it hurts, to enter into places of pain, to share in brokenness, fear, confusion, and anguish . . . to cry out with those in misery, to mourn with those who are lonely, to weep with those in tears.' For 'compassion requires us to be weak with the weak, vulnerable with the vulnerable, and powerless with the powerless. Compassion means full immersion in the condition of being human.'[24] Such compassion is the gift of the King who calls us to 'be compassionate as your Father is compassionate'.[25] Such compassion prevents us from merely talking about prayer and prompts us, instead, to translate our prayer into practice.

Epilogue

Just as my stay as a patient and the months since I had been discharged had changed me, so changes have taken place within St Luke's. Personnel have changed and new policies have been implemented. One of the staff changes was the retirement, at the age of seventy-three, of Jimmy. Just before this well-loved porter left to visit his family in Australia, Alan Brown arrived. Two resident doctors have been appointed to provide the patients with round-the-clock in-house care and Mrs Pam S Hutchence has become Appeal Director. With Matron and others, she is drawing up plans for the future.

Among the imaginative new policies is a nationwide network of Consultant Psychiatrists who have agreed to make themselves available locally to those eligible for care through St Luke's. All of these consultants have experience in the care of the clergy and their families and are sympathetic to the needs of those in Christian leadership.

The hospital has also established close links with The Westminster Pastoral Foundation with its fifty affiliated centres throughout the country. These offer individual counselling, psychotherapy, group therapy and a counselling service for people with serious physical illnesses and their relatives as well as a counselling service for clergy couples – particularly those with marital problems.

Meanwhile, as letters from patients testify, the ministry of the hospital continues to be as much appreciated today as when the original Hostel of St Luke's was founded. And God seems as eager as ever to prove that the hospital comes under his caring eye. In his latest letter to me, Peter Nicholson says: 'God has done it again!' and refers me to the paragraph in the Staff Bulletin which reads:

> *God will provide.* 'It always happens! Just as the workmen were laying the last pavement slabs to complete the work which will cost at least £15,000, we received a cheque for over £14,000 – a legacy from the estate of a Mrs Dyer. Give thanks!'

We past patients do give thanks: to God and all those who, for one hundred years, have made the ministry of St Luke's possible. We echo Lord Runcie's claim that 'St Luke's Hospital is one of the best things in the Church of England.'

Notes

Poem

1. Macrina Wiederkehr OSB, *A Tree Full of Angels*, San Francisco: Harper and Row, 1988, pp.49–50.

Chapter 1

1. Macrina Wiederkehr OSB, op. cit., pp.49–50.
2. Luke 8:3.
3. Macrina Wiederkehr OSB, op. cit., pp.49–50.
4. Gerard Manley Hopkins, *God's Grandeur*, London: Penguin, 1981, p.27.
5. Sheila Cassidy, *Sharing the Darkness*, London: DLT, 1988, p.17.
6. Ibid., p.28.

Chapter 2

1. Macrina Wiederkehr OSB, op. cit., p.4.
2. Henri Nouwen, *The Genesee Diary*, New York: Doubleday Image Books, 1981, p.88.
3. Henri Nouwen, *Reaching Out*, London: Fount, 1980, p.74.
4. John Sanford, *Ministry Burnout*, London: Arthur James Ltd, 1982, p.9.

5. Ibid., p.107.
6. Sheila Cassidy, op. cit., p.13.
7. Ibid., p.5.
8. Ibid., p.38.
9. Norman Autton, *Touch: An Exploration*, London: DLT, 1989, p.141.
10. Ibid., p.141.
11. *The Alternative Services: Ministry to the Sick*, quoted Autton, op. cit., p.140.
12. Morris Maddocks, *The Christian Healing Ministry*, London: SPCK, 1981, pp.122 and 121.
13. *The Alternative Services: Ministry to the Sick*, quoted Autton, op. cit., pp.49–50.
14. Macrina Wiederkehr, op. cit., pp.49–50.
15. Norman Autton, op. cit., p.5.
16. Macrina Wiederkehr, op. cit., p.47.
17. Henri Nouwen, *Out of Solitude*, Notre Dame: Ave Maria Press, 1974, page not traced.
18. Heather Ward, *The Gift of Self*, London: DLT, 1990, p.43.
19. Heather Ward, op. cit., p.12.
20. Eric Abbott, *The Compassion of God and the Passion of Christ*, Geoffrey Bles, 1963, p.16.
21. Adaptation of a prayer by the late Bishop of Bloemfontein, quoted Angela Ashwin, *Prayer in the Shadows*, London: Fount, 1990, p.121.
22. Macrina Wiederkehr OSB, op. cit., p.49.
23. Norman Autton, op. cit., p.5.

Chapter 3

1. Macrina Wiederkehr OSB, op. cit., p.2.
2. Sheila Cassidy, op. cit., p.16.
3. Ibid., p.19.
4. Taken from a leaflet called *The Patient's Round: Prayers for the Hospital Day*, produced by St Luke's Hospital for the Clergy from words written by the parish staff of St Luke's Charlton.
5. Macrina Wiederkehr, op. cit., p.xiii.

6. Ibid., p.49.
7. Michael Mayne, *A Year Lost and Found*, London: DLT, 1987, p.45.
8. Ibid., p.45.
9. Ibid., p.44.
10. *The Patient's Round*.
11. The Office of Compline quoted in *The Patient's Round*.
12. John Ellerton (1826–1893).
13. Report of Annual General Meeting 1895.
14. Report of Annual General Meeting 1899.
15. Letter written to Matron and the staff 1990.
16. Macrina Wiederkehr, op. cit., p.2.
17. Report of Annual General Meeting 1990.
18. Report of Annual General Meeting 1896.
19. Report of Annual General Meeting 1909.

Chapter 4

1. Henri Nouwen, *Compassion*, London: DLT, 1982, p.4;
2. Michael Mayne, op. cit., p.44.
3. W. H. Vanstone's phrase.
4. Flora Wuellner, *Prayer, Stress and our Inner Wounds*, Guildford: Eagle, 1991, pp.16–17, 23.
5. Ibid., p.99.
6. A. Tindal Hart, *Canon William Henry Cooper: A Memoir*, (No publisher. No date) p.2.
7. Ibid., p.5.
8. Quoted A. Tindal Hart, ibid., p.5.
9. Canon Henry Cooper, *The Mission Field*, London: SPG, 1867, pp.74–5.
10. Quoted A, Tindal Hart, op. cit., p.6.
11. Gustave Doré and Blanchard Jerrold, *London: A Pilgrimage*, Dover Publications Inc., 1970, p.120.
12. Ibid., p.120.
13. Quoted John Pollock, *Shaftesbury: The Poor Man's Earl*, London: Hodder and Stoughton, 1985, p.23.
14. Ibid., p.132.
15. Gustave Doré and Blanchard Jerrold, op. cit., p.143.
16. Blanchard Jerrold's phrase (1870).

17. Wordsworth, *Upon Westminster Bridge*, quoted Doré and Jerrold, op. cit., p.xxiii.
18. Millicent Rose, Introduction, Doré and Jerrold, op. cit., p.ix.
19. Jeremy Taylor (source untraced), quoted Michael Mayne op. cit., p.ix.
20. Michael Mayne, op. cit., pp. 46–47.

Chapter 5

1. Flora Wuellner, op. cit., p.17.
2. John Sanford, op. cit., p.1.
3. Ibid., p.4.
4. William Henry Cooper, *Mission Field*, SPG, June 1st, 1883, p.210.
5. Ibid., p.210.
6. Ibid., p.211.
7. Ibid., p.211.
8. Ibid., p.212.
9. William Henry Cooper, *Mission Field*, SPG, August 1st, 1883, p.278.
10. Ibid., p.278.
11. William Henry Cooper, *Mission Field*, SPG, September 1st, 1884, p.288.
12. William Henry Cooper, quoted A. Tindal Hart, op. cit., p.14.
13. Report of the Annual General Meeting 1894.
14. A. Tindal Hart, op. cit., p.20.
15. Ibid., p.20.
16. Ibid., p.20.
17. Ibid., p.22.
18. Ibid., p.23.
19. Ibid., p.27.
20. Extract from a letter from Canon Cooper dated March 17th, 1893, now at St Luke's Hospital for the Clergy.
21. See Alan Haig, *Victorian Clergy*, London: Croom Helm, 1984.
22. Flora Thompson, *Lark Rise to Candleford*, London: Oxford University Press, 1968, p.245.

23. Report of the Annual General Meeting 1902.
24. Report of the Annual General Meeting 1894.
25. Ibid.
26. Cecil Woodham-Smith, *Florence Nightingale*, The Reprint Society, 1950, p.348.
27. Ibid., p.349.
28. Ibid., p.351.
29. Ibid., p.351.

Chapter 6

1. Flora Wuellner, op. cit., p.20.
2. Report of the Annual General Meeting 1895, now at St Luke's.
3. Report of AGM 1897 – St Luke's.
4. Report of AGM 1909.
5. Report of AGM 1906.
6. Report of AGM 1896.
7. Sarah Horsman, *Living With Stress: A Guide for Ministers and Church Leaders*, Lutterworth Press, 1989, p.24.
8. Ibid., p.25.
9. John Sanford, op. cit., p.5.
10. The Rt. Rev. Michael Whinney, unpublished sermon preached on June 29th, 1986.
11. Sarah Horsman, op. cit., p.31.
12. Henri Nouwen, *Compassion*, London: DLT, pp.16–17.
13. Luke 8:45, 46.
14. John Sanford, op. cit., p.7.
15. Sarah Horsman, op. cit., p.30.
16. Michael Whinney, *Episcopacy Today and Tomorrow*, August 1989, p.6. Available from the author at: 173, Harborne Park Rd., Harborne, Birmingham B17 0BQ, priced £3.00.
17. Lord Runcie, Foreword to Esther de Waal, *Seeking God*, London: Fount, 1984, p.9.
18. Encounter Programme, *Clergy Stress*, Central Television.

19. Unpublished script for Encounter Programme, *Clergy Stress*.
20. John Sanford, op. cit., p.8.
21. Jack Dominian, *Cycles of Affirmation*, London: DLT, 1977, p.130.
22. Ibid., p.154.
23. Mary Anne Coate, *Clergy Stress*, London: SPCK, 1989, pp.126–127.
24. Joyce Huggett, *Marriage Matters*, Guildford: Eagle, 1991.
25. Derek Nimmo, Broadcast Appeal: February 4th, 1973.
26. Evelyn Underhill, *Concerning the Inner Life*, London: Methuen, 1947, pp.1–2.

Chapter 7

1. Noreen Riols, *When Suffering Comes*, Milton Keynes: Word Publishing, 1990, p.261.
2. Sheila Cassidy, op. cit., p.48.
3. Ibid. p.48.
4. Esther de Waal, *Seeking God*, London: Fount, 1984.
5. Ibid., p.86.
6. Ibid., p.85.
7. Ibid., p.119.
8. Thomas Merton, quoted ibid., p.30.
9. Ibid., p.78.
10. Ibid., p.92.
11. Jean Vanier, *Community and Growth*, London: DLT, 1979, p.220.
12. Sheila Cassidy, op. cit., p.118.
13. Paul Gurr, *Come as You Are*, Richmond, Australia: Spectrum Publications Pty Ltd.
14. Joyce Huggett, *Prayer Journal*, London: Marshall Pickering, 1990.

Chapter 8

1. Jean Vanier, *Treasures of the Heart*, London: DLT, 1989, p.14.

2. Esther de Waal, op. cit., p.107.
3. Ibid., p.118.
4. I have told this story in detail in my chapter in Ann England's book *We Believe in Healing*.
5. Joyce Huggett, *Marriage Matters*, Guildford: Eagle, 1991, p.90.
6. Peter Nicholson, *Caring for the Carers*, Article in Chichester Theol. Coll. Magazine 1989, p.33.
7. Thomas Merton, *The Seven Storey Mountain*, London: Sheldon Press 1975, pp.303, 302.
8. Garth Lean, *God's Politician*, London: DLT 1980, page number not traced.
9. Matthew 25:31, 36.
10. Quoted Esther de Waal, op. cit., p.108.
11. Ibid., pp.111, 110.
12. Peter Nicholson, op. cit., pp.31, 32.
13. Peter Nicholson, op. cit., p.32.
14. Galatians 5:22
15. Esther de Waal, op. cit., pp.91–92
16. Ibid., p.145.
17. Ibid., p.145.
18. Ibid., p.153.
19. 1 Corinthians 12:27
20. 1 Corinthians 12:14
21. 1 Corinthians 12:15
22. Luke 10:37

Chapter 9

1. Abraham Schmitt, *The Art of Listening with Love*, Abingdon Press 1977, p.169.
2. Gerard Hughes, SJ, *Walk to Jerusalem*, London: DLT, 1990, p.31.
3. Joyce Huggett, *Listening to Others*, London: Hodder and Stoughton, 1989.
4. See Psalm 121:1.
5. Gordon McDonald, *Restoring Your Spiritual Passion*, Crowborough: Highland Books, 1986, pp.127, 152–153.

6. 1 Peter 5:7.
7. John 17:20–23.
8. 2 Corinthinas 12:9.

Chapter 10

1. Henri Nouwen, *The Genesee Diary*, Doubleday Image Books, 1976. p.14.
2. Ibid., p.13.
3. Ibid., p.14.
4. Roger Hurding, *Coping with Illness*, London: Hodder and Stoughton, 1988, p.19.
5. Norman Autton, op. cit., pp.40–41.
6. Jack Dominian, quoted ibid., p.40.
7. David Watson, *Fear No Evil*, London: Hodder and Stoughton, 1984, pp.9 and 42.
8. Sheila Cassidy, op. cit., p.88.
9. Maria Boulding, *The Coming of God*, London: SPCK, 1982, p.7.
10. Anne Long, *Listening*, London: DLT, 1990, p.56.
11. Joyce Huggett, *Just Good Friends?*, Leicester: IVP, 1985, p.142.
12. James L. Johnson, quoted Nicky Cruz, *Lonely But Never Alone*, London: Pickering and Inglis, 1981, p.86.
13. Sheila Cassidy, op. cit., p.90.
14. R. A. Lambourne, quoted Peter Speck, *Being There: Pastoral Care in Time of Illness*, SPCK 1988, p.79, brackets mine.
15. Jean Vanier, *Treasures of the Heart:* Daily Readings with Jean Vanier, London: DLT, 1989, p.14.
16. Henri Nouwen, *Reaching Out*, London: Fount, 1975, p.44.
17. Ibid., p.31.
18. George Appleton, *Prayers From a Troubled Heart*, London: DLT, 1983, p.11.
19. Quoted Nicky Cruz, op. cit., p.142.
20. Roger Hurding, op. cit., pp.18, 19.
21. Ibid., p.36.
22. Peter Speck, *Being There: Pastoral Care in Time of*

Illness, London: SPCK. 1988. Chapters 5, 6 and 7 deal most helpfully with the subject of visiting.
23. Jo Anne Kelly Smith, quoted Peter Speck, op. cit., p.67.
24. Charles Causley, quoted Peter Speck, op. cit., pp.90–91.
25. Charles Causley, *Collected Poems 1951–1975*, London: Papermack Macmillan, 1983, p.245.

Chapter 11

1. Canon Cooper, quoted A. Tindal Hart, op. cit., p.23.
2. Unpublished taped interview with Canon Peter Nicholson.
3. A. Tindal Hart, op. cit., p.16.
4. Sir Charles Petrie, *The Victorians*, Cambridge: Eyre and Spottiswoode, 1960, p.231.
5. See Alan Haig, op. cit., p.314 for some specific examples of this.
6. Report of the Council for the year ended December 31st, 1898.
7. Ibid.
8. James Wolvin, *Victorian Values*, London: Andre Deutsch Ltd, 1987, p.96.
9. Gustave Doré and Blanchard Jerrold, op. cit., p.184.
10. James Wolvin, op. cit., p.99.
11. Florence Nightingale, quoted Cecil Woodham-Smith, op. cit., p.53.
12. Ibid., p.64.
13. Ibid., p.35.
14. Ibid., p.64.
15. James Wolvin, op. cit., p.99.
16. Ibid., p.107.
17. Ibid., p.105.
18. Ibid., p.100.
19. Cecil Woodham-Smith, op. cit., p.14.
20. Quoted John Pollock, op. cit., p.23.
21. Gustave Doréand Blanchard Jerrold, op. cit., pp.181–182.
22. Ibid., pp.183–184.

23. Peter G. van Breeman, S.J., *As Bread That Is Broken*, New Jersey: Dimension Books, 1974, p.114.
24. Gerard Hughes, S.J., *Walk to Jerusalem*, London: DLT, 1990, p.56.

Chapter 12

1.   John Powell, *He Touched Me*, Argus, 1974, p.35.
2.   Macrina Wiederkehr, op. cit., p.49.
3.   Dominique Lapierre, *City of Joy*, London: Arrow, 1985, p.44.
4.   Jean Vanier, *The Broken Body*, London: DLT, 1988, p.72.
5.   Ibid., p.92.
6.   Jim Wallis, *Call to Conversion*, Oxford: Lion, 1981, p.51.
7.   Micah 6:8.
8.   Luke 6:36.
9.   James 2:14 ff.
10. John Stott, *Issues Facing Christians Today*, London: Marshalls, 1984, pp.13–14.
11. Ibid., p.14.
12. George Carey, Enthronement Sermon.
13. Jean Vanier, op. cit., p.73.
14. Psalm 46:10.
15. Thomas à Kempis, *The Imitation of Christ*, London: Penguin Classics, 1976, p.50.
16. Kenneth Leech, *Spirituality and Pastoral Care*, London: Sheldon Press, 1986, p.19.
17. Ruysbroeck quoted ibid., p.33.
18. Jean Vanier, op. cit., p.123.
19. Jim Wallis, op. cit., p.6.
20. Sheila Cassidy, op. cit., p.115.
21. Alec Dickson, *The Glasgow Herald*, June 28th, 1965, quoted Campbell R. Stevens, *An Anthology of Hope*, Stirling: Jamieson and Munro, 1990, p.24.
22. Michael Griffiths, quoted, ibid., p.22.
23. Henri Nouwen, *Compassion*, London: DLT, 1982, p.18.
24. Ibid., p.4.
25. Luke 6:36.

Photographic Credits for
Under the Caring Eye of God

Hardback Edition

All photographs are by Lorenzo Lees, London, and used with permission, with the exception of:

p1	top: Frontages and Garden Committee, Fitzroy Square, from the 1982 report.
p1	below: prints by Gustave Dore from *London: a Pilgrimage* (Grant and Co, 1872).
p2	Print by Gustave Dore, *op. cit.*
p4/5	Scene from the Oberammergau Passion Play 1990, © Foto Huber, D-8100, Garmisch.
p6	Below: Canon K W Coates, St Helens.
p7	In Deine Hande, statuette by Dorothea Steigerwald, © Brendow Verlag, D-4130 Moers 1.
p8	Canon K W Coates, St Helens.
p9	Müde, statuette by Dorothea Steigerwald, © Brendow Verlag, D-4130 Moers 1.
p11	Awaiting Admission to the Casual Ward, by Sir Luke Fildes (1844–1927). Used by permission, the Bridgeman Art Library.
Front Cover:	*Young Girl Reading to an Invalid* by Eva Bonnier (late 19th century). Used by permission, the Bridgeman Art Library.

Paperback Edition

All photographs by Lorenzo Lees, London, and used with permission, with the exception of:

p1	Detail from Awaiting Admission to the Casual Ward, by Sir Luke Fildes (1844–1927). Used by permission, the Bridgeman Art Library.
p2	Scene from the Oberammergau Passion Play, 1990, © Foto Huber, D-8100, Garmisch.
p5	Müde, statuette by Dorothea Steigerwald, © Brendow Verlag, D-4130 Moers 1.

Joyce Huggett

GOD'S SPRINGTIME

A book-cassette pack providing readings and prayers for Lent.

This complementary book and cassette will help the reader and listener live through Lent in a uniquely deep and fruitful way. The book contains a Bible passage for each day, a comment and a prayer or meditation, written in Joyce's unique and personal way. The cassette features six programmes of prayers, readings and discussion material interspersed with music by the Jane Lilley Singers.

God's Springtime will be appreciated by people from a variety of walks of life and church backgrounds; the book and cassette combination is ideal for Lent study groups.

Joyce Huggett

MARRIAGE MATTERS

An affirmation of the power of God's healing love to transform, renew or redeem any and all marriages. Joyce Huggett has met and counselled couples who have been rescued through God's grace from the brink of divorce. Sharing these stories, the author shows how we can recommit our life and our partner to God. Previously entitled *Marriage on the Mend*.